An Introduction to Staff Development in Academic Libraries

An academic library's single most valuable resource is its workforce. Without educated, well-trained, and motivated librarians and library staff, an academic library program is ill-prepared to meet the needs of its clientele or the challenges that face institutions of higher education. Presenting case studies from a wide range of academic libraries internationally, *An Introduction to Staff Development in Academic Libraries* is geared toward librarians involved in teaching, orienting, training, mentoring, and developing librarians and library staff at colleges and universities.

The ideas and methods described in this book are intended for readers to modify and use in a variety of settings. By understanding the importance of staff development, and adapting and building on some of the approaches described here, librarians, no matter their roles, can move their careers and organizations forward. By relating staff orientation, training, and development to the library's mission statement and strategic plan, an academic library can remain relevant, focused, and results-oriented. The book is supplemented by exercises designed to educate, train, and develop library school students, entry-level librarians, mid-career librarians, and library administrators alike.

Elizabeth Connor is Associate Professor of Library Science at the Daniel Library of The Citadel, the Military College of South Carolina. She is a distinguished member of the Academy of Health Information Professionals (AHIP), serves as the book review editor of *Medical Reference Services Quarterly*, and coedits the *Journal of Electronic Resources in Medical Libraries*. Recent publications include *An Introduction to Instructional Services in Academic Libraries*; *An Introduction to Reference Services in Academic Libraries*; *Evidence-Based Librarianship: Case Studies and Active Learning Exercises*; *A Guide to Developing End User Education Programs in Medical Libraries*; and *Planning, Renovating, Expanding, and Constructing Library Facilities in Hospitals, Academic Medical Centers, and Health Organizations*.

An Introduction to Staff Development in Academic Libraries

Edited by Elizabeth Connor

Routledge
Taylor & Francis Group

NEW YORK AND LONDON

First published 2009
by Routledge
270 Madison Ave, New York, NY 10016

Simultaneously published in the UK
by Routledge
2 Park Square, Milton Park, Abingdon, Oxon OX14 4RN

Routledge is an imprint of the Taylor & Francis Group, an informa business

© 2009 Taylor & Francis

Typeset in Sabon by
HWA Text and Data Management, London
Printed and bound in the United States of America on acid-free paper by
Walsworth Publishing Company, Marceline, MO

Library of Congress Cataloging in Publication Data
An introduction to staff development in academic libraries /
    edited by Elizabeth Connor.
        p. cm.
        Includes bibliographical references and index.
        [etc.]
    1. Academic librarians – In-service training. 2. Library education
    (Continuing education). 3. Academic librarians –Training of.
    4. Academic libraries – United States – Personnel management – Case
    studies. 5. Library education – United States – Case studies. 6. Career
    development. I. Connor, Elizabeth, MLS.
Z682.4.C63I58 2009
020.71´55–dc22   2008032526

ISBN10: 0-7890-3844-7 (hbk)
ISBN10: 0-7890-3845-5 (pbk)
ISBN10: 0-2038-8300-4 (ebk)

ISBN13: 978-0-7890-3844-9 (hbk)
ISBN13: 978-0-7890-3845-6 (pbk)
ISBN13: 978-0-2038-8300-6 (ebk)

Contents

Figures

Tables

Contributors

About the Editor

Elizabeth Connor, MLS, AHIP is Associate Professor of Library Science at the Daniel Library of The Citadel, the Military College of South Carolina. She earned her ALA-accredited MLS at the State University College at Geneseo in 1978, has worked as a community college librarian, medical librarian at teaching hospitals and medical schools in three states (Maryland, Connecticut, and South Carolina) and two foreign countries (Kingdom of Saudi Arabia and Commonwealth of Dominica), and now works as the Science Liaison in an academic library. She is a distinguished member of the Academy of Health Information Professionals (AHIP), serves as the book review editor of *Medical Reference Services Quarterly*, and co-edits *Journal of Electronic Resources in Medical Libraries*. Research interests include how case studies and audience response systems can be used to engage and sustain learning, especially in science undergraduates. Recent publications include *An Introduction to Instructional Services in Academic Libraries*; *An Introduction to Reference Services in Academic Libraries*; *Evidence-based Librarianship: Case Studies and Active Learning Exercises*; *A Guide to Developing End User Education Programs in Medical Libraries*; and *Planning, Renovating, Expanding, and Constructing Library Facilities in Hospitals, Academic Medical Centers, and Health Organizations*.

Contributors

M. Sue Baughman, MLS is Assistant Dean for Organizational Development at the University of Maryland Libraries in College Park, Maryland.

Phillip M. Edwards, MSI is a Doctoral Candidate at the Information School of the University of Washington in Seattle, Washington.

Donna F. Ekart, MS, MLS is New Technologies Librarian in the Digital Initiatives Department at Kansas State University Libraries in Manhattan, Kansas.

Dolores Fidishun, EdD is Head Librarian at Pennsylvania State Great Valley School of Graduate Professional Studies in Malvern, Pennsylvania.

Shawn R. Fields holds an MLS degree from Southern Connecticut State University and a BS in Business Management from the University of Connecticut. Before joining Huntington Branch Library in Shelton, Connecticut as Branch Director, Mr. Fields was Communications & Outreach Librarian at Small Town University, and has worked in other academic libraries.

Priscilla Finley, MA, MLS is the Humanities Librarian at the University of Nevada, Las Vegas Libraries.

Michael Fosmire is Associate Professor of Library Science and Head, Physical Science, Engineering, and Technology Division at Purdue University Libraries in West Lafayette, Indiana.

Jennifer Heikkila Furrey, BA is Communications and Outreach Coordinator at Kansas State University Libraries in Manhattan, Kansas.

Susan Hamburger, MLS, MA, PhD is Manuscripts Cataloging Librarian at The Pennsylvania State University in University Park, Pennsylvania.

John H. Heinrichs, PhD is Assistant Professor in the Library and Information Sciences Program at Wayne State University in Detroit, Michigan.

Paul Holland, MSc, PGCE is Head of Customer Services at St. Martin's College (now known as University of Cumbria) in Lancaster, United Kingdom.

Suzanne E. Holler, MLS is an independent consultant and contract trainer, working primarily with the Central Florida Library Cooperative in Maitland, Florida.

Elaine Z. Jennerich, MSLS, PhD is Director of Organization Development and Training at the University of Washington Libraries in Seattle, Washington.

Carol P. Johnson, MSIS, MA is the Director of Libraries, Media Services, and Archives at the College of St. Catherine, St. Paul, Minnesota.

Jane Kinkus is Associate Professor of Library Science and Mathematical Sciences Librarian at Purdue University Libraries in West Lafayette, Indiana.

Jennifer Kinniff is a graduate assistant in the Staff Development department at the University of Maryland Libraries in College Park, Maryland.

Cynthia M. Kisby, MALS is Head, Regional Campus Libraries at University of Central Florida Libraries in Orlando, Florida.

Bin Li, PhD is Assistant Professor in the Library and Information Sciences Program at Wayne State University in Detroit, Michigan.

Jeen-Su Lim, PhD is Professor of Marketing at the University of Toledo in Toledo, Ohio.

Kee-Sook Lim, PhD is Lecturer of Information Operations Technology at the University of Toledo in Toledo, Ohio.

Sidney Lowe, MS, MLS is the Government Information Librarian at the University of Nevada, Las Vegas Libraries.

Julie Meyer is the Instructional Designer in the Library at Pennsylvania State Great Valley School of Graduate Professional Studies in Malvern, Pennsylvania.

Mary Murray is a Library Assistant at Pennsylvania State Great Valley School of Graduate Professional Studies in Malvern, Pennsylvania.

James M. Newsome is currently Head of Public Services at the College of St. Catherine Libraries, Media Services and Archives. He received a BA from St. Olaf College in 1971, an MA in Library Science from the University of Minnesota in 1979 and an MA in Theology from the College of St. Catherine in 2005.

Rebecca Richardson is Technology Training Specialist at Purdue University Libraries in West Lafayette, Indiana.

Lisa Rile is Business Manager of Executive Offices at Purdue University in West Lafayette, Indiana.

Carol Riley is Head of Circulation in the Library at Pennsylvania State Great Valley School of Graduate Professional Studies in Malvern, Pennsylvania.

Maggie Z. Saponaro is Manager, Staff Learning and Development at the University of Maryland Libraries in College Park, Maryland.

Susie Skarl, MLS is the Urban Studies Librarian at the University of Nevada, Las Vegas Libraries.

Lisa Toner, BA (Hons), Dip Lib, MCLIP is Site Library Manager at St. Martin's College (now known as University of Cumbria) in Lancaster, United Kingdom.

Ellen R. Urton, MLS is Visual Arts Librarian in the Social Sciences/ Humanities Department at Kansas State University in Manhattan, Kansas.

Diane VanderPol, MLS is the Head of Instruction at the University of Nevada, Las Vegas Libraries.

Jennifer L. Ward, MSLIS is Head of Web Services at the University of Washington Libraries in Seattle, Washington.

Margaret Weaver, MSc, BA, MCLIP, FHEA is Head of Learning and Information Services at St. Martin's College (now known as University of Cumbria) in Lancaster, United Kingdom.

Sandra G. Yee is Dean of University Libraries at Wayne State University in Detroit, Michigan.

Preface

An academic library's single most valuable resource is its workforce. Without educated, well-trained, and motivated librarians and library staff, an academic library program is ill-prepared to meet the needs of its clientele or the challenges that face institutions of higher education. This work presents case studies from a wide range of academic libraries in the United States and United Kingdom, and is geared toward librarians involved in teaching, orienting, training, mentoring, and/or developing librarians and library staff at colleges and universities.

The ideas and methods described in this book are intended for readers to modify and use in a variety of settings. By understanding the importance of staff development, and adapting and building on some of the approaches described here, librarians, no matter their roles, can move their careers and organizations forward. By relating staff orientation, training, and development to the library's mission statement and strategic plan, an academic library can remain relevant, focused, and results-oriented.

The book is supplemented by exercises that can be used to educate, train, and develop new and current library personnel. Based on an adaptation of Bloom's taxonomy, these exercises are designed to teach and enlighten library school students, entry-level librarians, mid-career librarians, and library administrators alike.

Many efforts, great and small, can be made to welcome and orient new employees, and to develop the knowledge base and skill sets of existing employees. The workplace should be as welcoming and nurturing to new library faculty and staff as it is to administrators, faculty, students, and visitors. Invest time and effort in librarians and library staff by supporting their educational growth, and retain valued employees by appreciating and recognizing their intellectual contributions. Academe's most valuable resource depends on it.

Elizabeth Connor

1 Welcome! Creating an Effective New Employee Orientation Program at Kansas State Libraries

Donna F. Ekart, Jennifer Heikkila Furrey, and Ellen R. Urton

Introduction

Investment in individual success is essential to the health of any organization regardless of size, type, or mission. When a person enters a new job, the earliest days and weeks provide an opportune time to lay the groundwork for eventual success; thus, working as an organization to ensure that new employees feel welcome should be a top priority. By taking the time to properly acculturate an incoming hire to the work environment, the organization provides the tools not only for his or her daily tasks but also for career achievements and contributions to the organization. Having invested time, energy, money, and forward planning into hiring employees, it is vital to sustain this investment with equal orientation resources, and take care in preparing for a new employee's first day on the job. In return, the organization will benefit from a workforce that is motivated, well informed, and communally invested in accomplishing even the largest of goals. Kansas State Libraries (KSL) is one such organization, committed to making a strong initial investment in its new employees through development of a new employee orientation program. Designed and implemented by three current employees who sought to address some of the unique needs of the organization, KSL's program stands out as a simple and effective orientation plan that increases communication, strengthens the organization's identity, and should ultimately improve retention rates.

This orientation program provides early support, guidance, and the basic tools necessary to strengthen the foundation upon which new hires build their careers. The program's aims were to establish a consistent, organization-wide orientation program that would:

- organize essential tasks and package fundamental information for both new employees and their supervisors;
- encourage employee support and connections beyond their immediate work area;

- promote a holistic perspective on the organization;
- help the employee place himself or herself in the context of the organization;
- offer a polished end product that still allows for customization.

Many of the aims flowed from the transitional era at KSL into which the orientation program was introduced.

Setting

Located in the town of Manhattan, Kansas State University had a 2006 enrollment of more than 23,000 students. The Libraries are comprised of a main library (Hale) and five branch libraries: Fiedler Engineering Library, Math/Physics Library, Paul Weigel Library of Architecture Planning and Design, Veterinary Medicine Library, and K State at Salina Library. Print holdings total more than 1.8 million volumes, over three million government documents, and more than 2.5 million microforms. Electronic subscriptions total more than 12,000 titles. The Libraries employ approximately 125 non-student staff, the majority of whom work in Hale Library.   Departments are spread throughout Hale's 550,000 square feet and across six floors; the building's design limits interaction among units and departments. Partly due to the challenges created by lack of proximity, the organization continually struggles to optimize effective and efficient communication.

When KSL's orientation program was developed, the organization had recently entered a period of substantial transition. The arrival of a new Dean of Libraries prompted a redesign of the organizational structure, and KSL began a shift from an administrative body consisting of one dean and three interim associate deans to a more flattened structure. This opened the culture to some innovative approaches to shaping the future. With the reorganization, KSL found itself in the interesting position of initiating a hiring boom while simultaneously vacating the Director of Human Resources position. These two factors threatened to leave a large group of new employees adrift without formal guidance. With the hiring boom reaching nearly every department and unit, the organization as a whole was affected by the leadership void. Several supervisors were newly appointed with the redesign, and many of those with experience had not needed to train a new employee for years. Deciding to embrace the new organizational *Zeitgeist* and initiate change from a lower level, an *ad hoc* task force of three staff members stepped forward to create, implement, and manage a new employee orientation program until a human resources director could be hired.

Literature Review

Looking to the literature, much exists regarding employee orientation in academic libraries. In his mock memo piece, Schott highlights how *not* to treat new hires. Schott advises against overwhelming individuals with too much highly detailed information too quickly, unreasonable expectations, intimidating tasks, cumbersome bureaucracy, or the "sink or swim" approach to professional success.[1] In accordance with Schott's position, KSL's program provides a balanced, gradual transition over a reasonable period of time with sufficient personal attention and assistance along the way.

Mossman speaks to similar sensitive concerns by summarizing how a real-life orientation for NextGen librarians can help individuals "avoid trauma."[2] Bird recommends that library managers actively support "newer librarians by providing them with the experience and training needed to become the next generation of managers and leaders."[3] Weingart, Kochan, and Hedrich outline the myriad ways by which an orientation mechanism strengthens the business of academic librarianship.[4] In contrast, KSL's program developed from personal experiences and compassionate insight, rather than specific knowledge or understanding of business matters related to the high cost of employee turnover. These various discussions focus on individuals who hold an MLS or other advanced degree whereas KSL's program applies to all new employees regardless of rank or title. In addition, other orientation schemes tend to center on the specifics of daily job performance expectations, while KSL's program seeks to establish fundamental feelings of comfort and familiarity for both the new employee and his or her colleagues.

Many orientation discussions limit focus to a particular category of employee, type of library, or specific proficiency required of everyone regardless of unique job duties. Recognizing the inherent value and indispensable functions performed by students employed in academic libraries, Kathman and Kathman focus on training student employees to provide quality customer service, and teaching them one or more detailed aspects of their jobs.[5] They place this orientation responsibility on supervisors and highlight the inherent benefits to job performance quality. Yessin shares how he and his colleagues met the challenge presented by staffing a new law library.[6] His example of an all-encompassing basic orientation was designed to create a common knowledge base and high-quality patron service by familiarizing all employees with legal materials and terminology. Cooper concentrates on one vital aspect—technology training—of an employee's continual development.[7] Cooper's focus, although universal and necessary, is narrower than the needs at KSL.

Another thread in orientation writings is the implementation of an orientation program. DiMarco speaks to new employee orientation in academic libraries, and takes a broad approach by outlining some essential elements of an orientation program.[8] Yet DiMarco does not discuss personal attention and the principles of one-on-one interaction considered fundamental at KSL. Omidsalar and Young present an orientation scheme for reference librarians, carefully considering practical benefits and cost savings, and emphasizing the importance of obtaining the full support of library administration.[9] While the KSL orientation program received the complete backing of the Libraries' leadership prior to implementation, it favors individuals over pecuniary concerns. In another how-to article, Ballard and Blessing present their personal experiences at North Carolina State University Libraries.[10] Their program developed over many years and was implemented in stages. Firmly rooted in theory, this formal, highly structured orientation scheme pays particular attention to issues of diversity. As it developed, they incorporated feedback and eventually hired a staff development librarian to fully implement the program. In contrast, the KSL program developed rapidly to fill an immediate need as the organization faced a tide of new hires, as well as to lay a foundation for a more complex, long-term solution.

Davis developed an extensive and formal how-to manual for libraries, and his program outline resembles KSL's project in various ways.[11] Similar to Davis, the KSL group began by assessing the existing organizational structure, and identifying the essential elements and program goals. In part, this assessment was informed by surveys of relatively new staff. Other similarities include the role of the immediate supervisor, a flexible timeline, and documentation such as checklists. The KSL program adds training for volunteer guides and various tours. Additionally, the KSL guide program substantially differs from the role of a permanent "mentor" who would be responsible for more long-term professional development and advising over the career lifespan. Guides are assigned to every new employee based on very deliberate criteria, and paired across departments and professional classifications for a short period of time. The differences between Davis's program and KSL's are significant, as they highlight the primacy of the unique needs of K-State Libraries at the time of the creation of the orientation program. KSL required a program that could function with no human resources' apparatus to prop it up, handle a rapid influx of many new employees, and come to fruition in a highly condensed period of organizational transition. These needs informed the objectives the task force set out to meet.

Objectives

The KSL task force had rather informal beginnings among staff members. During these casual conversations, it became apparent that a good deal of vital information, although readily available, was not passed on to new employees in any systematic manner. Rather, new employees seemed to stumble upon useful policies, procedures, or contacts through random chance, or not at all. Task force members began to survey new staff, asking the question, "What do you know now that you wish you'd known when you started?" Pages and pages of notes later, it became apparent that something had to be done. The weight of anecdotal evidence seemed solidly in favor of creating some sort of formalized orientation program.

The task force represented the three types of employees at KSL (classified, unclassified professional, and tenure-track faculty), and although they differed in terms of professional classification, position description, department affiliation, and level of experience working in academic libraries, they shared common concerns for the new employee experience. This unique combination of viewpoints helped to strengthen and broaden the scope of the overall program. The resulting multifaceted program design allowed for personal attention within a scheduled orientation, and built structure into the process without requiring an onerous time commitment from either new or current employees.

From this grass roots beginning, the task force endeavored to build a comprehensive orientation to assist individual new employees, their supervisors, and the organization. Additionally, the group hoped to establish a set of consistent practices, increase communication across the organization, and enable thoughtful attention to distinct requirements of each new employee. This program would fulfill a specific and immediate need and the task force hoped to see it flourish once the new human resources director was hired. As of this writing, seventeen individuals have been through the orientation program, resulting in a smoother integration of these individuals into the Libraries compared to those hired before the orientation program was in place.

Planning

Even with a fairly limited scope, it was apparent that the project would take considerably more time than any of the group had anticipated. Hoping to see project time validated, the members approached KSL's Library Leadership Council (LLC) and asked to be formally recognized as a task force. When approval was granted on September 13, 2005, it was agreed that the task force would gather some preliminary information and return to the LLC with a report and an implementation plan. The imminent arrival of three new hires drove a very tight time frame (less than four months) and the need for an immediately useful, focused outcome. The task force presented its planned orientation program to LLC on November 1, 2005, and it was approved for implementation.

Seeking evidence beyond their personal experience, the task force's work began with a survey of all fourteen staff members with less than one year's employment at the Libraries. This survey was created and distributed utilizing the university's online survey system, <https://online.ksu.edu/Survey/>, which allowed employee anonymity. The seven-question survey was a combination of multiple choice and free-response questions. Those surveyed were asked about specific activities during the initial weeks of employment (tours, training, etc.), orientation materials received, and the usefulness of those activities and materials. The survey also solicited suggestions for making future new employees feel more welcome and prepared to work. See Appendix 1.A for a complete list of survey questions.

Eight employees responded to the survey and the task force was not surprised to find a substantial lack of commonality in the new employees' experiences. Some seemed to get along fine, and the welcoming nature of other KSL employees was often cited in comments such as "the staff was very supportive and friendly" and "people are very nice and always willing to answer my questions without making me feel stupid." However, these positive comments were overshadowed by the disclosure of some negative experiences that conflicted with assertions of support. For example, some employees did not have basic supplies such as phone books and writing materials at their desks upon arrival, other employees still had questions about necessary tasks such as completing time sheets, and respondents also expressed the desire for more orientation with comments such as "didn't have much orientation, so in that sense it was all useful" and "I found all of the orientation materials useful. I just wish there was more."

Based on this feedback, the task force concluded that although KSL staff had the proper welcoming attitude toward new employees, the lack of a formalized program or understanding of what new employees might need were definite hindrances for the new employees as well as for the organization.

Rather than reinvent the wheel, the task force surveyed a similarly sized group of long-term KSL employees to determine whether pockets of relevant organizational knowledge existed, and ascertain whether or not there had been an orientation program in the past. This second survey was sent to fifteen employees with a range of three to twenty-plus years' employment at KSL. These individuals represented all KSL units and departments, and were likely to have taken part in orienting new employees at some point in their careers at Kansas State. The survey attempted to elicit actual current practice and identify needs as perceived by well-established personnel. This second survey was carried out using the same anonymous survey system as the one used for new employees. Out of fifteen employees, ten responded to the request. As with the responses from the new employees, the results were quite uneven, and reflected a lack of any centralized practice at KSL. The information gathered included many thoughtful suggestions for formal orientation program items, including basic help charts for computer and software information, and a structured way to learn about what other departments do on a daily basis. See Appendix 1.A for a complete version of the survey.

Program

After compiling survey results and notes from informal conversations, the task force determined that a three-pillared approach to orientation was warranted. The three pillars represent the layers of orientation necessary for a well-rounded acculturation into the organization, by addressing 1) the new employee's orientation to his or her new job, 2) the hiring department, and 3) the entire organization. Each of the three pillars is essential for the program's success. To support new employees with a multifaceted approach, these program components include tools and advice to be utilized by the new employee, his or her supervisor, a designated orientation guide from outside the new employee's department, and by the administrative arm of the Libraries.

Orientation Notebook

First, to orient the new employee to his or her job, each new employee is given a notebook presenting information universal to all KSL employees. This notebook is intended to serve as a reference tool that can be utilized beyond orientation, rather than an overwhelming, all-inclusive manual. It is organized into basic categories including fundamental facts about KSL, general policies and procedures, and some rudimentary computer training. The notebook also allows space for customization as necessitated by the unique demands of the new employee's position. The first page features a checklist of tasks and events that may be encountered during the first few weeks of employment. There is space to take notes during training or to add other useful information as discovered. By using a three-ring binder, information can easily be added, updated, or removed. Electronic versions of these documents are saved separately onto the KSL network so that notebooks can be easily updated. Names or phone numbers of individuals currently responsible for various tasks were purposefully omitted. Job titles and department designations tend to be more stable; in the event of a personnel change, or a shift of duties, the entire notebook needed not be changed. See Appendix 1.B for more information.

Orientation Checklist

The second pillar provides structure for the supervisor to properly welcome a new employee. Coordinating a new employee's workspace and pre-planning basic orientation activities prior to his or her arrival are atypical yet indispensable undertakings for all supervisors. Previously, orientation activities carried out by supervisors lacked standardization across the organization. To achieve consistency, supervisors are given a checklist of tasks and a rough timetable for their completion (see Appendix 1.C). This checklist includes tasks to be completed well before the new hire's arrival as well as those to be completed during the initial period of adjustment. The intention is to keep all training participants on the same page and identify the person responsible for each task. In addition to the checklist, supervisors receive their own copy of the orientation notebook. This gives the supervisors further information to cover with a new employee and provides a foundation on which to add important departmental policies or procedures.

Organizational Connections

The human aspect of orientation is based on a simple, yet commonly overlooked, thoughtfulness that should go into making a new employee feel welcome. The task force wanted to dispel the anxiety of being a new employee by capitalizing on an organizational strength identified in the surveys—a warm and welcoming attitude. This led to the third and final pillar: building a connection to the larger organization. This pillar has two facets, a friendly guide and a series of brief departmental orientations.

To provide an immediate, one-on-one connection, a staff member from another department is assigned as an orientation guide. Optimally, this guide would not only work in another department, but also be situated in a space physically removed from the new employee's immediate work area. Guides are deliberately paired with new employees based on contrasting job classifications (i.e. classified paired with faculty), in an effort to bring two people together and establish communication where it might not otherwise occur. For the first four to six weeks of a new employee's career, the guide acts as an informal resource and a conduit through which other KSL areas can be introduced.

Facilities Tour

The guide's first task is to take the new employee on an intensive facilities tour. Whether working in the main library (Hale) or in a branch library, every new staff person needs to become familiar with all KSL facilities. Tours are designed with time to answer questions, point out useful tips, and highlight "staff-only" information. Guides also conduct a tour of the campus and provide basic, informal information regarding local traditions and culture. This cultural orientation is especially important to employees new to the region as well as to the Libraries. For those employees hired locally, the guide draws attention to some of the unique features of the organization and its relationship to the campus and local communities. As with the new employee and supervisor, the guide receives a copy of the orientation notebook. The guide's copy includes a building tour checklist and an orientation activities checklist in addition to the basic information received by all new employees. By providing all participants with essentially the same resources, this coordinated effort ensures that orientations are well-rounded, consistent, and thorough.

Department Orientations

In addition to the one-on-one contact the guide program provides, the new employee's orientation involves a series of one-hour orientations to various KSL departments and units. These departmental orientations were designed to create context for the larger organization, connect faces with functions, and give at least a vague idea of future contacts for various requests and projects. Designed as overviews of a department's primary role, these sessions are a way to start understanding what other departments do and how that relates to other work at KSL. Very little of what happens in one department stays in that department; work and ideas filter out and affect the workflows of almost every other department. Since every position is different, the functions of specific departments need to be shared with respect to their relevancy to the new employee. Knowing what other departments do and having connections in them allows the new employee to feel comfortable communicating openly and equips them with an early appreciation of how the organization is put together.

Functional Orientation Sessions

Initially, eighteen supervisors were approached to participate by creating a short functional orientation for their respective areas. Basic topics were suggested, but each supervisor was free to tailor the orientation to the functions and personalities of the department or unit in question. The only firm requirements were sessions shorter than one hour presented by a permanent, non-student employee. With the tight schedule, units were given just over one month to prepare the orientation. Additionally, each was asked to choose a time and day each month to serve as a fixed orientation time (e.g. each second Tuesday at 2 p.m.). This allowed multiple new employees to be scheduled at a single orientation time for a department or unit, and reduced each unit's time commitment to no more than one hour per month.

    A chart was created to log each orientation slot to avoid conflicts with other sessions or standing meetings involving a significant number of employees. In the end, some units chose to further subdivide themselves, and twenty-one orientation times were established. The complete schedule can be found in Appendix 1.B. It should be noted that since each new employee was expected to approach the orientations with consideration for the immediate needs of his or her position, no firm order was prescribed or implied by the schedule. Thus, a new employee in Circulation might need to meet with related areas such as Preservation or General Reference fairly soon, while orientation to Library Instruction or Digital Initiatives could be deferred.

Building the Orientation Guide Program

With the notebook, checklist, and supporting documents for orientation guides and supervisors completed, and final approval granted by LLC, the task force turned its attention toward building the guide program. The task force estimated how many individuals they would require for the first round of incoming hires and sought a pool of proactive, encouraging volunteers from throughout the organization to be trained as guides. The KSL Dean issued a formal call for volunteers and some individual solicitations by the task force resulted in thirteen volunteers for the guide program.

These individuals were given guide notebooks and they provided one hour of training to explain their areas of responsibility: the facilities tour, campus tour, and discussion of KSL organizational culture. Informal meetings could also take place over coffee or lunch, and the guides were available as an information source. The training also featured an introduction to the overall goals of the orientation program, and suggested various ideas for helping an individual feel welcome. Three guides were matched immediately to individuals who began employment in October and November 2005; the rest remained in the pool for future hires. So far, twelve volunteers have guided at least one new employee, with some guides serving as many as three times. Matching guides to new employees was one part formal cross matching of employment types and work areas, and one part informal brainstorming about who might be best suited for personality and scheduling factors. Due to this process, some guide names rose to the top of the list more frequently than others. As hiring patterns rise and fall and individuals come and go from the organization, it is anticipated that additional guides will be recruited and trained.

Supervisor Training and Staff Awareness

The next steps in the implementation process were supervisor training and staff awareness. To introduce the program, the task force made a brief presentation at an all-staff meeting in mid-November 2005. Drawing on a pre-existing culture of organization-wide participation in the hiring process, the task force asked for continued staff support once new employees arrived to work. The task force shared the rationale for the program, how it grew and evolved from staff suggestions, and summarized goals and expectations for the program's future. An invitation was extended to current employees to attend any department or unit-level orientation sessions. Current employees were also encouraged to request an orientation notebook for personal use. An article in the staff newsletter

summarized the all-staff presentation, highlighted upcoming supervisor training sessions, and introduced the guide pool.

To familiarize current supervisors with the orientation program checklist, the task force offered four one-hour sessions between November 21, 2005 and December 5, 2005; all but three supervisors out of a pool of approximately thirty were able to attend a training session. It was stressed that neither the contents of the notebook nor the full program was in any way intended to replace position-specific or task-related departmental training, but rather to allow supervisors more freedom to orient their new employees.

Upon completion of the supervisor training, the implementation phase was concluded and task force duties shifted to maintenance of the employee notebook and assignment of guides. This period of intermittent focus continued until early 2007, when administration of the program passed to the newly hired Director of Human Resources and her staff.

Outcomes

To date, seventeen individuals have been acculturated to the organization using the orientation program as a framework. These individuals were surveyed to gain general impressions of the program's scope and implementation. See Appendix 1.D for survey questions. Surveys were conducted at two separate points—one at six months after implementation (five individuals), and a second round after one year (twelve individuals)—and used the same campus survey system as the pre-program surveys. In all, fourteen people completed at least part of the survey. It may be worth noting that not only did all five orientees in the first group respond, but also that their responses were more uniformly positive than those from the second group. Whether this is due to some dilution of the program over time, or idiosyncrasies of the supervisors and/or new employees is unclear.

Overall, the new employees surveyed seemed to find the program useful, but occasionally too broad in scope. A typical response showing this mixed impression was:

> The entire program is ambitious, very useful, but also overwhelming for a new employee ... There are a large number of employees in the Hale Library system and a lot of names to remember. The notebook is a great idea and is very useful because it lists the teams and their members.

The majority of individuals completing the survey reported that the basics of the program were completed: they received notebooks, spent time with their guides, attended many of the departmental orientations, and completed most of the checklist items. Without exception, responses that showed aspects of the program were not being carried out came from the second group of respondents.

What may not have been conveyed to training participants, however, were the philosophy or intentions of the orientation program as a whole. One employee commented:

> I wasn't sure exactly at what point it was that I was expected to be "oriented." I wonder if instead of the process being drawn out over two months a lot of the orientation could be concentrated into a couple of weeks. Even if I didn't get to meet with every "head" person in their area, surely one could speak with another person in a given area and that might be sufficient. Then instead of feeling like I didn't "really" work here or fit here or belong here for the first two months—because I was not oriented yet—it could be two weeks, intense and then, "you have completed boot camp!" and feel officially part of things more quickly.

It seems that the program's goal of drawing employees in, rather than excluding them until orientation was "complete," was not conveyed to this individual. Another employee echoed the task force's philosophy, apparently unaware that it existed at all:

> Above all, the goal of the program should be to accompany the new employee as s/he acculturates to the new work environment. Relying on the employee's department to do this is risky, especially until more is known about which departments and people do well at orienting their employees.

This same employee suggested a feedback mechanism by which both guides and supervisors could be evaluated, which would be an excellent idea for the human resources staff to implement, but one probably inappropriate for the task force, as it would involve employee performance evaluations.

From these and similar survey responses, it seems likely that when asked to accomplish something that did not quite make sense, some participants (supervisors, guides, and new employees alike) would continue to move forward without clarification. Consequently, parts of the orientation program were skipped or glossed over simply because someone did not understand how it contributed to the overall program's effectiveness. Involving human resources staff directly in the individual steps of the orientation program should work to answer these questions as they arise. These findings also indicate the need to document each step of the program to remove any ambiguity about the reasons for inclusion. Thorough descriptions of and instructions for all parts of the orientation program should lead to a better overall understanding of the role the program plays.

The survey results also illustrated that no two employees will perceive their orientation experience the same. While some found it overwhelming, others suggested that it was too brief. The task force learned from casual conversations and survey results alike that there is no single program that would adequately accommodate the idiosyncrasies of individual personalities. In trying to please a majority of participants, it is inevitable that some will still feel alienated. The task force therefore strove for the middle ground, and incorporated as much flexibility as possible.

Several questions and issues arose during the implementation of the orientation program that fell beyond the scope of the task force. Working through the various training sessions with supervisors and guides, the task force discovered a lack of supervisor training in general, especially with regard to accommodating new employees. Since the task force included neither supervisors nor human resources staff, and intended only to create an interim solution to a problem that was tied to a specific moment in the organization's history, comprehensive supervisor training was not an issue the task force could tackle. This lack of programmatic training also suggested the need for refresher training as the program continues to grow and develop in the future.

The human resources staff are on the front lines of hiring, therefore the orientation program finds a natural home with them. They have access to all of the relevant information and will be poised to begin orientation planning for each new employee on the same day an offer is accepted. The task force's efforts were often hampered because they had to track down bits and pieces of information in order to put together a full packet of information for new employees. Most of the information that is specific to the orientation program originates in human resources; updating and maintaining this information will be a much easier job for them and make the overall program more current.

Conclusion

Looking to the future, it is essential to preserve the spirit that originally conceived the program while continuing to build upon its foundation. With a director of human resources in place, tasks and training can be developed that could not have been carried out by the task force alone. Collaboration among the human resources staff and the task force should ensure that future developments and changes do not compete with the original intentions of the program. Since the program addresses some perennial, systemic problems such as communication difficulties, it should not be assumed that any of the main pillars of the program will ever become obsolete.

KSL's orientation program is intended to increase communication, strengthen organizational identity, and improve retention rates by setting an appropriate tone from the first moments of employment. Several key

14 Donna F. Ekart, Jennifer Heikkila Furrey, and Ellen R. Urton

elements arise that point toward this effort's eventual success. First, the program is flexible and customizable yet based on a strong framework. For example, supervisors can add information to the notebook, or employees can attend department orientations in any order, yet the fundamental information that makes the program valuable to all employees remains. A second strength of the program is its intention to introduce a cross-organizational view. In any given department, an employee will receive training regarding a specific job. Taking this idea of a deep understanding of a set of tasks, and pairing it with a larger organizational orientation allows employees to understand how their pieces fit within the entire puzzle, leading to a more nuanced, multifaceted view of the organization. Third, KSL's program emphasizes the need for human connections with the guide program. It is pivotal to make these kinds of connections within the first month of working in a new job. These three elements combine to provide a firm foundation for the new employee, and offer the organization a plan for investing in individual success. Sustaining the investment will lead to a compounded return, as these well-informed, communally invested individuals will likely seek to give back to future new employees, thus creating a cycle that can only lead to organizational success. Since "[few] have curiosity or benevolence to struggle long against the first impression,"[12] an organization that provides a thoughtful, well-conceived, and continually renewed orientation program will long see rewards from that positive first impression.

References

1. Schott, Michael J. "Memo: New Librarian Orientation." *Library Journal* 131 (April 15, 2006): 54.
2. Mossman, Katherine. "Good Orientation Counts." *Library Journal* 130 (June 15, 2005): 46.
3. Bird, Jason. "Ready and Waiting for the Future: New Librarians and Succession Planning." *Feliciter* 51 (2005): 36–37.
4. Weingart, Sandra J., Kochan, Carol A., and Hedrich, Anne. "Safeguarding Your Investment: Effective Orientation for New Employees." *Library Administration & Management* 12 (Summer 1998): 156–158.
5. Kathman, Jane M., and Kathman, Michael D. "Training Student Employees for Quality Service." *The Journal of Academic Librarianship* 26 (May 2000): 176–182.
6. Yessin, Gary. "Orienting New Employees: Law Libraries 101." *Law Library Journal* 96 (Winter 2004): 193–203.
7. Cooper, Eric A. "Managing Change to Enhance Technological Orientation and Knowledge Among Library Staff." *The Electronic Library* 16 (August 1998): 247–251.
8. DiMarco, Scott R. "Practicing the Golden Rule: Creating a Win-Win New Employee Orientation." *College & Research Libraries News* 66 (February 2005): 110–113.
9. Omidsalar, Teresa P., and Young, Margo. "Orientation to Reality." *The Reference Librarian*, 72 (2001): 21–32.

10. Ballard, Angela, and Blessing, Laura. "Organizational Socialization through Employee Orientations at North Carolina State University Libraries." *College & Research Libraries* 67 (May 2006): 240–248.
11. Davis, H. Scott. *New Employee Orientation: A How-To-Do-It Manual for Librarians*. New York: Neal-Schuman Publishers, 1994.
12. Johnson, Samuel. *The Rambler* 166(October 19, 1751). Vol. V. New Haven: Yale University Press, 1969, p. 117.

Appendix 1.A: Pre-program Surveys

Pre-program Survey – Recent Hires

1. In what orientation activities did you participate during your first month at K-State Libraries?
2. What welcome/orientation materials did you receive upon being hired at K-State Libraries?
3. What office supplies/materials were at your desk on your first day?
4. What orientation materials or activities did you find most useful?
5. What orientation materials or activities did you find least useful?
6. What, if any, orientation materials or activities were lacking that you wish were included?
7. What one thing would you do to make new employees feel more welcome at K-State Libraries?

Pre-program Survey – Long-Term Employees

1. Does your department or unit have a formal orientation program in place for new employees?
2. If you answered yes to question #1, please describe the types of orientation activities currently in place.
3. Have you personally participated in any informal orientation/mentoring activities with a new employee? Please describe.
4. One idea under consideration for the employee orientation program is to assign each new employee an orientation "buddy" for the first month of employment. Would you be willing to be a buddy, or allow those you supervise to be buddy? Is there a limit to the amount of time you'd be willing to commit?
5. Are there any activities or materials you would like to see included in a library-wide orientation program?
6. Do you have any other thoughts about the Libraries' orientation program, past, present, or future?

Appendix 1.B: Department and Unit Orientation Schedule

	Day	*Time*	*Department/Unit*	*Contact*
1st	Monday	10am	General Reference	Erma
	Tuesday	10am	Math/Physics Library	Barbara
	Wednesday	9am	Weigel Architecture Library	Jeff
		10am	Library Instruction	Sara
		2pm	Multicultural Resource Center	Rhondalyn
	Thursday	10am	Digital Initiatives	David
		1pm	Cataloging & Serials	Char
		3pm	Government Publications	Debbie
	Friday	9am	Sciences	Mike
2nd	Monday	3pm	Veterinary Medical Library	Gayle
	Tuesday	10am	Microforms	Debbie
	Wednesday	9am	Special Collections	Lori
		10am	Interlibrary Loan Services	Kathy
	Thursday	1pm	Preservation	Marty
		2pm	Binding	Terrell
3rd	Tuesday	10am	Administration	Stella
	Thursday	4pm	Annex	Max
	Friday	9am	Social Sciences/Humanities	Marcia
4th	Tuesday	2pm	Circulation/Reserves	Janice
	Wednesday	9am	Fiedler	Alice
		10am	Acquisitions	Eric

Appendix 1.C: Supervisor Checklist

	Task	To Be Done by/ with	Done
Prior	Welcome letter/packet	Admin	
	Assign & confirm orientation guide	Admin	
	Schedule meetings: (summary list – items are also in appropriate checklist section) Lunch with dept/others (1st day) HR paperwork (1st day) Computer orientation with DSP (1st day – 2 hrs) Guide introduction (2nd day – 1 hr) Meet & Greet tour with dept member (2nd day – 2 hrs) Ergonomics evaluation with Admin (1st week – ½ hr) Voyager/Systems overview with DI rep (1st wk – 1 hr) Voyager login with Merry (1st wk – ½ hr) Building tour with Guide (1st week – 1 hr) Unit/dept orientations (1st-8th wks, list below) Dean (2nd-3rd wk – 1 hr) AD/Dept Head (2nd-3rd wk – 1 hr)	Supervisor	
	Request LAN access as appropriate (select W:/folder access)	Supervisor/DSP	
	Establish GroupWise accounts and group list assignments	Supervisor/DSP	
	Submit computer request	Supervisor	
	Submit phone/data jack requests (allow 4-6 wks)	Supervisor	
	Order basic desk supplies	Supervisor	
	Order magnetic name tag	Supervisor	
	Order name plate for desk	Admin	
	Prepare HR paperwork, including signed key card	Admin	
	Schedule benefits orientation with KSU HR	Admin	
	Schedule New Faculty orientation if applicable	Admin	
	Complete LAN account application	Admin	

continued …

Appendix 1.C continued

	Task	To Be Done by/ with	Done
1st day	Complete HR paperwork	Admin	
	Update staff phone directory/website	Admin	
	Welcome Lunch	Dept/Others	
	Desktop/LAN/GroupWise/Intranet orientation (allow 2 hrs)	DSP	
	Get KSU id card (photo required)	Supervisor	
	Telephone/Audix training	Supervisor	
	Tour/staff introduction in immediate work area	Supervisor	
	Orientation notebook	Supervisor	
	Job description/Employee's position within the unit and department/Role of dept & unit within library	Supervisor	
	Emergency/security guidelines for work area (building-wide procedures on intranet)	Supervisor	
	Supply storage/requests/procedures/ check desk	Supervisor	
	Lunch times/break times/staff lounge/ work schedule	Supervisor	
2nd day	Evaluation forms/process	Supervisor	
	Meet & Greet tour	Supervisor	
	Meet orientation guide/discuss orientation program & notebook	Supervisor/Guide	
	Pay periods/leave policies/holidays	Supervisor/Admin	
1st week	Key assignment	Admin	
	Workstation ergonomics evaluation	Admin	
	Voyager login/modules access (supervisor attends)	Merry	
	Building Tour	Guide	
	Library culture/traditions/history	Guide	
	Handbooks (dept, faculty, university, etc.)	Supervisor	
	Library hours/service point schedules/ building schedules	Supervisor	
	Library organizational chart	Supervisor	

	Task	To Be Done by/ with	Done
	Library committees/teams overview	Supervisor	
	Library policies/procedures not covered elsewhere, if applicable	Supervisor	
	Begin unit/dept orientations	Various dept/unit representatives; see schedule.	
2nd/3rd wks	Order business cards	Supervisor	
	Training plan	Supervisor	
	Committees participation	Supervisor	
	Opportunities & challenges within the organization/Major library-wide projects review	Dean	
	Strategic Plan/Mission statement	Dept Head/AD	
	Professional development opportunities/requests, as applicable to position	Supervisor/ ProfDev Committee rep/ Classified Council rep, as appropriate	
	Campus tour	Guide	
	Community items/campus perks	Guide	
	Interview for Staff Bulletin article	Staff Bulletin writer	
1st month	All Staff meeting introduction	Supervisor/Dean	
	KSU Benefits orientation	Admin	
2nd month	Review orientation list with employee – request refreshers/additional orientation as desired	Supervisor	

Appendix 1.D: Post-Program Survey

Post-Survey: employees who participated in the orientation program, 14 respondents total, number choosing each response in parentheses, not all respondents answered every question.

1. Did you receive a black New Employee Orientation notebook?

a. Yes, on my first or second day. (10)
b. Yes, within my first two weeks of work. (2)
c. Yes, after I had been working for more than two weeks.
d. No. (2)
e. I don't know.

2. Looking at the checklist at the front of your orientation notebook, how many of the items have you completed?

a. All of them. (4)
b. Most of the items, less than 6 things skipped. (6)
c. About half of the items. (1)
d. Very few of the items, no more than 5 things completed.
e. None of them.

3. Was there a particular group or category of items from the checklist that you have not completed (check any that apply)?

a. Unit/Department orientations (1)
b. Activities with my guide (1)
c. Computer/systems items (1)
d. No, nothing specific (5)

4. Is there anything additional you'd like to see as part of the orientation program?

5. Are there any checklist activities you completed that you think could be left out of the orientation program or that you did not find particularly valuable?

6. What activities did you do with your orientation guide (check all that apply)?

a. Guide took me on a building or campus tour. (11)

b. Went to coffee/lunch with my guide. (6)
c. Used guide as a resource when I had a question. (5)
d. Attended library gatherings/social events with guide. (5)
e. No activities with my guide.
f. Other activities.

7. Please identify yourself using the categories below.

a. Classified employee (5)
b. Unclassified professional (3)
c. Tenure-track faculty (3)

2   Improve Your Circulation

Does Your Library Have a Family History of Poor Service? Staff Development at Small Town University

Shawn R. Fields

Introduction

Many academic libraries never achieve their full potential because of poor organizational structures. Having the wrong staff, in the wrong place, at the wrong time can be devastating to operational plans and to service promises alike. The most deadly place to have a non-functioning or underachieving department is in Circulation. A university library with an untrained, underperforming, and unhappy Circulation Department can not survive in the twenty-first century.

Even with the great increase over the last two decades of electronic patron traffic, personal interactions between library staff and patrons are still extremely important.[1] The Circulation Desk in particular has the ability to powerfully effect patron perceptions and experiences. Patrons often interact with Circulation staff immediately upon entering the building,[2] perhaps to ask for directions, operating hours, or for proto-reference help such as "Do you have this book?" More importantly, Circulation is usually the last department that a patron interacts with, either by returning materials or checking them out.

The influence of Circulation extends beyond the physical library walls, as the department often has one of the most prominent library phone numbers in public displays. Circulation also frequently has a high-profile library e-mail address. As Michael Gorman points out, indirect service can be just as important as direct service.[2] Circulation is involved in both types and is the locus of patron interaction.

Setting

The Library on the campus of Small Town University (STU) has unfortunately experienced the ill effects of a poor Circulation Department. The purpose of the school, founded in 1963, was to service the local community by providing a morally sound and student-focused place of higher education. The school was originally only one step above the community college level in academic rigor, with a small number of academic programs and a commuting student body.[3]

STU met with a fair amount of success throughout the 1960s and 1970s following the model of small class sizes, compassionate faculty and staff, and a high level of individual attention for students. Unfortunately, by the mid-1980s, STU was in dire economic straits. The administration failed to keep up with the educational times, and the institution was teetering on the brink of bankruptcy.

Fortunately for Small Town, the cavalry arrived in 1988. A new and energetic leader was named as the University's fifth president. The school was quickly converted into an economically sound institution of vibrant activity. Dormitories were built, and laptops were issued; admissions scores were raised and sports programs were elevated. By 2007, STU was the second largest university of its type in the region, with 5,800 students[4] enrolled on a main campus covering 65 acres. There are also satellite campuses, including two on the European continent.[5]

As the university leapt into academic success with increasing numbers of students, higher test scores for incoming students, and more rigorous academic programs in the 1990s, the Library was left behind. The budgets became very small, the collection outdated and irrelevant, the technology within the library became anachronistic, and the skills and attitudes of a fair portion of the employees were not ideal. The University realized that it was not going to achieve its strategic goals for the twenty-first century without making the library the recipient of some added attention and revised expectations.

A new and visionary University Librarian joined the staff in 2002. He outlined a unique ten-year plan that would put the Library at the forefront of academic innovation. A new organizational structure was drawn up, complete with new roles and opportunities for library staff. The plan also incorporated the sound ideas of flexibility, feedback, and accountability. The STU Board of Trustees intelligently accepted the plan, and provided the funding to ensure success.

Initially, the ten-year plan was met with a small degree of enthusiasm. Staff members were appropriately embarrassed by the appearance of the library, the archaic systems and collection within, and the general ambience of malaise. Initial phases of the plan, including some organizational changes, were accepted by the staff. These early changes were defined as "low hanging fruit" by the University Librarian, meaning that the changes were obviously and immediately needed and they involved virtually no extensions by the staff out of their zones of comfort.

By year three of the ten-year plan, the University Librarian was getting a great deal of pushback from the staff for the middle phases of change. His plans for revolutionary library services and increased community contact with librarians were being stalled by the difficult and negative attitudes and behaviors of a portion of the professional and non-exempt staff. The Circulation Desk became a rallying point for contumacious employees.

Patrons were ignored and frustrated; processes were codified, multiplied, and documented *ad nauseam*; progress was shunted; good plans and people were criticized; inter-staff fights simmered and erupted; and proper organizational processes were ignored in favor of random decisions made by ever-changing groups of librarians and staffers. Personal convenience became the benchmark for decision making, and the rolling train of progress had been stopped dead in its tracks.

The Circulation Department was run by a non-librarian supervisor when the University Librarian first arrived on the scene. When this individual ceased working at STU, the University Librarian began to supervise the department himself. He empowered the non-exempt employees who worked in the department to manage and revise circulation policies, schedules, and issues. These changes were seemingly positive, but unfortunately a portion of the staff at the time turned the lack of direct attention by administration into a negative.

By year four of the ten-year plan, a strange situation had arisen in Circulation. There were three Circulation staff members responsible for covering the desk, supervising the Student Library Assistants (SLAs), and monitoring the building. All Circulation employees had desks away from the public Circulation Desk in the private and semi-secluded Public Services area. Because the Circulation staff spent so little time at the actual desk, borrowed employees from the Interlibrary Loan, Reference and Technical Services Departments covered the desk for approximately 30–40 hours a week out of a 93.5-hour weekly schedule. SLAs were frequently left at the desk to cover additional hours by themselves.

Twenty-five to thirty SLAs were hired each year to assist with Circulation duties. Two or three students were scheduled to work at the same time, with the hopes that at least one of them would actually come into work. Since they were allowed to sign up for their own hours, there were either too many or too few students working throughout the schedule. Students were given performance evaluations at the end of each academic year but they were also given a $0.25/per hour raise simply for returning to work at the library the next year regardless of their actual performance.

While there were some self-motivated and competent students, most SLAs became products of their environment. They were used to covering the desk while their supervisors engaged in negative activities with other staffers in the public area. They also spent large amounts of time chatting with their supervisors about library gossip. Patrons were often ignored in preference to homework worked on by the SLAs, and tasks were performed incorrectly and half-heartedly.

In addition to staff issues, the technology used in the Circulation Department was also woefully inadequate. The powerful integrated library system was poorly deployed, and often malfunctioned. No part of the Circulation process was automated, with the exception of checking materials in and out, and sending notices (and this only worked partially). Date stampers were given heavy use, and handwritten notes instead of printed ones were used with abandon. Even frequently reproduced forms were copied from copies, instead of creating electronic masters to print from.

Objective

The Library's ten-year plan could not be advanced without the successful implementation of a new phase of organizational restructuring. The Circulation Department was the keystone in this revitalization, and the mission of the department needed to be refocused. Circulation was made the "tip of the spear" in the latest set of library changes. The goal was to change the attitude and performance of the staff, which included full-time, part-time, and student workers.

Methods

Proper organizational culture needs to be created and nourished by the library's leadership. The first step in Circulation's rebirth was the establishment of some departmental values[2] and a mission statement.[6] To foster this area of growth, and to provide the driving force behind the Circulation changes, the University Librarian created a new position. A Reference Librarian was assigned to work as the new Circulation Librarian, who would function as a department head going into the fifth year of the ten-year plan.

The Circulation staff anticipated this change prior to the University Librarian even producing the idea, and any potential candidates for the position of Circulation Librarian were treated poorly by a portion of the staff. As the University Librarian began to entertain the concept, he assigned Sunday Circulation Desk coverage to the eventual Circulation Librarian, as well as two major projects. The first project involved the first inventory of the circulating collection, and the second involved shifting the entire circulating collection to allocate the proper amount of space for each discipline.

The Circulation staff often fought with each other; however, in this instance, they made a collective effort to put a halt to the two new projects. Consequently, they were given heavily supervised and diminished roles in each project. Five SLAs were hired to assist with the projects that were under the direct authority of the Project Manager, and had no ties to the Circulation staff. The first two months of the projects were extremely successful, despite a great deal of staff pushback. When the University Librarian arrived in January 2006, a new leadership structure was announced. Unfortunately, some library staff members were less than enthusiastic about the announcement.

As mentioned previously, the first step in changing the culture and performance of the department was to codify a set of departmental values, which would culminate in a departmental mission statement. This process was to take about six months in total, but was hindered by the reluctance of the staff to commit to being held accountable for upholding the values. The process involved frequent individual and group meetings in conjunction with "homework" intended to get each individual's input and buy-in into the process. The mission and initial top values were presented in a training module intended for new staff and SLAs in July 2006, and are represented in brief in Figures 2.1 and 2.2.

Once the continued process of forging the mission statement and cultural values began, the second step in the process was started: changing attitudes and activity levels. It is very difficult to modify the attitude and activity level of employees.[7] Attitude in this case relates to a worker's general behavior, outlook on work and life, reaction to adversity, and flexibility. Activity level pertains to an employee's work ethic. Is their motor always running? Do

The Library **Small Town University**
The Library provides information services of many types to students, faculty, staff, and guests.
Our mission in the Circulation Department is to provide a personalized experience for any patron that enters the building, or who directly approaches us for assistance.

Figure 2.1 Circulation department mission statement

What service means
Any person who enters the library building, calls us on the phone, or enters our Web site is a patron.
A patron should be made to feel like the most important person in the world when they have contact with us.
Our building, our actions, our speech, and our attitude communicate our level of concern.

Figure 2.2 Circulation department values

they work as quickly as they can, even when it is not required? Do they look for new challenges and activities to participate in?

The transparent process of creating development plans, rewards structures, and procedures became much more difficult when the focus of those changes was placed solely on improving attitude and activity. It is easy to train people to perform a set of tasks when there is good leadership and a good trainer. Even without these conditions, most workers will eventually absorb the better portion of what is being conveyed. It is very difficult and often uncomfortable for all parties involved, however, to include behavior modification and personal development into a management program.

Typically, US Marine Corps drill instructors make statements to groups of young recruits in boot camp to the effect that, "I can't change how you've been for eighteen years in three months. If you were a punk before you joined the Corps, you may change while you are here, but you will probably go right back to being a punk after boot camp. Only a small number of you will make a positive change." This is a powerful statement, as the behavioral development of recruits is attempted in an atmosphere that is totally controlled by the instructors. If drill instructors cannot change behavior in a situation that is under their control 24 hours a day for three straight months, how can change be effected in employees during a 35- to 40-hour work week?

A combination of three concepts was utilized to attempt to change the thinking of the Circulation Department. The three concepts were: principle-based decision making, a service-based culture, and a merit-based reward structure. Only by modifying the thought process of the Circulation employees would the attitude, activity, and general performance of the department be raised to acceptable levels.

Principle-based Decision Making

To foster an atmosphere of principle-based decision making, departmental cultural values and mission were first outlined and emphasized. The next step was to physically clean out the Circulation area. Over the years, large, disorganized piles had accumulated in the drawers, shelves, and desks. In these piles were myriad policies, procedures, notes, and general instructions. Anytime an unusual issue arose, there was a clamor to develop a procedure that addressed every possible variation of the issue with an accompanying solution. Some of these procedures found their way into binders that were supposed to function as manuals. These binders were jam-packed with reams of paper, often with handwritten notes accompanying the printed instructions.

Unfortunately, when issues arose, employees either could not find the exact situation and solution in the manual, or simply ignored written procedures in favor of solutions that were personally convenient at the time. The binders, as well as the drawers, shelves, and desks, were brimming with outdated and irrelevant information. The Circulation Librarian engaged in three separate "garbage days," in which the Circulation area was ransacked and all unnecessary materials were removed.

In conjunction with the cleaning, new electronic forms were created and distributed for easier reproduction. Procedural documents gave enough information to be helpful, but they did not get into painstaking detail that would have to be repeatedly revised. The new documents were collected in a new, clearly marked, and clean binder.

When issues arose that the Circulation staff members were unsure about answering, the Circulation Librarian asked a series of questions intended to help evaluate the situation and make decisions based on the departmental values. These situations were reviewed, and the principles behind them were analyzed at bi-weekly Circulation staff meetings. Some employees were particularly challenged when they could not fall back on forms to explain their actions.

This new emphasis on a service-based culture was instituted along with the principle-based decision-making process. Too often in the past, decisions based on tradition or existing policies negatively affected library patrons.[1] Although adopting fleeting service fads and catering to every illogical whim of patrons must be avoided, the needs and wants of the patron must factor into the structure of a functioning Circulation Department.

Service-based Culture

The goal of achieving the highest level of customer service was set at the very first Circulation staff meeting in 2006. Almost anyone is capable of providing fair to good customer service. This level consists of generally being nice to patrons, knowing the basics of the job, and logically approaching problems. Fantastic customer service means working on patron wants and needs before they ask, taking care of problems before they occur, subconsciously influencing patrons by keeping work areas clean and cared for, and making each experience feel highly personalized.[1]

All patrons should be made to feel that each member of the library staff is a personal friend, and that the staff is genuinely interested in satisfying their needs. The most obvious way to build patron–staff relationships is to provide consistent staffing. Instead of having desk coverage consisting of randomly rotating shifts involving many non-Circulation staffers, the schedule was changed to provide consistency for all parties involved.

Circulation staff members were given desks directly behind the Circulation Desk, instead of the backroom out of public view. The schedule was modified a few times to keep moving toward the goal of consistent staffing. After a second Circulation member left the university, the final arrangement was arrived at. A new staff member was hired who was competent, pleasant, and willing to put service first.

Going forward, the Daytime Supervisor was tasked with opening the library five days a week, Tuesday through Saturday, and working (generally) from 8 a.m. to 4 p.m. The Evening Supervisor was scheduled to work Sunday through Thursday from 4 p.m. to 12 a.m. The Circulation Supervisor continued to cover the Sunday daytime shift. The back-up Circulation staff covered the Monday day shift and the closing shift on Fridays. Each back-up staff member was given the same two hours to cover the Circulation Desk each week. Students were only used to cover the Circulation Desk in the event of lunches, meetings, or unexpected days off. The goal of the new schedule arrangement was for patrons who kept regular schedules to see familiar faces and to get more consistent service.[1] The level of service at the Circulation Desk was also raised, as a regular staff provides more knowledgeable service. The amount of fill-in time was reduced from the aforementioned 30–40 hours down to 10 hours.

To go along with the new schedules, staff members were encouraged to have service as the primary focus when dealing with patrons. The directive was given that each patron should be greeted. Another directive instructed staffers to be proactive, and to approach and assist patrons who look confused and who had not yet asked for help. A "no pointing" law was also instituted. In the past, if a patron asked a reference question, the staff member would point toward the Reference Desk and say "go there." In accordance to the new rule, the Circulation staff member would walk the patron over to the Reference Librarian, introduce the patron to the Reference Librarian, and repeat the patron's question.

Staff members were also instructed to look at the library rules differently. For example, if a patron wanted to borrow a video for a class that would take place five days from check-out, in the past, the patron would have been told to come back later in the week to perform the transaction, as videos circulate for only three days. Under the new service-minded policy, staff members are empowered to change due dates or to make alternate arrangements for special needs. A training table used to clarify library rules is featured in Figure 2.3.

Merit-based Rewards

Even the greatest amount of personal charm usually fails to turn around employees that are headed in the wrong direction. Nevertheless, an important part of the change process is to reinforce proper behavior. Accordingly, a merit-based system of responsibility, accountability, and reward instituted in the Circulation Department. A clearly defined set of responsibilities were established in conjunction with the existing formal job description. An agreement was also drawn up between the Circulation Librarian and each Circulation employee to further emphasize expectations. These documents established a clear set of job responsibilities, which would be used for evaluative purposes (see Appendix 2.A).

Rules
Rules are there for a reason.
Do not let rules ruin good service!
Say no first.
Get a staff-member/superior.

Figure 2.3 Library rules

Based on the newly established responsibilities, Circulation employees were empowered to fulfill their duties within the confines of the departmental mission. Workers were invited to propose new ideas for better service and procedures, and to question existing policies and procedures to ensure the best possible service. In frequent feedback sessions, employees were held accountable for individual portions of the department's operational plan. Points of accountability were worked into the annual evaluation that each STU employee was given before the end of the fiscal year.

In years past, an automatic percentage of an employee's salary was granted as a "merit" raise. The process failed to acknowledge any merit as everyone was given equivalent raises. But now Circulation staff evaluations were directly connected to the departmental goals and values, and a critical eye was used to score each employee's progress. With the cooperation of the rest of the library administration and department heads, a system-wide standard for leveled raises allowed the new process to reward true merit.

A system that focuses attention on those who underperform, those who simply do their jobs, and those who overachieve puts a great deal of pressure on the underperforming employees.[8] This pressure was intended to be relieved by a formal training and development program, which provided the double benefit of keeping good employees engaged and interested. A continuous series of training classes were developed to provide formal, consistent education in important areas such as systems usage and advanced customer service.

At the end of the evaluation process, each employee was assigned one major issue to work on for the next year. Specialized training sessions were developed to assist the employees in developing a skill or addressing a weakness. Typical sessions included "The Millennial Generation and Their Social Technology," and "The Triumphs and Tribulations of Returning to the Full-Time Work Force."

Over time, each Circulation worker was assisted in developing future career interests that could be facilitated by prior training. The environment of open and honest communication allowed employees to be vocal about their wants and needs, and for the library to be prepared to assist them in their new internal positions or to recover from their departure.[9] Special attention is paid in this area to the library's overall strategic and operational plans.

A similar pattern of deconstructing old vices and building new virtues was implemented with the SLAs. Each shift was limited to one student worker. The schedules were set by the Circulation Librarian in conjunction with Circulation Assistants. The level of expectations was raised to that of full-time employees in the areas of attendance, responsibility, and attitude.

Students were placed into a four-grade pay structure. Each higher grade paid $0.50 per hour more than the last. Students were given the opportunity to learn about their jobs and the quality of their work by having an increased number of evaluative sessions with their supervisors. Instead of getting one formal evaluation at the end of the year, students were given one informal verbal evaluation in the middle of each semester, and one formal written evaluation at the end of each semester. They were given the incentive of mid-year promotion, which enticed meritorious students to work harder in each individual semester because of the more timely reinforcement that was provided (see Appendix 2.B).

The students were also placed on a perpetual ranking list, which rated them for attitude and capabilities. Before the beginning of each semester, students could choose special projects and work schedules based on these rankings. For example, the highest ranking student chose first, then the second, and so forth down the list. This added benefit placed a non-monetary reward for their performance, which is important as studies have shown that money is not the only effective motivator.[10]

The students were also given more consistent and comprehensive training. A department-wide training class was held for the SLAs at the beginning of the fall semester, which is the time of the largest influx of new employees. The meetings provided the opportunity for mass training for the Circulation basics, as well the opportunity to form bonds with fellow workers and staff members. The rest of the SLA training was conducted by the Circulation Assistants, who train, test, and retest students in all of the different areas of their jobs. A form was developed to keep track of each student's progress.

Students were given job descriptions, a specialized library policy to sign, and a security compliance statement, also to be signed, which drew their attention to the importance of patron privacy. Each form was reviewed with the SLAs at the beginning of their term of employment, and was later reinforced during the duration of their positions at the Library. A copy of the SLA training schedule is featured in Appendix 2.C.

Happy workers make effective workers, and an effort was made to tie in the concept of having "fun" in the workplace to the new departmental culture.[11] A great deal of time is spent at work, and while a place of employment is not supposed to be constantly entertaining, it can be made more interesting and invigorating. Non-exempt employees were allowed to put personal touches into their positions. For example, one Circulation Assistant began decorating the desk for each holiday.

An effort was also made to engage the SLAs in some fun activities. A student rewards committee was founded to give a student of the month award. The award is ongoing, and during five months of the school year, an SLA is rewarded for meritorious service to the library with a $25 gift certificate to a local entertainment store. At the end of the year a student of the year is chosen and given a $100 gift certificate and a framed certificate of merit.

Prizes were also awarded for participating in an SLA Halloween contest. The most impressive costume was judged by the Circulation staff and awarded a $25 gift certificate to the University's bookstore. In a further effort to bring fun into the workplace, SLAs were given specialized nametags. In the past, students griped and grumbled about their simple nametags listing their first name and last initial. In the new structure, after their first year they are awarded a new nametag with a staff-assigned nickname at the fall SLA meeting. One example is the nickname "Dusty," assigned to an inventory student of the previous year because of the large amount of dust disturbed by the process.

Other Changes

To support the new attitude and way of thinking in the Circulation Department, technology upgrades were implemented. Magnetic strip readers were purchased to allow the swiping of student identification cards to bring up their records. Receipt printers were obtained allowing for the elimination of the process of stamping due date cards. The integrated library system was revamped to be more efficient, more secure, and to function properly in all areas. The Circulation Desk computers were also rearranged (and one was replaced) to present a cleaner appearance and a better workspace.

The recruiting process was also changed within the department. Traditionally, Circulation employees were hired by a large committee of library staff from across the organization. Emphasis was placed on prior experience and existing library skills. In the new system, the Circulation Librarian conducted the interviews, and enlisted the help of a few selected managers and staff to add their opinions to the decision. Attention was then focused on the candidate's attitude and activity level.

Finally, more attention was paid to the security of patron information. Each employee who worked at Circulation at any point, including the Reference Librarians who only infrequently backed up the desk, was directed to sign a university-approved patron confidentiality form. A shredder was placed under the desk for immediate destruction of unneeded personal information. Training sessions were also conducted to teach staff about being conscious of protecting patron privacy, such as closing open records on the computer, and not leaving patron information on the Circulation Desk where it could be viewed by other patrons.

Results

Although some employees decided to leave the library due to the new level of expectations, fantastic replacement staff members were hired through a revamped hiring process. The department flourished. The integrated library system was modified to provide maximum functionality. All Circulation policies and procedures were examined and revised to emphasize personalized customer service, individualized accountability and responsibility, and having fun in the workplace. New training programs and materials were created to suit departmental and individual needs in order to meet annual developmental goals.

The Circulation Desk and areas under its responsibility looked neater and services were easier for patrons to use. Circulation became a center of positive thought and discussion, a place of new ideas and action. Problems with patrons decreased substantially, and the new attitude of positive helpfulness was returned by the patrons with patience and appreciativeness. The quality of the SLA workforce increased dramatically. Students became motivated, happy, and energized. It was not difficult to keep them busy given the rapid pace of work.

The concepts of a mission statement and cultural values have resonated with the staff, and not a single meeting goes by without the mission or values being referenced. Increasingly, Circulation staffers have made difficult decisions based on departmental values and the idea of service first. The merit-based system has encouraged the staff to set realistic goals, and to fervently work toward them. A healthy level of competition has arisen in the minds of the SLAs and regular staffers; they compete with each other to win prizes, more responsibilities, and praise. The members of the department also view themselves as an elite unit, serving as an example to other library departments for what a motivated group can accomplish.

SLAs have commented on the changes:

> So this is what a real job is like ... The staff is nicer and more willing to help both patrons as well as other staff members in any way they can ... I don't hate coming to work anymore.

Patrons have also shared their feelings:

> The staff is so nice and very helpful ... The stacks look incredible ... I feel like I am welcome to ask questions now, whereas before I always felt like I was interrupting.

Communication is now carried out through the proper channels, and the appropriate hierarchy is followed when making decisions. Circulation staff members feel valued and comfortable, as the system of frequent meetings, both individually and as a group, and frequent feedback sessions have allowed them to be better informed about their situation and surrounding environment. They are also very pleased to be able to individualize their developmental plans to accomplish long-term goals. Since staff members no longer feel threatened by the success of others, they now cooperate with each other, share ideas, and give compliments. They are also more mindful of departmental confidentiality and the importance of protecting the personal information of patrons.

The strategy of revitalizing ways of thinking along with equipment and procedures has led to a visible improvement in patron relations. Circulation statistics increased by 18 percent compared to the previous year. Some months posted statistical increases of over 40 percent. During the same time, the library headcount increased by just a few percentage points.

Non-vacation-related time off has also decreased considerably. Employees are amenable to attending events and meetings outside of their normal schedules, even when these events are unpaid. Most importantly, the Circulation Desk is now a magnet for positive attitudes and efficiency. Students and staff all look forward to new challenges, new learning opportunities, and new chances to serve patrons.

Conclusion

A strong development plan is needed to restructure a bad situation. This plan must include organizational restructuring, strong leadership, principle-based decision making, a mission statement, cultural values, patience, and some luck. Major changes can be accomplished in short periods of time, even in a slow-moving academic climate. To accomplish changes of this magnitude, the support of the library administration, other department heads, and the university is needed. The most rapid way, and realistically the only way, of remedying a bad situation is through intensive staff development.

Librarians and library staff are very special people. In general, they love to help others, to contribute, and to progress in their professional development. It is important not to let people with negative attitudes ruin the opportunity to achieve world-class service, especially in such an important area like Circulation. The behavior and thought processes of the Circulation staff are the most important issues to address in attempting to achieve great things.

References

1. Woodward, Jeannette. *Creating the Customer-Driven Library: Building on the Bookstore Model*. Chicago: American Library Association, 2005.
2. Gorman, Michael. *Our Enduring Values: Librarianship in the 21st Century*. Chicago: American Library Association, 2000.
3. Clish, Herbert C. *Small Town University History*. c. 1973.
4. Division of Institutional Advancement, *Small Town University. 2006 Annual Report*.
5. Office of Institutional Research, Small Town University. Fact Sheet – Small Town University – Fall 2006 (October 2006).
6. Toftoy, Charles N., and Chatterjee, Joydeep. "Mission Statements and the Small Business." *Business Strategy Review* 15 (Fall 2004): 41–44.
7. Nicholson, Nigel. "How to Motivate Your Problem People." *Harvard Business Review* 81 (January 2003): 57–65.
8. Walker, Alice G. "Is Performance Management as Simple as ABC." *T+D 61* (February 2007): 54–57.
9. Crawford, Dough. "How to … Inspire Your Staff." *People Management* 12 (May 18, 2006): 46–47.
10. Walters, Suzanne. *Customer Service*. New York: Neal-Schuman Publishers, 1994.
11. Lundin, Stephen C., Paul, Harry, and Christensen, John. *Fish!* New York: Hyperion, 2000.

Appendix 2.A: Circulation Assistant Agreement

The following agreement outlines the expectations that the Circulation Librarian and the Circulation Assistant (Daytime Supervisor) have for each other during the course of employment under the current situation.

CA expects from CL:

- A clear job description
- The resources required to perform her duties
- To be paid
- To be held accountable
- To have an experience that is equivalent to the first step of learning in a long library career
- To be trained.

CL expects from CA:

- To perform your duties as directed
- To be honest
- To expect frequent feedback
- To be held accountable
- To expect scheduled evaluation
- To be confident that you will be heard
- To expect training and development
- To be patient.

Circulation Assistant... Date ....
Circulation Librarian.. Date ....

Appendix 2.B: Student Evaluation Form

(Student)

Department:... Supervisor: ....
Semester:... Evaluation Date:.......................

Rating Guide:

1 = Excellent
2 = Good
3 = Satisfactory
4 = Unsatisfactory
NA = Not Applicable

Please rate your student in the following areas using the rating guide above.

1   Performance of general Circulation duties:
2   Performance of individual duties on permanent assignment:
3   General attitude:
4   Customer service:
5   Punctuality:

Current Rank:

Recommended Rank for the Following Semester and Reason:

Comments (on back):

Student... Date ....
Supervisor .... Date ....
Circulation Librarian.. Date ....

Appendix 2.C: Student Library Assistant Training Program

The purpose of this program is to ensure that all SLAs are well versed in all of the library functions that they are responsible for.

	Initial Training:	Tested:	Retested:
Customer Service:			
Greeting patrons			
Attitude			
Nametags			
At the Desk:			
Answering the phone			
Borrowing policies			
Checking materials in			
Checking materials out			
Renewals			
Holds			
Recalls			
Alarms			
Reference questions			
Copies/printing			
Fines			
Receipts			
Office supplies			
Reserves			
Enterprise			
Interlibrary Loan			
Assisting patrons			
Locating staff			
Equipment:			
Cash register			
Computers			
Receipt printers			
Printers			
Copy machines			
Microfilm machines			

Continued...

	Initial Training:	*Tested:*	*Retested:*
DVD player			
VCRs			
CD players			
Away from the Desk:			
Library layout			
Sweeps			
Patron count			
Count use			
Mail			
Slashing			
Recycling			
Overdue notices			
Inventory			
Handling books			
Shelving materials			
Shelf-reading			
Facing			
Policies:			
Lost and found			
Guests			
Food and drink			
Emergencies			
Opening and Closing:			
Gate count			
Newspapers			

3 Library Techno Day at College of St. Catherine Libraries

James M. Newsome and Carol P. Johnson

Introduction

Staff development has never been more important in libraries than it is today. Change is rapid and new technologies with potential library applications appear constantly. User expectations grow as new formats for information transfer occur and competition from other information providers gives library users a variety of options. These customers expect libraries and their staffs to provide up-to-the-minute service, using the latest technologies. In today's information marketplace, libraries must move quickly to understand the new technologies as they become available. When they are relevant and cost-effective, librarians must learn their usage and implement them. To do this, library staff must be made aware of new products and services and how they work in a practical sense. At the same time, library personnel need to know where the future of technology is heading. Continuing education becomes essential for this learning process.

Yet many smaller libraries do not have the budget to send their employees to expensive training programs or national conferences.

This case study offers an example of how one smaller academic institution and its libraries addressed these issues by creating an on-site "Library Techno Day." This annual program provides opportunities for staff to learn and develop technological skills and understanding. By employing local talent and developing expertise from within this event also fosters presentation and training skills for a variety of staff members. Younger staff members are encouraged to become technology experts, and many do.

Setting

The College of St. Catherine is a small academic institution in the Twin Cities of Minneapolis and Saint Paul, Minnesota. It has two campuses, each with its own library. Founded as a liberal arts college, the larger St. Paul campus offers undergraduate programs for women, while the Minneapolis campus offers associate-degree and certificate programs in health care and human services. Both campuses offer graduate programs for women and men. Ten librarians, four administrative staff, and eight support personnel (including Media Services and Archives positions) staff the College of St. Catherine libraries. Together they serve 5,000 students, 256 faculty, and a comparable number of staff. The libraries are members of a library consortium of eight academic institutions in St. Paul and Minneapolis. This organization, the Cooperating Libraries in Consortium (CLIC), shares an online library system and provides twice daily delivery of library materials among members.

The St. Catherine Libraries' staff development budget for off-site workshops and training opportunities is modest, although faculty librarians do have access to faculty development funds. The libraries are not large enough to afford on-site professional training staff, or to develop and maintain a defined staff development program. Participation in state and national professional association activities is encouraged whenever possible. Many staff give presentations or participate in panels or poster sessions at these conferences. As members of the CLIC consortium, staff also participate in planning for system upgrades, and devote time to learning the new software features of a dynamic integrated library system.

The Problem

How does a small academic library maintain its edge with new software and research tools? How can it improve staff understanding of developments and trends that are likely to be important in the future? How does it create a way for younger staff to develop expertise and presentation skills? And how does it provide staff with opportunities for innovation and empowerment within the organization?

Staff Involvement in Continuing Education

As is true in many libraries, the majority of the librarians and staff at the College of St. Catherine Libraries can be characterized as in mid or late career stages, and, in recent years, turnover has been minimal. The few younger librarians and staff want opportunities for professional growth and the chance to influence and affect policy. Since they are technologically adept, it is in the libraries' interest to create a setting that allows these newer library workers ways to contribute their expertise. Younger staff are much more likely to be familiar with and use innovative technologies including social networking services, course management software, etc. They are very comfortable with the shift to electronic formats for library resources and services. This is not always true of the more experienced staff.

History of Continuing Education Opportunities for College of St. Catherine Staff

Over the past two decades, continuing education at the College of St. Catherine Libraries was deemed essential, but opportunities occurred in a piecemeal manner. Some librarians attended national conferences. Others made use of workshops in the local metropolitan area. The state library association's annual conference contained a mixture of programs, many dealing with management issues. The state's library resource-sharing network, MINITEX, sponsored continuing education opportunities that brought national speakers to Minnesota for broad speculative views of the library future. These were all useful, but, unfortunately, not all staff could attend these events. Many could not find affordable continuing education opportunities outside the library that both inspired and empowered them in their work. Often, presenters at state-wide workshops did not offer the topics most desired by library staff.

Internally, the library had also long made efforts at continuing education. Monthly library staff meetings sometimes included a guest expert, usually someone from another on-campus service or department. Examples included directors of Computing Services, Campus Security, the Tutoring Center, and Counseling Services. These presentations tended to be FYI (For Your Information) sessions designed to help library workers know what others on campus did. Sessions were usually productive, opening dialogue between the library and other departments. There was usually a discussion as to how cooperation and referral might be enhanced with each speaker's department. Though the guests were interesting and outcomes positive, actual discussion at the meetings tended to be dominated by senior members of the library's staff. Younger library employees usually took a back seat.

The library's Public Services Department also sponsored reference update seminars. Each month an individual St. Catherine librarian would take a turn updating people on developments in the presenter's area of concentration or expertise. As a typical example, the Music Librarian taught a session on strategies for doing Music Research. Over time, several concerns arose with this method. First, it was difficult to find a time each month for such updates. A choice often had to be made between interruptions in reference service versus leaving one Reference Librarian at the desk to miss a session. Library staff from the smaller Minneapolis campus library often could not attend because of tight staffing needs there. Also, these training opportunities, like the other library staff meetings mentioned above, tended to be dominated by senior librarians with the most collection development and reference experience, with little opportunity for newer staff or non-professional staff to contribute at a significant level. It was a top-down situation in most cases. Moreover, each monthly topic was almost always related to reference collections and materials, and was usually of little interest to staff beyond those doing reference. At busy times of the semester, the updates were often postponed as Public Services Librarians became busy with library instruction, meetings, and other necessary activities. By fall 2005, a number of staff at the library increasingly felt that a new way of doing continuing education was necessary.

Outside Trends Affecting the Library

At the same time new technologies were affecting the workings of libraries and their staffs. These technological innovations created enhanced means for information transfer. The transformation of print resources into networked electronic information continued. Besides new databases, federated search services, and electronic versions of texts, a whole new range of telecommunication methods was emerging. These included wikis and blogs, PowerPoint presentations, classroom management software like Blackboard, MySpace, Facebook, and so on. Traditional library vendors increasingly offered new technological add-ons to standard library products. Talk began of Library 2.0 and Web 2.0.[1] In academic libraries, Millennial or NextGen students brought new information-seeking behavior to the research process.[2, 3]

In this context, staff realized that the continuing education milieu within the Libraries needed to change. The old methods used for continuing education seemed insufficient to meet the training challenges related to the constant emergence of new technologies. The responsibility to serve an emerging generation of students, who were increasingly more native to the technologies than most library staff (especially the older members) needed to be addressed.

Literature Review

The library literature contains a large body of research on library staff development. Two sub-themes resonate on this topic: 1) adult education theory (the study of the characteristics of the adult learner and the setting in which learning occurs), and 2) current research on generational differences as they affect the workplace and libraries.

Adult Education Theory

Malcolm Knowles, one of adult education theory's most important thinkers, is cited frequently in the research on staff development. Knowles characterized adult learners as self-directed, with experience in a number of work and life roles that they bring to the learning experience. They are motivated to learn when the experience is of a practical or useful nature that can improve their performance or solve a problem.[4] Knowles also noted that important elements for learning include establishing an optimal "climate setting" that includes mutual respect and trust, collaboration, supportiveness, openness and authenticity, pleasure and humanness.[5] Those experienced in creating and providing staff development programs in libraries encourage the creation of environments that promote continuous learning and the development of systems to ensure continuous learning.[6] They advocate active engagement for adult learners in activities such as "spotting" the future and thinking systematically beyond boundaries.[7, 8]

Generational Differences

The second issue, generational differences, has been a feature of library literature for about ten years. The research on generational differences between the "boomers" and successor generations, and the demographic shifts that will affect libraries in the future provides interesting reading. Whether library staff belong to or identify with the "NextGen," "Millennial," or "Gen Y" generation (born 1977–1994), or the latter part of "Gen X" (born 1965–1976), it is apparent that younger librarians bring talents and skills that libraries will need as their elders retire in the next twenty years.[9] Rachel Singer Gordon regularly contributes to a column titled NextGen in *Library Journal*. Gordon's "In Our Own Words" acknowledges the creativity and energy of the "NextGens" and their wish to be given opportunities to learn and contribute.[10] Gordon encourages libraries, in their own self-interest, to recognize the importance of this generation to their future. With their talents and skills, they will be important players in the future transformation of the profession.[11] In another article, she warns that libraries need to mentor and encourage younger librarians. Libraries will need to cultivate their skills and enthusiasm as they become the next generation of library managers. Libraries must therefore provide creative opportunities for their learning and development.[12]

For "NextGens," computers have always been a part of their lives. Meredith Farkas writes about this generation's comfort with technology and online socializing. They are "constantly connected to and immersed in it."[13] These are the librarians who will successfully integrate new and future social networking software into library services. Farkas advocates viewing mentoring as a two-way activity, providing opportunities for both the younger and the older librarian to learn from each other.[14] Carolyn Wiethoff writes about managing "Gen X" staff, and also comments on their ease and comfort with technology. She advocates that managers find ways to tap into the Gen X and Y creativity, creating a climate that welcomes them and values their contributions.[15]

While a library may not be large enough to design, support, and run a formal staff development program, it can use the insights from adult education research and the research on generational differences to create a climate that supports adult learners in the workplace. The College of

St. Catherine's Library Techno Day, as it has been developed, provides such an environment: a setting for librarians and staff to share their skills and talents, while developing new ones. For all staff, new software and technologies are presented at the point of "need to know." Creativity and a willingness to experiment have been the result. The following section describes the history, logistics, and content of the first two Library Techno Day events.

The Solution: Library Techno Day

Developing a Rationale

In September 2005, the St. Catherine Public Services Librarians met to plan their traditional continuing education monthly sessions for the 2005–2006 academic year. It quickly became apparent to all present that the program of monthly reference updates had become cumbersome, and no longer adequately addressed the needs of the broader library staff. As one librarian argued, in order to inject new life into an increasingly tiresome mode of continuing education, something different was needed. The first decision made at the planning meeting was to eliminate the monthly sessions, replacing them with a more carefully planned once-a-year event.

Several reasons were given for replacing the monthly sessions with a special day. Primarily, the event could happen during a quieter part of the academic year. January was selected since the College operates with a significantly reduced teaching schedule during that month. January is also when many students study abroad or work on special projects off campus. With library usage significantly lower in January than during the rest of the year, scheduling a continuing education day then would be less disruptive to library service. All library staff could attend at least portions of the day's activities. If scheduled carefully, a day-long January event would also be easier for Minneapolis-campus library staff to attend. Planning the event for later in the year also allowed more lead time for session preparation. The general consensus was that a superior experience would be had by everyone involved if there were one event scheduled for later in the year.

Topic Selection: Technology

The second group task was to decide which topics to cover. Almost immediately, the Public Services staff agreed that emerging new technologies would be the ideal subject matter on which to focus. One Reference Librarian coined the phrase Library Technology Day, quickly shortened to Library Techno Day. Another decision rapidly reached was to take the event beyond public services. Involvement would include all library staff, not just as audience, but in the planning and presenting as well. A check with the Library Director revealed she was completely behind the idea, although she noted that as the budget year had already begun in June, there was nothing budgeted for the event or for bringing in an outside keynote speaker or paid expert. It soon became apparent that the library staff, especially the younger members, were eager to participate and further develop their expertise. In addition, a cornucopia of librarians existed at nearby libraries with a consortial tradition of sharing experiences and skills. And with a library science program on campus, the two campus libraries could find or create plenty of experts locally upon which to draw for program content. The lack of budget became irrelevant.

The First Library Techno Day

The Head of Public Services was selected to organize the Library Techno Day. In early October, he distributed an e-mail message to all library staff soliciting their ideas for specific technology topics of interest, as well as sessions they might want to lead or to which they might contribute. Soon, several responses helped set the tone for the workshop. One responder remarked that it would sure be great fun if some of the sessions were futuristic and imaginative. Another volunteered to lead a very practical session on instant messaging (IM) training for the soon-to-be inaugurated reference IM service. Another person suggested that sessions be about an hour long, and that staff be allowed to pick and choose which ones they would attend. The Library Director realized that a new digitization project two members of the library staff were developing was not well known to the rest of the staff. One of the digitizers was extremely new to the process, while the other had been involved early on with the Minnesota Digital Library Coalition. They were asked to co-present a current awareness update on their project.

After this initial flurry of responses, the rest of the input for the program was received piecemeal. Informal discussions during breaks and lunches led to one librarian volunteering to demonstrate some of the untapped possibilities for a library presence on Blackboard, the course management software used by the college. The library's administrative assistant later suggested that someone speak in a fun way about the "communication tools of the future" such as wikis, blogs, and RSS feeds. The young technology assistant in the Library Science Department immediately came to mind as a potential presenter. The Head of Public Services wanted to recruit someone from the college's Instructional Technology Department to teach ways of improving PowerPoint presentations. He also hoped to use the session as a bridge for developing closer ties with that department. The final segment of the day's content emerged after one librarian attended a meeting at another library where she heard enthusiastic reports about federated searching. While some meeting attendees expressed skepticism about the dangers of "Googlizing" the library search process, she thought a demo by an enthusiastic proponent of federated searching, followed by a frank discussion of its implications, would be exciting. The discussion might help set directions for the libraries' future in the information retrieval area.

Once the topics were agreed upon, the day was organized with the first presentation being Instant Message Reference Training, a topic not germane to all. Since not all staff needed to attend this session, scheduling it earlier in the day allowed those not interested to arrive later. A long lunch period was set aside to allow leisure time for reflection and networking about the morning's sessions.

The library's instruction classroom was chosen as the site for the day's activities. This room contained ample computers for hands-on training. Most Library Techno Day sessions allowed participants to practice or follow along on PCs. For example, the PowerPoint audience was able to create pages "on the fly" following the lead of the IT presenter. Her presentation was augmented by that of a young library staff member, who showed PowerPoint slides created for student employee training. These slides incorporated catchy music, sound effects, and a wide variety of humorous graphics.

Once the day's content and presenters were set, the Head of Public Services decided to treat presenters as speakers at a conference, soliciting biographical sketches for the introductions to each session and its speakers. In addition, a sign-up sheet for each session was created to determine numbers of attendees so that room demographics and an ample number of handouts could be determined ahead of time. See Appendix 3.A for the agenda that was distributed about ten days before the event (note: names of presenters have been removed).

On January 19, 2006 the big day arrived. Each session went well, with an average of about a dozen audience members. Most staff from both campuses attended at least a couple of presentations, and some attended all. Several times during the day the Head of Public Services was told that this should be an annual event. Though no formal evaluation form was distributed, anecdotal evidence was overwhelmingly positive for the day, and for each of the sessions. People appreciated the hands-on opportunities, as well as the excitement of a new event. Planning for a second Library Techno Day was set for the following September, although at a general staff meeting held in the spring, staff were encouraged to begin thinking of sessions they might like to do, and emerging technologies that might lend themselves well to group exploration.

The Second Annual Library Techno Day

A Second Annual Library Techno Day planning meeting was held in September 2006. At this brainstorming session, several new ideas emerged. One brainstormer suggested that the best sessions from the past year be repeated. However, it was decided that this would shrink the potential audience at those sessions to the small number of staff who had not attended previously. It would also cut into the number of new sessions possible. So the idea was withdrawn. A second idea was to make use of the local population of library science graduate students. This was met with enthusiasm, and several talented students were mentioned as possible speakers or demonstrators. Another librarian suggested including a keynote presentation focusing on a broader view of technology. The college's Assistant Director of Academic Computing was known to have spoken to a group of alumnae about "technology and the future of higher education." Reports had reached the Techno Day planners that she was a great speaker, with many fascinating insights into future technology scenarios. She was immediately contacted and agreed to modify the presentation for a library audience. The Head of Public Services asked whether planners had included all potential groups in the demographics of the presenter pool. At this point, the Access Services Librarian suggested that one of the more knowledgeable student employees would be a good choice, if one could be found who "knew something useful or innovative about technology." One student was identified who seemed well versed in social networking software such as Facebook and MySpace.

As the fall semester moved forward, a date was chosen. For the first Techno Day, January had been picked as the quietest month for in-person library traffic. Further analysis of gate traffic and reference desk transactions revealed that the last Friday of January 2006 had the fewest reference transactions and on-site patrons of any weekday of that month. Assuming the same pattern would again hold true, the last Friday of January was chosen for Library Techno Day Two. A general call for more proposals went out to the library staff. At the same time, informal recruiting began within the Library Science Department for students who had done worthwhile technology projects and would be willing to speak about them.

Gradually, proposals came to the Head of Public Services for a variety of presentations. All were deemed appropriate, and enough were received to fill the day with a balanced selection. The program was to start with a practical hands-on introduction to the new College Portal, and especially to the libraries' channel on it. The next presentation scheduled was the student expert on Facebook and MySpace, working in tandem with the newest librarian. Together they would lead the audience through a discussion of how the library could best use either, both, or neither of the services. The keynote speaker on the technology future would follow. After lunch, the afternoon would be devoted to presentations by library science students, in a section of the day called MLIS (Master of Library and Information Science) Student Technology Showcase. Two students were chosen to demonstrate Flickr and del.icio.us, and to moderate

Table 3.1. Technology topics explored

Library Techno Day	Instant Messaging
	Digitization projects update
	Library presence on Blackboard
	Communication tools – wikis, blogs, RSS
	Improving PowerPoints
	Federated Searching
2nd Annual Library Techno Day	Future of Academic Computing & Higher Education
	Facebook & MySpace
	Folksonomies – Flickr, del.icio.us
	College Portal & Libraries' Channel
	Media Site Software for Research Instruction

a conversation on their library implications. Two more students would teach how they created library instruction sessions using software called Media Site.

As in the previous year, the room with hands-on computer capabilities was reserved. Appendix 3.B duplicates the agenda for the day (names of presenters removed). As with the first year's event, the day was "glitch free." Speakers showed up prepared and on time; an enthusiastic audience appeared; and the technology functioned as advertised. The Head of Public Services introduced the presenters and kept the day moving as scheduled.

Several weeks later at a general staff meeting feedback was solicited from attendees. Again it was highly positive of the format, location, topics, and presenters. It was proposed that the event become a regular part of the library year, and continue to be organized by the Head of Public Services for the foreseeable future. See Table 3.1 for a list of technology topics explored on the two events.

Results

Library Techno Days Helped Mediate Change

For the College of St. Catherine, Library Techno Days have been opportunities for library employees to learn about new technologies in a non-threatening collegial environment. As a result of the first Library Techno Day, library staff who received hands-on training on advanced PowerPoint techniques quickly used newly learned skills as they developed presentations of their own. The sessions on direct linking of articles from subscription databases into classroom management software caused several attendees to adopt the practice, once they saw the process demonstrated. Instant messaging became a regular part of reference following that training segment.

The session on federated searching was an introduction to the concept for many in attendance. It rapidly became a high priority, resulting in the purchase of a federated searching option for eighty online databases. This service is now available to the academic community. Although the library did not adopt an official blog or wiki, the technology was explored and several staff members helped create blogs or wikis outside of the library.

With the second Library Techno Day it is too early to see how all the technologies will be adapted to the St. Catherine Libraries' setting. However, the portal is already live for some members of the college's community. Interestingly, it has been the consensus of the staff in attendance that at this time, neither MySpace nor Facebook would justify large amounts of staff time in developing a major presence there. However, St. Catherine Libraries did develop a basic profile on MySpace, <http://www.myspace.com/stkateslibrary>, as part of its general marketing and outreach to undergraduates. The presentation on the future of technology in higher education was deemed useful and great fun, and the presenter went on to be the keynote speaker for the local library consortium's annual meeting. Several younger library staff have since come forward with innovative ideas for future topics, and for new technology innovations in the library. At staff meetings there is now more input from NextGen and Gen X staff members, for whom Library Techno Days have been a way to gain experience, confidence, and expertise.

Conclusion

In summary, Library Techno Day has accomplished its goals. It does provide an improved way of delivering staff development, as well as helping the library's workforce better envision the possibilities of many emerging technologies. Just as importantly, it opens the door for newer and younger staff to develop expertise and share it with the more entrenched library employees; this annual technological gathering works as a method of staff development and training. It also creates a stronger community while solving the logistical problems of older continuing education methods. Though it cannot totally replace all other in-house staff development, and while staff participation at external workshops and conferences will always be strongly encouraged, Library Techno Day is now the centerpiece for staff education and renewal in the College of St. Catherine Libraries.

References

1. Stephens, Michael. *Web 2.0 & Libraries: Best Practices for Social Software.* Chicago: ALA SoftTech, 2006.

2. Howe, Neil. *Millennials Rising: The Next Great Generation.* New York: Vintage, 2000.

3. Tapscott, Don. *Growing Up Digital: The Rise of the Net Generation.* New York: McGraw-Hill, 1998.

4. Knowles, Malcolm. *Andragogy in Action: Applying Modern Principles of Adult Learning.* San Francisco: Jossey-Bass Publishers, 1984.

5. Deiss, Kathryn J. "Introduction to Staff Development." In *Staff Development: A Practical Guide* 3rd ed. Edited by Elizabeth Fuseler Avery, Terry Dahlin, and Deborah A. Carver. Chicago: American Library Association, 2001.

6. New Strategist Editors. *Millennials: Americans Born 1977–1994.* Ithaca, NY: New Strategist Publications, 3rd ed., 2006.

7. New Strategist Editors. *Generation X: Americans Born 1965 to 1976.* Ithaca, NY: New Strategist Publications, 5th ed., 2006.

8. Gordon, Rachel Singer. "In Our Own Words." *Library Journal* 129, no.19 (November 15, 2004): 38.

9. Gordon, Rachel Singer. "Secure Our Professional Future." *Library Journal* 131, no. 3 (February 15, 2006): 50.

10. Farkas, Meredith. "Balancing the Online Life." *American Libraries* 38, no. 1 (January 2007): 43-45.

11. Wiethff, Carolyn. "Management Basics: Managing Generation X." *Indiana Libraries* 23, no. 2 (2004). Available: <http://vnweb.hwwilsonweb.com/>. Accessed: March 28, 2007.

Appendix 3.A: Library Techno Day Agenda

Library Techno Day, January 19, 2006.
St. Paul Campus Library, Room 110.

Agenda

8:45–9:30 a.m.
Instant Messaging (IM) Training – For those who will be working evenings or weekends at the reference desk. Library staff (Note: Others may attend, but this is really a pre-conference for those doing IM at the desk).

9:30–10:30 a.m.
Jazzing UP Your PowerPoint Presentations – Improve PowerPoint presentations with better graphic design, animation, sound, incorporation of screen captures, and much more. Computing Services and Library staff.

10:30–10:45 a.m.
Break

10:45–11:45 a.m.
Digitization at the CSC Libraries and Archives – What's going on, and plans for the future. Library staff.

11:45 a.m–1 p.m.
Lunch on your own

1–2 p.m.
Federated Searching – What is it? Should we do it? How do we do it? Outside Library expert and Library staff.

2–2:15 p.m.
Break

2:15–3:15 p.m.
Blogs, RSS Feeds, and Wikis – Communication tools of the future are here now. MLIS Dept. Instructional Technology Expert.

3:20–4:20 p.m
Incorporating Direct Links to Articles from our Subscription Databases into Blackboard – A great leap forward for a library presence on Blackboard.

Library staff:
Important Note: Different people will be interested in different sessions. To help presenters plan their sessions, please RSVP to the Head of Public Services by the end of the day on Tuesday, January 17 as to which sessions you plan to attend. Just list the numbers of the sessions, 1-6 above. Thanks in advance.

Appendix 3.B: Second Library Techno Day Agenda

2nd Annual Library Technology Day, Friday, January 26, 2007.
CSC St. Paul Campus Library, Room 110.

Agenda

8:50–9:45 a.m.
Kateway and College Portal Training (hands-on) — Library staff lead us into the brave new portal world.

9:50–10:35 a.m.
Social Networking Software Playoffs: MySpace vs. Facebook – a demo and discussion. – Library staff and student presenter.

10:35–11:00 a.m.
Break

11:00 a.m.–Noon
Technology and the Future of Higher Education – Assistant Director of Academic Computing gazes into her electronic crystal ball, and offers her vision of future technology trends in higher education.

12:00–1:30 p.m. Break For Lunch
MLIS Student Technology Showcase

1:30–2:30 p.m.
Folksonomies R Us.
Demo and discussion of Flickr and del.icio.us websites that allow users to organize photographs and other information (with implications for libraries) — Two MLIS student presenters (invited) share personal experiences with folksonomies.

2:35–3:30 p.m.
Media Site
Demo and discussion
Two MLIS students lead a discussion of how they used Media Site software to create training web casts for RefWorks and CLICnet.

4 Formalizing Staff Development from Inception to Implementation at University of Central Florida Libraries

Cynthia M. Kisby and Suzanne E. Holler

Introduction

This case study traces the formalization of staff development activities at a large public university library. While every organization offers some variety of training to meet its needs, the degree of formal structure can vary greatly. The arrival of a new Director of Libraries brought this function and others into the spotlight by creating task forces charged with examining needs and outcomes. This case study examines one library's staff development structure with a long lens, since available historical documents allow reporting of events prior to, during, and subsequent to the work of the task force—from inception to implementation and beyond.

Setting

The University of Central Florida Libraries (UCFL) is a system that supports a rapidly growing metropolitan university in a region with a population exceeding two million. The 1,445-acre campus is located thirteen miles northeast of downtown Orlando. UCFL includes a Curriculum Materials Center on campus, a subject-specific library focused on hospitality materials located near the Disney attractions, and several joint-use libraries around the state. The main library, housed in a 200,000 square foot facility, has a collection of 1.6 million volumes, 16,000 serial subscriptions, 7,400 electronic journals, and is a partial depository for US and Florida documents and US Patents. The 2006 library budget is approximately $12 million. The student population in 1999 (when the Staff Development Task Force discussed herein was convened) was 30,000; in the fall of 2007, it approached 47,000. Library staff increased during that time frame from 100 to 130 full-time equivalents (FTEs).

Historical Background

As early as November 1992, staff development concerns were being discussed in various areas of the Libraries. Minutes from an Access Services

Department meeting identified the following needs and issues related to training:

- provide ongoing training for support staff;
- consider adult learners' needs;
- develop content for library basics and call numbers as well as advanced topics;
- gather staff input on their needs;
- define acronyms;
- identify a list of essential skills that all staff would be expected to learn or update;
- specify training responsibilities and propose a coordinator position or distribute the work among employees;
- have librarians and support staff work together to create training in each area.

Individuals responded to these identified needs by arranging programs, but no formal coordination was built into the organization and no additional resources were allocated. UCFL had a long history of sporadic and uneven support for staff development and training. Administrative financial support for travel, conferences, and workshop activities was available at various levels upon request and with a supervisor's approval. The annual discretionary travel budget for each librarian was fairly well established and had increased over the years. UCFL provided release time and registration fee support for various off-campus events such as attendance at the state library association meetings. "In-house" sessions ranged from casual events such as monthly brown bags ("bring your own lunch" discussion meetings) to sponsorship of campus-wide affairs, including invited speakers or subsidized teleconferences. The Staff Orientation Series for new employees was coordinated by the Libraries' Personnel Officer as needed on an infrequent basis.

Objectives

In January 1999, the Director of Libraries created several task forces to address various issues. The relevant one for this discussion was the Staff Training and Development Task Force, which immediately changed its name to the Training and Employee Development Initiative, thus allowing members to refer to themselves as the TEDIs and use a bear logo as a unifying icon for their work, incentives, snacks (Teddy Grahams®), rewards, etc. The TEDI charge was to conduct a needs assessment of staff development and training issues. TEDI was to look at types of programs (orientation, ergonomics, technical, non-technical, etc.); types of venues (on- and off-site workshops); "train the trainer" sessions, expert consultants, local and campus organization offerings, etc.); and audience (student assistants, staff, supervisors, managers, etc.).

By May 1999, the Director expected the group to have prepared a report with recommendations about what was currently lacking, what should be done about it, what should be included in a comprehensive program, who would coordinate the efforts, and who would participate. He emphasized that the task force should not limit its vision by predetermining what might be possible in terms of budget or staffing. The Director also stressed that the task force should continuously share information and progress with the entire library staff. He suggested the possibility of group meetings or focus groups during the needs assessment phase, seeking out what worked elsewhere or what new staffers felt was lacking during their own orientations.

The task force members began their deliberations by conducting a literature review and discussing information gleaned about the fundamentals of staff development. A number of comprehensive sources covered program essentials, including planning, funding, sponsorship, needs assessment, curriculum content, core competencies, training methods, and training evaluation.[1–8] This background reading informed decisions throughout the work of the task force.

At subsequent task force meetings, the group created ground rules for successful team work, identified another group goal of stimulating staff interest in training, and finalized methods for conducting a needs assessment. The preliminary needs assessment took the form of a staff survey (see Appendix 4.A), which was distributed with pay checks to all faculty, support staff, and student assistants. The task force conducted other, smaller surveys, identified issues and core curriculum preferences, and reported recommendations as requested. The Director and department heads reviewed, approved, and supported selected recommendations.

Methods

The needs assessment survey was distributed to 254 employees, including student assistants, and 60 completed surveys were returned. The low return rate of 23.6 percent did concern TEDI; however, the returned surveys represented 50.7 percent of support staff. The committee chose to proceed by interpreting the results primarily in terms of support staff recommendations. In future library-wide assessments, student assistants would not be included. A review of the returned Preliminary Needs Assessment surveys generated the following observations from TEDI members:

• All the content items were checked as important. (Lesson learned: the yes/no option would be replaced on future surveys by a Likert rating scale.)

- Comments on surveys were more about the process of training than about training content.
- Employees used this as an opportunity to vent about non-training related issues. Some comments were forwarded to the Vision and Program Review Task Force.
- In evaluating barriers to training, there were obvious differences among library departments.
- As a result of comments about specific supervisors, the TEDIs realized that they needed to discuss supervisors' participation at some point, perhaps as part of implementation.
- Student assistants' training needs were better evaluated departmentally, not library-wide.
- Terminology needed to be considered for uniformity and sensitivity. If the term "staff" was used generically, it left people wondering if faculty were specifically excluded. Using the term "professional" to refer to MLS librarians caused problems for some people because it implied that others were not professional. (Lesson learned: future surveys referred to "faculty," "staff," and "faculty and staff.")
- Frequent reference to lack of time revealed this as an underlying problem.

Survey and Follow-up

TEDI shared the general survey results with the entire library staff, but distributed only the numbers of responses to yes/no questions while excluding the very numerous comments and suggestions. The entire detailed results, however, were available in a public location to anyone who wished to view them. TEDI learned that follow-up surveys would be more meaningful if they required employees to rank and prioritize content offerings. Additionally, the task force discovered that it is important for people to be given information about both delivery methods and the process for providing training when they are making decisions about training content.

Staff Development Implementation Issues

TEDI evaluated implementation issues that would need to be addressed in terms of the realities of budget and staffing. While the Director did not want the group's visioning to be inhibited by financial constraints, experienced members were aware of the difference between visioning without limits and implementing within realities.[9] Three main issues dominated the implementation discussions: responsibility, content delivery, and accountability.

In terms of responsibility, the main issue was that the library did not have a training officer at the time of the survey and existing personnel expressed concerns about accepting additional duties. As to content delivery, TEDI members favored the idea of purchasing a special collection of multimedia training materials, since that provided a multiplicity of delivery options, including self-study. For accountability, the concepts of a core curriculum, grouped "tracks" of information similar to conference organization, and possible certificate programs were all considered. The group realized that if a certificate program could not be linked to financial rewards, it would probably not be considered an incentive.

In order to encourage maximum participation in programs, TEDI favored a mandatory core curriculum with required courses noted on job descriptions. The concept of required courses including a mandated core curriculum did not survive administrative review, however. TEDI later acknowledged that even if training were incorporated as part of the position description, it would be better implemented as an annual goals-based discussion between the employee and the immediate supervisor.[10]

TEDI Final Report and Recommendations

Desired Outcomes

As part of the final report to the Director, TEDI identified a number of anticipated outcomes that would be advantageous to both the organization and its employees. With a formalized approach to new employee orientation, UCFL would benefit from increased interdepartmental cooperation, understanding, and awareness among staff of the interrelationships and functions of the various activities and services of the Library. Through appropriate application of cross-training, there would be improved departmental flexibility and coverage. Formal structure would also increase the participation of all employees (director through students) in training opportunities, provide equitable opportunities for all staff to participate in training, and involve supervisors and department heads in employee development. Additional expected rewards to the organization would include increased ability to meet current and future needs of users and employees; efficient use of resources; provision of better service; improved staff morale; increased employee retention; and more creative and capable employees.

UCFL employees, for their part, would experience improvement in morale, confidence, and job satisfaction plus a reduction in stress. They would also enhance their job performance, broaden their vision, upgrade their skills and abilities, and heighten their ability to change and to take advantage of new career opportunities.

Methods to Achieve Desired Training Outcomes

TEDI identified two primary mechanisms for realizing the desired outcomes. The first recommendation was to create a new department that would assume responsibility for staff development. The second was to recognize staff training and development as a UCFL goal that would be strongly supported and implemented by department heads until a new department charged with staff development could be organized.[11]

Recommendation 1: Create a Staff Development Department

TEDI felt strongly that there should be a unit designated with the responsibility for staff development and it offered options about reporting structure and possible areas of responsibility for the new department. In many libraries, including UCFL, it would be a luxury to have an entire department dedicated solely to staff training. Other duties considered by TEDI that could be combined with training included new employee orientation, library instruction, distance learning, electronic resources, research consultations, or coordination of written pathfinders. All these options would depend on the unique talents of the person selected to coordinate staff development.

Staffing options considered included filling the proposed department head position with a current faculty librarian in an "acting" status, hiring a temporary adjunct librarian, or starting a national faculty search immediately. The group also suggested the possibility of employing a staff person who would work half-time in the Systems and Technology Department and half-time as a technical trainer in a new Library Instruction and Training Department. TEDI acknowledged that coordinators for some or all of the broad areas in the new department would be needed, as would administrative support staff. The task force also recommended that the existing TEDIs would continue to serve in an advisory capacity for input, not evaluation or control, for at least one year.

TEDI identified two possible goals and objectives of a new Library Instruction and Training Department related specifically to staff development and training. The first broad goal would be to manage the staff development and training program activities. That would involve planning additional needs assessments, goals, and a budget, as well as monitoring and reporting outcomes. Managing would also include developing a curriculum and programs, plus coordinating activities, promotion, and publicity. This goal also includes actually providing training, training other trainers, mentoring, and facilitating use of self-study resources. The second broad goal would be to serve as the liaison with local and regional training organizations, the University's Human Resources Department, UCFL department heads, supervisors, and staff.

Delivery Methods

Based on the preliminary survey and other input gathered by TEDI, the following list was created of possible delivery methods or projects specifically related to staff development:

- multimedia "training library" for self- or group-study;
- one training session developed per year, per supervisor;
- web page for centralized publicity and calendars;
- web-based training;
- "Do-Drop-In" (scheduled training not requiring pre-registration);
- "Quick Flicks";
- journal clubs;
- new employee checklist;
- orientation information packets;
- staff recognition awards;
- training "tracks";
- training newsletter;
- "field trips" within and outside of the library;
- invited speakers.

Content

Several broad categories of subject content were identified from the needs assessment survey: managerial/supervisory; personal/professional development; job-specific or technical library skills; electronic library resources; basic computer hardware and software; new employee library orientation; and health and safety. For a detailed list of course topics, see Appendix 4.B.

Recommendation 2: Formalize Training Goals

The second proposed method for achieving the desired outcomes (if a new department could not be created) was to recognize staff training and development as a UCFL goal that would be strongly supported and implemented by department heads. TEDI proposed that this would be accomplished by having the Director support the plan and communicate its importance to department heads. TEDI would explain the plan and seek input from department heads and would then communicate the plan to and solicit feedback from all staff. The Director and department heads would individually discuss goals regarding staff development and training for each department for the following evaluation year. The department head would be evaluated in part based on successful achievement of staff development and training goals set at the beginning of the evaluation year.

Results

Staffing, Budget, and Evaluation

UCFL partially implemented TEDI's recommendations, based on resources available at the time. Although the task force proposed a full department with various optional responsibilities, the actual implementation consisted of creating a coordinator-level position within the existing Administration Department with support from department heads as described above.

A Staff Development Coordinator (SDC) position description (see Appendix 4.C) was created for a 0.4 FTE librarian; this position was filled in January 2000. In this case, the staff development functions consumed approximately 40 percent of the librarian's time, or approximately sixteen hours per week, while 60 percent was dedicated to other human resource functions such as recruiting, hiring, separation, evaluations, and supervision of payroll. Additionally, the original TEDI members continued to serve in an advisory capacity for the first year of implementation.

A budget was provided to acquire a collection of materials, which are advertised on an internal website. A record 60 programs, more than one per week, were offered during the first year. An interactive, online shelving training website was produced the second year. The staff development website continues to function as an organizing tool to convey both policy and operational issues such as the purpose and scope of the program, curriculum and calendar, types of training, and links to specific course materials.[12]

Programming was evaluated and adjusted according to feedback in succeeding years. The first follow-up survey was conducted in February 2002, with 115 surveys distributed and 52 returned, for a 42.5 percent response rate. The most notable result was the request for more live training. This is understandable since the initial programming emphasized use of the purchased collection of training videos primarily published by CareerTrack.[13] The second follow-up survey was conducted as part of the Administration Department's customer survey in December 2005. The survey design compared how effectively the service was delivered to how important the service was to staff members. The survey also allowed for comments; however, it only contained three questions related to staff development. The notable result from this survey was dissatisfaction with timely scheduling of new employee orientation.

Orientation

New employee orientation at UCFL continues to be a challenge despite experiments with a variety of approaches.[14, 15] A very detailed checklist that was being used even before TEDI convened was updated and revised by the SDC. The checklist (see Appendix 4.D) identifies items that should be prepared before a new employee arrives, information that needs to be shared on the first day, and other information and meetings that vary with the hiring department. In addition to the checklist, the SDC also arranges orientation meetings with UCFL administrators and with representatives of all other departments. These sessions normally last 60 to 90 minutes on five days, spread over one to two weeks. The typical orientation would begin with half an hour dedicated to the Administration Department. The same session might proceed to Acquisitions, Collection Management, and Special Collections Departments for ten to twenty minutes each. On day two, the new employees would visit the Interlibrary Loan, Circulation, and Cataloging Departments. Day three might consist of Reference, Government Documents, and Curriculum Materials Departments, and so on. Special sessions would also be scheduled to demonstrate the online catalog, databases, and web pages.

Depending on the number of newly hired employees and the amount of time elapsed between hire dates, the orientation sessions could be less than cost-effective. Even with a full-time staff of 130 FTEs, turnover is neither predictable nor regular. On many occasions the SDC would be scheduling administrators and department heads to meet with a very small group of new employees. Even though the sessions were not optional, there were times when only one new person would attend. On other occasions, if sessions were only scheduled when a large enough group of attendees might be assembled, then the sessions were not viewed as timely and relevant by the new employees.

In mid-2006, the New Employee Orientation schedule was changed from "as needed" to a regular monthly arrangement. According to the new plan, each of the twelve months would be assigned to a different department to host an educational open house. New employees were expected, and seasoned employees were encouraged to attend these orientations offered by the "department of the month." This program was reevaluated after seven months. Scheduling issues and small attendance continued to plague the orientation sessions. The UCFL management team at that point agreed that orientations would be the responsibility of the hiring supervisor. New faculty librarians (not support staff) continue to have individual meetings with each of the Libraries' department heads, but the group departmental orientations have not taken place since August 2006. This method works as long as department heads are accountable for the successful orientation of all their new employees.[16]

One very helpful by-product of the TEDI work is a detailed staff directory entitled *Who Does What?* This continues to be a helpful orientation tool since it is arranged alphabetically by department and includes all names and phone numbers. Along with the directory information, the major department functions are grouped and defined and the initials of the appropriate contact person are included. This makes it easy for new employees to look at the Administration Department page, for example, find the Human Resource functions, and next to that, locate the initials of the person who can help with payroll or training questions. The initials match the full names and contact information at the top of the departmental page.

Programming

TEDI successfully obtained approximately $10,000 to purchase a collection of books, pamphlets, CDs, videos, and cassette programs, some with facilitator's guides. These materials are listed on a staff development web page and can be checked out by individuals or departments for three weeks. The SDC immediately began previewing the programs in open "lunch-and-learn" sessions that all library employees were free to join in. In the first year, fiscal year ending 2001, 60 programs were offered, including 31 video discussions and 29 guest presenters. In subsequent years, 30 to 40 programs have been offered. With assistance from the Library Systems and Technology Department, the SDC created a database to track training and to record and report attendance. The database enables inputting and tracking of all types of training, including department-specific programs. With the recent implementation of a new integrated library management system, the emphasis has migrated away from managerial and developmental training topics to unit- and technology-specific training.

The education, background, and personal preferences of the SDC allowed for the creation of a variety of customized training sessions. With input from various librarians and department heads, the SDC led the development of UCFL Service Standards training and pamphlets. The Coordinator created customized programs on communication skills, meeting management, job and process analysis, training, delegation, goal setting, job satisfaction, and change management.

Given that the staff development program at UCFL is open to contributions from all library employees, supervisors, and committees, a wide variety of interests can be met in-house. In summer 2007, for example, the Digital Services Librarian instigated and coordinated a summer-long interactive Web 2.0 training program[17] based loosely on Helene Blowers' Learning 2.0 project.[18] This particular librarian's initiative, paired with her interest in and exposure to the newest technologies, formed the basis for UCFL's current self-paced learning experience. Similarly, the faculty mentoring committee has organized and delivered many programs specific to faculty promotion needs.

Partners in Programming

As a result of high demand for broad "soft skills" programming with a library perspective (such as the Service Standards sessions mentioned earlier), the SDC was able to expand the audience for some of the specific programs developed for UCFL to other local libraries' employees through a relationship with the Central Florida Library Cooperative (CFLC), one of six regional Multitype Library Cooperatives covering all of Florida. CFLC, in turn, is a remarkable source of high-quality library-specific training. UCFL has availed itself of CFLC programs, both by bringing their offerings to the campus and by encouraging staff to attend sessions at CFLC training sites. CFLC programs cover all the latest technology and applications, including Web 2.0 function (blogs, podcasts, wikis, folksonomies, and the collaborative web); the full range of the more traditional Microsoft Office products plus other software (Dreamweaver, Adobe Acrobat); Web authoring topics such as HTML, XML, RSS, Flash, cascading style sheets, and more; plus many other library-specific topics not necessarily related to technology.

Other sources of formal programming include many campus offices such as the Human Resources Department, Continuing Education Department, Diversity Office, Faculty Center for Teaching and Learning, and Disputer Resolution Services. The SDC also arranges library training such as book repair, cataloging, and service assessment through the southeast regional provider Southeastern Library Network (SOLINET). Using today's technology, Webinars and teleconferences with nationally recognized speakers are scheduled for individual and group viewing through the American Library Association, the Association of College and Research Libraries, Sirsi/Dynix, WebJunction, and the College of DuPage.

More Shared Learning

One other innovative experiment was a monthly program specifically envisioned as a "Supervisor's Tool Box" series designed to be a working group for front-line managers. The program content was designed to explore problems, but the real focus became the name of the group, "Solution Seekers." The topics in this series included: new employee orientation, clarifying expectations, training before delegating, performance evaluations, situational leadership, student hiring procedures, and so on. The scheduled classes and descriptions were announced on the UCFL intranet site and twenty-seven employees attended the first session. The sessions were largely interactive and were planned around content and handouts designed to stimulate discussion. The intent was for experienced administrators and department heads to share knowledge with newer supervisors using a loosely structured agenda. After about six months, the audience had dwindled to an enthusiastic few, not many of whom were experienced managers. The regularly scheduled discussion group meeting times were gradually converted into other prearranged programs and the work group concept was not revived.

Conclusion

A formal strategic planning process at UCFL concurrent to the work of
TEDI generated two specific statements in the 2000 UCF Libraries Mission,
Values, and Vision document[19] that were most relevant to creating a
formal Staff Development Program: 1) to build an organizational structure
and processes that anticipate and accommodate change and growth,
encouraging feedback at all levels, and 2) to enrich the work experiences
of library employees. The declared purpose of organizing the formal Staff
Development Program at UCFL described herein was to guide all library
employees in identifying and fulfilling their training and development needs
in order to ensure individual and organizational success. The allocation
of resources for staff development was one method used to support and
realize action items identified in the strategic planning process.

The role of supervisors, managers, and administrators is critical to the
success of a staff development initiative, given that they retain primary
responsibility for job training for their employees. Only library directors
can ensure consistent commitment, positive attitude, and participation in
such formal programs by linking training goals to the evaluation process.
The supervisors determine training needs and communicate to employees
why they should participate. Supervisors also facilitate participation by
finding replacements to cover for the employee and by being flexible
in scheduling release time. It is also essential for supervisors to coach
employees and help them transfer training back to the work unit to use
what they learn. Training efforts have the most lasting and beneficial effects
when the supervisor follows up by engaging the employee in discussion
about how the training has impacted job performance or workflow.

Balanced and relevant staff development programming can be provided
on a broad and consistent basis when it is the major responsibility of a single
individual. The primary role of a coordinator is to assist, guide, support,
and encourage supervisors and employees in identifying and meeting their
needs. Scheduling rooms, equipment, and speakers; announcing events; and
arranging refreshments, evaluations, and follow-up might be intimidating to
some, but are handled with ease and efficiency by an experienced coordinator.
The coordinator can provide programming ideas and suggestions based on
available resources and is also in a position to find appropriate sources when
the topic is identified by others. Affordable resources are available from a
wide variety of providers, including local librarians and teaching faculty,
campus offices, library cooperatives, and professional associations.

UCFL is fortunate that staff development is recognized as a priority
by the Director of Libraries. Without support from administrators and
managers, program attendance would undoubtedly suffer. With the
participation and enthusiasm of leaders, staff training can indeed increase
skills, confidence, and morale for employees while enhancing user
satisfaction and operational efficiency for the organization as a whole.

References

1. Lipow, Anne G., and Carver, Deborah A., eds. *Staff Development: A Practical Guide.* Chicago, IL: American Library Association, 1992.
2. Trotta, Marcia. *Successful Staff Development: A How-To-Do-It Manual.* New York: Neal-Schuman, 1995.
3. *Staff Training and Development: A SPEC Kit 224*, compiled by Kostas Messas. Washington, DC: Association of Research Libraries, 1997.
4. Shaughnessy, Thomas W. "Approaches to Developing Competencies in Research Libraries." *Library Trends* 41 (Fall 1992): 282–298.
5. Giesecke, Joan and Lowry, Charles. "Core Elements of ARL Library Staff Development Programs." *ARL: A Bimonthly Report* 221 (April 2002): 9.
6. Grealy, Deborah, Jones, Lois, Messas, Kostas, Zipp, Kathleen, and Catalucci, Lise. "Staff Development and Training in College and University Libraries: The Penrose Perspective." *Library Administration and Management* 10 (Fall 1996): 204–209.
7. "An 'Otter' Librarian. Support Staff Training: Why and How?" *Journal of Education for Library and Information Science* 36 (Winter 1995): 33–34.
8. Beard, William Randall. "Staff Development and Training: A Model." *Journal of Education for Library and Information Science* 36 (Winter 1995): 35–37.
9. Casey, James B. "The 1.6% Solution: Continuing Education and Professional Involvement Are Small But Crucial Budget Items." *American Libraries* 33 (April 2002): 85–86.
10. Creth, Sheila D. *Effective On-the-Job Training.* Chicago, IL: American Library Association, 1986.
11. Paterson, Alasdair. "Ahead of the Game: Developing Academic Library Staff for the Twenty-first Century." *Library Career Development* 12 (1999): 143–149.
12. Brandt, D. Scott. "Writing a Library Training Policy." *Computers in Libraries* 22 (June 2002): 37–39. Available: <http://www.infotoday.com/cilmag/jun02/brandt.htm>. Accessed: April 23, 2007.
13. CareerTrack, a division of PARK University Enterprises, Inc. Shawnee Mission, KS. Available: <http://www.pryor.com/index_body.asp>. Accessed: August 21, 2007.
14. Allerton, Haidee. "Professional Development the Disney Way." *Training and Development* 51 (May 1997): 50–56.
15. Starcke, Alice M. "Building a Better Orientation Program." *HRMagazine* 41 (November 1996): 107–113.
16. Creth, Sheila D. "Staff Development and Continuing Education." In *Personnel Administration in Libraries.* Edited by Sheila Creth and Frederick Duda. New York: Neal-Schuman, 1989.
17. Dotson, Lee. "Fun in the Socially intrigUing techNologies." Available: <http://funinthesunatucf.wordpress.com/>. Accessed: August 21, 2007.
18. Blowers, Helene and Reed, Lori. "The C's of Our Sea Change: Plans for Training Staff, from Core Competencies to LEARNING 2.0." *Computers in Libraries* 27 (February 2007): 10–15. Available: <http://www.infotoday.com/cilmag/feb07/Blowers_Reed.shtml>. Accessed: April 23, 2007.
19. *University of Central Florida Libraries Mission, Values, and Vision.* Orlando, FL: Vision and Program Review Taskforce, University of Central Florida Libraries, 2000. Available: <http://library.ucf.edu/Administration/FactsFigures/MissionStatement.asp>. Accessed: August 20, 2007.

Appendix 4.A: UCFL Training and Employee Development Initiative

TEDI

Preliminary Needs Assessment

A task force has been formed to evaluate training needs and to prepare recommendations regarding possible programs and implementation. The task force is interested in input from all library staff and student assistants on what information would help you do your job better or improve your personal skills. This is only the first phase in developing a training program. You will have future opportunities for questions and additional input.

If you would prefer to talk to a task force member rather than fill out a questionnaire, contact any member: [names deleted].

Status: Librarian _____ Staff _____ Student Assistant_____
Supervisor: No _____ Yes _____
I supervise: Librarians ____ Staff_____ Students _____

Please indicate importance for yourself and others. Feel free to make comments and add suggestions where appropriate or as necessary.

Potential Training Areas

[NOTE TO READER: Be sure to change yes/no ratings to 5 = most important, 1= least important. See paragraph under METHODS for reasons.]

Important		Content	Examples/Other Suggestions
Yes	No		
—	—	New Employee Library Orientation	Library Policies & Procedures; Department Descriptions; Phone Use _____ _____
—	—	Personal/Professional Development	Communication; Writing Skills; Meeting Management _____ _____
—	—	Basic Computer/Software	MS Office; Web Browsers; Windows; E-mail _____ _____

Important	Content	Examples/Other Suggestions
— —	Public Services/Reference	Library Policies and General Information; Dealing with Difficult People; Phone Skills
— —	Electronic Library Resources	EBSCOhost; WebLUIS; INNOPAC
— —	Managerial/Supervisory	Skills for Supervising; Dealing with Different Personalities
— —	Health & Safety	Ergonomics; Emergency Procedures
— —	Technical or job-specific skills	Preservation of Materials; OCLC

Other subjects of interest:

_____

_____

_____

Delivery Method

Prefer

Yes   No

— —   In the library/On site

— —   Off site

— —   Self-instruction: video, audio cassette, Web, CD-ROM, e-mail

— —   Brown Bag

— —   Internal Instructors

— —   Outside Experts

— —   "Train the Trainer" (one person learns how to teach others)

Comments:

_____

_____

_____

Reasons and Incentives for Participating in Training

What training have you attended in the last twelve months? Please also indicate where, e.g. CFLC, Human Resources, etc.

_____

_____

_____

What would encourage you to participate more in training activities? Examples: tuition waiver, flex time, content to help me do my job better, professional CEUs, required by supervisor, etc.

_____

_____

_____

Reasons for *Not* Participating in Training

What currently discourages you from taking advantage of training opportunities:

Important

Yes   No

—   —   Lack of release time

—   —   Too much work even with release time

—   —   Not interested in subject

—   —   Inconvenient location

—   —   Supervisor not supportive

Other:

_____

_____

_____

Appendix 4.B: Staff Training and Development Task Force

1999 Proposed Courses – DRAFT

Note: This list was compiled from suggestions collected during various needs assessment surveys and discussions and it was never ranked, prioritized into Curriculum Core & Electives, or adjusted to eliminate duplicates. There is also no attempt to explain acronyms or local specifics herein, as it is simply provided to give an idea of what could be included in general areas by a library. This list was never finalized, as administrators opted to go a different route than supporting a required core curriculum (see paragraph above under 'Staff Development Implementation Issues' for details).

Managerial/Supervisory Courses

UCF Quality Commitment Series
UCF Quality Coaches Training Session
UCF Interviewer Certification

Skills for Supervising: (Supervisor's Tool Box Series)
    Conflict Management
    Counseling for Performance Problem Improvement
    Mentoring/Coaching
    Discipline and Documentation
    Performance Appraisal
    Creating a Motivational and Supportive Work Environment
    Motivating
    Goal Setting
    Delegating/Assigning Work
    Encouraging Innovation & Creativity
    Managing Absenteeism

Managerial Skills: (SUS Department Heads Sessions, ARL Managerial Skills Workshop)
    Budgeting
    Decision Making
    Efficiency
    Establishing Goals, Objectives, and Priorities
    Ethical Leadership/Management
    Flexibility and Adaptability
    Leadership Development
    Managing Change
    Meeting Management
    Organization Skills
    Problem Solving
    Process Improvement & Streamlining

Professional Ethics
Project Management
Records Management
Self-assessment Techniques
Time Management

Personal/Professional Development

Communication Skills
   Oral
   Phone
   Presentation
   Written
Writing Minutes and Policies & Procedures
Listening Skills
   Mediation Skills
   Multicultural Communication
   Assertiveness
Negotiation Skills
   Communicating in Difficult Situations
How to Work in Groups/Team Building
   Dealing with Different Personalities (Myers-Briggs)
   Dealing with Difficult People or Situations
   Creative Thinking
   Risk-Taking
How to Build Self-Esteem (for self and others)
Organizational Skills
   Time Management/Planning
   Goal Setting
   Meeting Management
   Facilitation Skills
   Office Proficiency Series
UCF Quality Commitment Series:
   Customer Service Program
   Products & Services That Meet Customer Needs
   Set Measures & Standards for Performance
   Process Improvement Tools

Technical/Job-Related – Library Specific Training Organized By Department Head/Supervisor:

(Training for each department will vary at the supervisor's discretion)
These are examples only:
Preservation of Materials
Collection Development Techniques
Accounts Payable/Receivable

Purchasing Procedures
Overview of each department, procedures, cross-training
OCLC
Technical Aspects of OPAC
MARC Records
INNOPAC

Electronic Library Resources

Library Self-guided Audio Tour
WebLUIS (OPAC) tutorial
Internet Workshop Series - Basic & Advanced
EBSCOhost
INNOPAC
Online tutorials (i.e. The Help Web)
Database-specific sessions
Vendor demos
CFLC workshops
Specialized Library Instruction Classes

Basic Computer/Software

Windows
MS Office instruction classes
    Excel Spreadsheets (Intro & Advanced)
    Microsoft Word (Intro & Advanced)
    PowerPoint (Intro & Advanced)
    Access Database (Intro & Advanced)
    Publisher
    FrontPage
Netscape/Web Browsers
HTML Editor/Creating Home Pages
Desktop Publishing
GroupWise Instruction: E-mail, Calendaring, Organizing Your Work,
E-mail Etiquette

Library and University Orientation – New or Review

Library – General Information:
    Library Policies & Procedures
    Department Descriptions
    How Departments Affect the Total Picture – Students
    Library as Part of the University
    Branch Campus Tours/Meetings
    Main Campus Tour
    Phone Use
Rights and Responsibilities of Employees
    Benefits Packages

    Employee Incentives
    Employee Assistance
    Mentor Program
    Job-Sharing
Policy/Procedure Awareness and Training
Understanding the Library's Long-Range Plans
    University Policies/Procedures
    Purchasing Policies/Procedures
    Human Resources Policies/Procedures
    Discipline and Documentation
    Travel Policies/Procedures
    Position Descriptors: Faculty
    Position Descriptors: USPS

Health and Safety

Environmental Issues:
    Sick Building
    Safety of Water Supply
    Workplace Injury
Security & Emergency Procedures
    Workplace Violence
    Safety Measures on Campus
    Evacuating Building/Fire Drills
    First Aid Responses – employees/patrons
    CPR Training
Ergonomics – Comfortable Work Surroundings (computers, desks, chairs, lighting, etc.)
Stress Management/Desk Yoga
Counseling – Grief/Personal Problems
Sensitivity Training
    Work Attitude – Humor
    Handling Discrimination and Diversity
    Handling Intimidation and Harassment
    Cultural Awareness
    AIDS Awareness
    Alcohol/Drug Awareness
    Dealing with Difficult People/Getting Along With People
    Disability
    Equal Opportunity & Affirmative Action

Appendix 4.C: Staff Development Coordinator

Original Position Description Draft Developed 4/11/2000

Duties

A. Establishes Staff Development goals and policies in consultation with the Director of Libraries.
B. Develops and provides for evaluation of the curricula and programs.
C. Schedules and facilitates training programs.
D. Develops and maintains access to a collection of staff development materials.
E. Maintains training records, statistics, and files.
F. Promotes and publicizes staff development and training.
G   Serve as liaison with training organizations, the University's Human Resources Department, Library Department Heads, supervisors, and staff.

Performance Objectives

H. Establishes and monitors uniform procedures for access to developmental opportunities.
I. Encourages managers and employees to participate in training opportunities.
J. Oversees new employee orientation.
K. Conducts needs assessments and program evaluations.
L. Chairs meetings with the Staff Development Advisors.
M. Supervises clerical staff and student assistants in the unit.
N. Maintains an awareness of developments in the field and plans for growth and improvement in the service.
O. Provides budget, attendance and other program information to the Library Director.

Other roles added later:
Ex officio on faculty mentoring committee and faculty promotion committee.
Coordinator of internship activities.

Appendix 4.D: UCFL – New Librarian Orientation Checklist

Prepared for: _____ Date of Hire: _____

Mentor: _____

Before Arrival	*Assigned To/ Date Completed*
Computer Accounts Requested	_____
Workstation Stocked	_____
Need new telephone or computer?	_____
Keys	_____

Orientation Information Packet	*Assigned To/ Date Completed*
Library Mission, Values, Vision	_____
Library & Department Organization Chart	_____
Maps: Library & Parking	_____
"Who Does What?" List (staff directory)	_____
Emergency Contact Form to Personnel Librarian	_____
Time Sheet, Instructions & Pay Schedule	_____
Conflict of Interest Form	_____
Telephone Directory, Tips & Helpful Hints	_____
Employee Orientation Checklist	_____
Confidentiality	_____

Home Department Information	*Assigned To/ Date Completed*
Department Info, Meetings, Resources, etc.	_____
Department Policies & Procedures	_____
Letters of Assignment & Accomplishment	_____
Promotions & Evaluations	_____
Evacuation/Fire Map	_____
Work Schedule	_____
Time Sheets	_____
Departmental Leave Procedures	_____
Supply Ordering & Location	_____
Business Cards & Notepads Ordered	_____
Telephone Logs & Dialing Instructions	_____
Staff Lounge Combination	_____
Technical Support	_____
Email, Knightline (listserv), Pegasus, Directories	_____
WebLUIS (OPAC), Library Homepage…	_____
Evaluations	_____
Training Opportunities	_____
Travel procedures & forms	_____

Library Staff Book Accounts   _____
Birthday in staff lounge   _____
Meeting Schedules: Faculty, Dept Heads, etc.   _____

Library Visits & Introductions   *Assigned To/*
                                                              Date Completed

Administration   _____
— Director   _____
— Associate Director for Administrative Services   _____
— Associate Director for Public Services   _____
— Associate Dir for Collections & Tech Services   _____
— Assistant Director Systems and Technology   _____
— Travel Procedures   _____
— Personnel & Staff Development   _____
Cataloging   _____
Circulation/Periodicals   _____
Collection Mgmt Acquisitions/Serials Binding   _____
Curriculum Materials Center   _____
Interlibrary Loan   _____
Reference   _____
— Ask A Librarian   _____
— Government Documents   _____
— InfoSource (fee-based service)   _____
Information Literacy & Outreach   _____
Special Collections & Archives   _____

Attend Library Meetings   *Assigned To/*
                                                              Date Completed

Department Heads   _____
Technical Advisory Group   _____
Director's Advisory Group   _____
General Staff – twice annually   _____
Librarians Personnel Advisory Committee – LPAC   _____
Faculty Senate   _____

Other   *Assigned To/*
                                                              Date Completed

UCF HR Orientation   _____
Tour Campus   _____
UFF Rep – Collective Bargaining   _____
UCF Annual Faculty Orientation   _____

5 Supporting a Culture of Library Research at the University of Washington at Seattle

Phillip M. Edwards, Elaine Z. Jennerich, and Jennifer L. Ward

Introduction

The University of Washington (UW) is a public research university with a large, comprehensive library system and a graduate program in library and information science within an Information School (iSchool). The UW Libraries' administration has long believed that fostering a culture of research within the Libraries enhances the services provided to the campus. Basic research in libraries is "critical if the field of library and information science 'is to solve professional problems, develop tools and methods for analysis of organization, services, and behavior, to determine costs and benefits of our services, and, most importantly, to establish or develop a body of theory on which to base our practice.'"[1] Although general staff development efforts have been beneficial for those who work at the UW Libraries,[2] supporting original research by individual staff members and articulating a formal research agenda for the entire organization present unique challenges for the UW Libraries' administration.

Perhaps the most obvious challenges relate to the nature of the work environment and local reward structures because UW librarians are classified as academic staff rather than faculty. Nevertheless, the Librarian Personnel Code at UW enables promotions through several ranks: Assistant Librarian, Senior Assistant Librarian, Associate Librarian, and Librarian. As of this writing, there are five Assistant Librarians, twenty-five Senior Assistant Librarians, sixty-six Associate Librarians, and forty-one Librarians. The rank of Associate Librarian carries with it "permanent status" akin to the academic freedom associated with faculty tenure. Research and publication are not absolute requirements for promotion to permanent status. Nevertheless, these activities demonstrate professional engagement that can serve as evidence in support of a librarian's documentation for promotion. Original scholarship, therefore, is professionally valuable, but it remains only one of many criteria against which a staff member's performance could be evaluated.

Setting

In an attempt to raise the profile of library research and provide staff with the skills necessary to succeed in their scholarly efforts, the UW Libraries entered into a collaborative partnership with the iSchool. The iSchool is home to four distinct degree programs: an undergraduate degree in informatics, a master's degree in library and information science (MLIS), a master's degree in information management (MSIM), and a doctoral degree in information science. The tripartite mission of the iSchool is to prepare information leaders, to research problems and opportunities of information, and to design solutions to information challenges. These aims offered a foundation for a research-centered relationship between the iSchool and the UW Libraries.

Following a brief overview of writing- and research-related staff development programs at other academic libraries, this chapter 1) details the structure and development of the main vehicle for Libraries—iSchool collaboration at UW, the Research Program Steering Group (RPSG), 2) identifies specific areas of need among staff at the UW Libraries related to research support, 3) enumerates activities and program undertaken by the RPSG to address those needs, and 4) concludes with reflections on lessons learned, examples of successes, and suggestions for institutions where similar kinds of collaboration could be created.

Profiles of Research Support Programs Within Academic Libraries

Research support programs for academic librarians are often designed with the tenure process as the unifying theme. Whether academic librarians should hold tenure-track positions remains an active debate in the literature.[3-5] Similarly, tensions related to the nature of the tenure process for librarians[6-11] and the quality of research emerging from the profession[12] are also evident. Given the various demands under which many tenure-track academic librarians work, the professional literature reports numerous support programs among institutions.

Such programs often address individual, institutional, and financial challenges associated with library research. Citing that "most librarians have not received extensive training in research methodology, their work schedules lack flexibility, and they usually have limited access to research funds," Miller and Benefiel describe a Tenure Support Group for librarians at Texas A&M University, whose main activities were monthly "brown-bag" lunch meetings.[13] Hill suggests providing research leave, offering a research semester, and extending the tenure clock for librarians without doctorates as support mechanisms.[4] Mentoring programs in which entry-level librarians are paired with more experienced colleagues are also common in the literature.[14-16]

Sapon-White, King, and Christie discuss the Library Faculty Association (LFA) at Oregon State University.[17] This group was open to all twenty-four tenure-track library faculty, met in optional bimonthly meetings during the academic year, held a bimonthly seminar series, organized *ad hoc* in-house research presentations, and offered a research and writing group. According to one survey, tenured librarians rated the value of the LFA meetings more highly than their untenured colleagues. The formal writing group was perceived as less effective for getting feedback than informal interactions with specific colleagues. In a similar initiative, Tysick and Babb describe grassroots efforts to form a writing group for junior library faculty and to host a writing retreat at the University at Buffalo. They remark that:

> after the first year, although interest began to wane for 40 percent of the group, the remainder of participants reported the Academic Writing Group to be successful not only in its initial stated goals but also in the wider goals of mentoring and support. The success of this peer-initiated and peer-supported grassroots program lay in its ability to evolve and provide support where it was needed.[18]

Extending these reports from the professional literature to the specific case of the UW Libraries, several questions remain open: how to balance structure with flexibility in staff development efforts related to research and scholarship, how to sustain these efforts over time, and how to take into account the needs of librarians and library staff who are not driven by concerns about the tenure process.

Research Program Steering Group

In an approach similar to professional development activities at other institutions, staff at the UW Libraries began to meet informally to discuss personal interests in scholarly work. Since the early 1990s, the Association of Librarians of the University of Washington has been investigating better ways to support librarians' pursuits of research and writing as part of their professional duties. In late 2002, a Writer's Interest Group emerged within the Libraries to provide an informal support group for those interested in professional writing. Those attending a meeting early in the following year were interested in a wide range of topics, including steps for publishing an article, developing research skills, identifying which research is worth doing and writing about, and using research and writing as a valuable part of professional development. One additional meeting was held in May 2003, but this self-managed writing group disbanded shortly thereafter.

Concurrently, a more holistic and systematic approach to encouraging research and scholarship was underway. In February 2003, the Associate Director of Libraries for Information Technology (IT) Services penned an internal white paper, "Creating a Research Agenda for UW Libraries," which included a proposal to create an institutional research agenda. The research agenda was intended to support the Libraries' strategic initiatives through applied research. Initial conceptualizations involved assigning research problems to interested staff members for investigation. The white paper explicitly acknowledged the desire to forge collaborative relationships with other units on campus. An early proposal for a potential relationship between the iSchool and the Libraries is described:

> While there are certainly synergies with work going on in the iSchool, the research agenda needs to belong to the Libraries. We should, of course, look for strategic partnerships and alliances in our research enterprise just as we do in carrying out other aspects of our mission. Where our research needs and the research interests of the iSchool overlap, we can benefit from collaboration. We might also look to the iSchool to help us develop or upgrade the research skills necessary for the projects we wish to undertake. Some staff may wish to take classes in the iSchool to improve their research skills, while a more targeted project-specific approach would work better in other cases.[19]

The Associate Director of Libraries for IT Services originally shepherded these ideas forward in his additional role as the Administrative Officer for Research. From the outset, research activities have been considered supplementary to staff members' job descriptions, but they could be included in annual performance evaluations, reappointments, promotions, and merit-based salary increases.

The Libraries Cabinet, the UW Libraries' senior leadership group, devoted their August 2003 meeting to an in-depth discussion of the research agenda. The research agenda was intended to foster a culture of research, increase the visibility and prestige of the UW Libraries, build partnerships with other organizations, support applied research for strategic decision-making, and bolster organizational outcomes based on research findings. The Libraries Cabinet subsequently authorized the formation of an internal steering committee, the Research Program Steering Group (RPSG), which was initially composed of seven librarians.

The RPSG met several times from November 2003 to February 2004 and arrived at two important conclusions: 1) there was a need to understand what barriers UW librarians faced when attempting to conduct research, particularly with respect to any gaps in formal support mechanisms at the level of the organization, and 2) the research and teaching expertise of the iSchool would be an asset for creating a culture of research.

With some form of collaboration in mind, the Associate Dean for Research at the iSchool was asked to join the RPSG. Shortly thereafter, the RPSG proposed a joint meeting of Libraries Cabinet, faculty members from the iSchool, and RPSG members. The goals of the meeting were to address the following questions:

• Why does your organization have an interest in this partnership? How would it further the mission and goals of your organization?
• If this partnership were successful from the point of view of your organization, what would it achieve? What would the partnership help your organization accomplish that it could not accomplish without such a relationship?
• What are your fears/concerns in entering into this partnership? What things could go wrong that would jeopardize the success of this relationship?
• Are there any critical factors that you are aware of at this time that your organization is not able to compromise on that might impact this partnership?

A trained facilitator led a productive half-day meeting around these items, and a list of "next steps" for the RPSG was developed with the assistance of interested faculty, students, and staff. The group later added several iSchool doctoral students to its roster, and efforts to understand and address barriers to conducting research began in earnest.

Needs Assessment

The RPSG conducted a survey of UW librarians and professional staff in May 2004 and identified several barriers to conducting research: conceptual barriers (e.g. research methods/design), technical barriers (e.g. data analysis skills), and institutional barriers (e.g. salaried time for research). The electronic survey was available for a two-week period, and there were fifty-two respondents. Thirty-six (69 percent) were permanent librarians, twelve (23 percent) were non-permanent librarians, and four (8 percent) were non-librarian professional staff.

Librarians rated the importance of conducting research for the Libraries highly: twenty-nine permanent librarians, ten non-permanent librarians, and all of the professional staff rated these activities as "important" or "very important." The interest in actually conducting research was lower, with only twenty-two permanent librarians and eight non-permanent librarians responding "interested" or "very interested." Among all respondents, thirty-three individuals (63 percent) had conducted research during the previous five years, with the majority of that research disseminated either as a presentation or as a peer-reviewed journal article. Non-permanent librarians also used poster sessions as a dissemination method.

Uncertainty about research methodologies (76 percent) and insufficient data analysis skills (71 percent) were identified as personal barriers to conducting research. Among librarians without permanent status, the percentages were even higher, with 83 percent rating research methodologies and 75 percent rating data analysis skills as barriers. The most frequently reported institutional barrier was insufficient paid release time, with forty-four respondents (89 percent) mentioning it as a problem. Half of the non-permanent librarians also indicated that getting published, securing travel funding, and obtaining grant support were problematic.

When asked what support was needed to conduct research, release time was identified by 73 percent of the respondents. Qualitative responses to open-ended questions corroborated that the most significant personal and institutional barrier was the need for more time—especially release time—with many stating that there was not enough free time in a standard work week to conduct research and writing. Research methodology training followed closely behind, mentioned as a challenge by 65 percent of the respondents. Nevertheless, qualitative comments indicated that most of the respondents thought that exploring user needs and assessing programs and services should be major research activities at the UW Libraries. Based on the identified barriers to conducting research and bolstered by the expanded RPSG membership, the RPSG planned several initiatives to support librarians in these areas.

Responding to Staff Development Needs

The programs designed and promoted by the RPSG focused heavily on institutional support mechanisms, educational workshops, and social events. An existing but underutilized Time Grant Program was strongly emphasized as a means for providing compensated release time for librarians' scholarly pursuits. A series of workshops and periodic educational events were also designed to provide overviews of research methods, to craft research questions, and to showcase librarians' research projects. A social reception series was also established to foster the development of community among the UW Libraries and the iSchool. Each of these initiatives is discussed in greater detail below.

Time Grant Program

Any staff member who has been employed at the Libraries for over one year is eligible to apply for up to 240 hours of paid release time to support their writing, research, or other scholarly activity that benefits the Libraries. The anticipated outcome is some kind of scholarly product: an article, a bibliography, or a conference presentation. In order to reach this goal, the UW Libraries' administration will work with the individual to ensure comparable coverage to support workflow and services that might be affected by his or her temporary release. The staff member must prepare a brief written report of the results of the activity within a month of the end of the time grant. Included with the report should be a copy of the resulting product, such as an article, bibliography, presentation, or online resource. The complete documentation and guidelines for the Time Grant Program are provided in Appendix 5.A.

In addition to the Time Grant Program, librarians with permanent status may be granted professional leave with pay, a privilege modeled after sabbaticals for faculty members. Professional leave is granted for up to one year during a seven-year period and is intended to provide an opportunity for librarians to increase their knowledge, further their scholarship, expand their skills, and enhance their professional development. Given the additional restrictions placed on these kinds of requests, the Dean of the University Libraries and the Provost are both responsible for approving requests for professional leave with pay.

Research Explorations Panel Session

For staff members without previous experience in conducting original research, one of the more difficult steps in the research process is selecting and refining a particular topic of professional interest. As a warm-up to the subsequent "Framing the Question" workshop, a panel of UW Libraries' staff members who were experienced researchers discussed how they got started, where they discovered their research topics, and how they stayed motivated throughout the process. Panelists from a variety of subject areas spoke about projects ranging from translations of Slovak folk poems to doctoral work in civil engineering. The goal of this session was to offer staff members a chance to start thinking about possible research questions before the follow-up workshop.

Research Explorations: Framing the Question

In this interactive half-day workshop, eleven faculty members and doctoral students from the iSchool facilitated small-group discussions among library staff interested in further developing their research questions and topics. Small groups, each with one iSchool faculty member and one doctoral student, worked with library staff to articulate well-defined topics for research. Although it was not necessary for participants to come prepared with polished descriptions of their topics, prior to the session they were presented with several prompts designed to elicit curiosities, concerns, and confounding issues that emerge in daily practice:

- "I wish _____ were more successful."
- "I wonder if our users are more satisfied with the service they get from _____."
- "There's got to be a more efficient way to _____."

- "It sure would be good to know how much _____ is really costing us."
- "I wonder what library staff members think about _____?"
- "Can we measure _____?"
- "How do _____ seek information?"
- Have we ever done an analysis on _____?"

Throughout the session, iSchool participants helped library staff tease out and develop related research questions on individuals' topics. Project ideas, research questions, and other concerns were recorded on flipcharts, and transcribed and shared with attendees following the session. At the end of the workshop, most participants responded that they had made at least some initial progress toward viable investigations.

Heart of Research Workshop

During this session, held in February 2006, staff were introduced to processes for selecting appropriate research methods. An iSchool faculty member and the Library Assessment Coordinator described elements of various research methods including case studies, systematic reviews, and transaction log analyses. The presenters created scenarios related to library research for use during this workshop, and participants were tasked with selecting appropriate research methods for addressing each scenario.

"UW Librarians Present" Poster Sessions

Since many staff members reported presenting findings or information to the profession during poster sessions, the RPSG offered a venue for library staff to share their research with their colleagues. This two-hour session, held in April 2006, showcased four projects by staff at the UW Libraries as presented at several professional conferences: the IUFRO World Congress, the SPARC/SPARC Europe Workshop on Institutional Repositories, Music Library Association Regional Meeting, and the Medical Library Association Annual Meeting. Posters covered topics such as forest resources, institutional repositories, music librarianship, and health sciences liaison programs. Invitations for this event were circulated widely within the Libraries and among faculty, students, and staff at the iSchool. Library staff and other guests from the iSchool were encouraged to ask questions of the presenters, and this session has been useful as a "testing ground" for posters not yet shown at conferences.

Human Subjects Division Presentation

In February 2007, the RPSG offered a two-hour program about the UW policies and procedures governing protections for participants in library-related research. An administrator from the UW Human Subjects Division spoke about the process of human subjects application review. The presentation focused on review processes related to particular types of research studies—those that could claim exemption from full institutional review board (IRB) review and those that could be classified by the IRB as posing "minimal risk" to participants.

UW Libraries/iSchool Social Receptions

In addition to the insights gleaned from the staff survey, the members of RPSG decided that collaborations between the iSchool and the Libraries should also have a social component that would enable librarians, faculty, and doctoral students to connect, get to know each other better, and informally discuss research, teaching, and other professional interests. At the inaugural social in November 2005, UW Libraries' staff and iSchool faculty and students were invited to have refreshments late in the Winter Quarter. The overwhelmingly positive feedback from this initial event prompted a second social in the following year. At the second social, four iSchool doctoral students were invited to present brief summaries of their library-related dissertation projects: information-sharing in design teams, information behavior of students in educational settings, online searching in public-access catalogs, and scholarly communication.

Discussion

There were several notable successes as a result of this collaborative venture, namely the increased awareness of issues in research and practice across both units, and the emergence of several collaborative projects between iSchool doctoral students and staff members at the UW Libraries. While students in the MLIS program are perhaps the most visible connections between the UW Libraries and the iSchool from the perspective of service provision, the activities organized by the RPSG have created the expectation that the Libraries and the iSchool will engage in meaningful, sustainable collaborations around research, teaching, *and* service. Similarly, by centralizing research support issues within one group, the RPSG has been able to serve as a single point of contact for visitors to campus who were interested in discussing research initiatives at the UW Libraries. The RPSG was also well positioned to co-sponsor a student organization's campus-wide event that brought a well-known Information Architect to speak at UW.

A great deal of insight was obtained about work practices within the UW Libraries by observing how various staff members did or did not make use of the programs created by the RPSG. For example, throughout the period when the RPSG was promoting the Time Grant Program, only six requests were submitted. Later, the group discovered that a far more pervasive practice involved making informal arrangements between individual librarians and their supervisors to complete work-related research and writing projects in the context of their daily work responsibilities.

Attendance at RPSG-sponsored events also exhibited interesting patterns. Workshops and events were often attended by roughly twenty "core" participants. This could suggest that the enthusiasm among the Libraries Cabinet for developing a culture of research at the UW Libraries was not uniformly shared among the staff. To address the disparity, events and activities bifurcated into more specific research topics (e.g. the Human Subjects Division presentation) and awareness-focused events such as the social receptions. The flexibility of the arrangements in response to shifting needs and interests in research and scholarship among the staff is one of the primary strengths of the RPSG, supported in part by the diversity of this group's membership.

An informal online survey conducted in May 2007 offers additional insights and suggestions from staff at the Libraries. Staff were asked two questions: 1) if they had engaged in any scholarly activities (e.g. research, collaboration, assessment, writing, poster session, having a conversation about collaborating) as a result of events sponsored by the RPSG, and 2) if there were particular activities they wanted to see implemented in the future. The responses, which provide sufficient evidence for use in formative assessment, suggest that staff would like to see sessions repeated periodically, especially the interactive "Framing the Question" session. Suggestions for additional activities included compiling a bibliography of staff publications, offering a session on scholarly communication and how librarians' roles as authors can be developed, and facilitating a "Statistics for Dummies" session where staff can better learn how to analyze the data from any of the UW Libraries' numerous surveys.

Conclusion

The RPSG represents a unique collaboration that has been successful on several levels. It has increased awareness of issues emerging from research and practice in academic libraries. It has provided workshops and educational programs for library staff and members of the iSchool community. It has stimulated exchange and cross-pollination of ideas among librarians, iSchool faculty, and students. Key to the structure and approach of this kind of organizational group is flexibility in planning for an audience with diverse needs. This fruitful arrangement may serve as a model for similar collaborative efforts at other institutions. Based on experiences at the UW Libraries, it might be reasonable to assume that self-organizing groups of colleagues, formal educational workshops, informal social events, and the development of policy-based support mechanisms would each appeal to a particular audience in uniquely productive ways. Sustaining these multiple activities requires a stable set of group members from various units on campus who are willing to be responsive to diverse and changing needs among the Libraries' staff.

References

1. Powell, Ronald R., and Connaway, Lynn Silipigni. *Basic Research Methods for Librarians*. 4th ed. Westport, CT: Libraries Unlimited, 2004, pp. 6–7.
2. Jennerich, Elaine Z. "The Long-term View of Library Staff Development: The Positive Effects on a Large Organization." *College & Research Libraries News* 67 (November 2006): 612–614.
3. Hoggan, Danielle Bodrero. "Faculty Status for Librarians in Higher Education." *Portal: Libraries and the Academy* 3 (July 2003): 431–445.
4. Hill, Janet Swan. "Constant Vigilance, Babelfish, and Foot Surgery: Perspectives on Faculty Status and Tenure for Academic Librarians." *Portal: Libraries and the Academy* 5 (January 2005): 7–22.
5. Welsh, Jeanie M., and Mozenter, Frada L. "Loosening the Ties that Bind: Academic Librarians and Tenure." *College & Research Libraries* 67 (March 2006): 164–176.
6. Park, Betsy, and Riggs, Robert. "Tenure and Promotion: A Study of Practices by Institutional Type." *Journal of Academic Librarianship* 19 (May 1993): 72–77.
7. Bradigan, Pamela S., and Mularski, Carol A. "Evaluation of Academic Librarians' Publications for Tenure and Initial Promotion." *Journal of Academic Librarianship* 22 (September 1996): 360–365.
8. Meyer, Richard W. "A Measure of the Impact of Tenure." *College & Research Libraries* 60 (March 1999): 110–119.
9. Mitchell, W. Bede, and Reichel, Mary. "Publish or Perish: A Dilemma for Academic Librarians?" *College & Research Libraries* 60 (May 1999): 232–243.
10. Henry, Deborah B., and Neville, Tina M. "Research, Publication, and Service Patterns of Florida Academic Librarians." *Journal of Academic Librarianship* 30 (November 2004): 435–451.
11. ACRL Committee on the Status of Academic Librarians. "A Guideline for the Appointment, Promotion, and Tenure of Academic Librarians." *College & Research Libraries News* 66 (October 2005): 668–676.
12. Floyd, Barbara L., and Phillips, John C. "A Question of Quality: How Authors and Editors Perceive Library Literature." *College & Research Libraries* 58 (January 1997): 81–93.
13. Miller, Jeannie P., and Benefiel, Candace R. "Academic Librarians and the Pursuit of Tenure: The Support Group as a Strategy for Success." *College & Research Libraries* 59 (May 1998): 260–265.
14. Kuyper-Rushing, Lois. "A Formal Mentoring Program in a University Library: Components of a Successful Experiment." *Journal of Academic Librarianship* 27 (November 2001): 440–446.
15. Lee, Deborah. "Mentoring the Untenured Librarian: The Research Committee." *College & Research Libraries News* 66 (November 2005): 711–713, 724.
16. Level, Allison V., and Mach, Michelle. "Peer Mentoring: One Institution's Approach to Mentoring Academic Librarians." *Library Management* 26 (2005): 301–310.
17. Sapon-White, Richard, King, Valery, and Christie, Anne. "Supporting a Culture of Scholarship for Academic Librarians." *Portal: Libraries and the Academy* 4 (July 2004): 407–422.

18. Iysick, Cynthia, and Babb, Nancy. "Writing Support for Junior Faculty Librarians: A Case Study." *Journal of Academic Librarianship* 32 (January 2006): 94–100.
19. Jordan, William. "Creating a Research Agenda for UW Libraries." Internal white paper, University of Washington Libraries, Seattle, 2003.

Acknowledgments

The authors would like to recognize Steve Hiller and Steve Shadle, both members of the RPSG, for their thoughtful comments during the initial formulations of many themes expressed in this chapter. The authors are also grateful for the efforts of all of the current and former members of the RPSG in making the activities described in this chapter possible.

Appendix 5.A: Time Grant Program Documentation and Guidelines

Definition.

A time grant is time during which a staff member or group of staff members is released from normal work duties and compensated at the regular rate of pay in order to pursue a goal of writing, research, or other scholarly activity. Activities should be of benefit to the Libraries and result in a product, such as an article, bibliography, presentation, or the like. If two or more staff members are working on a joint project, they may apply for time grants as a group. The time grant program is administered by the Libraries Staff Development and Training Coordinator.

Eligibility.

Time grants are available to any staff member who has been employed at the University of Washington Libraries for a period of one year.

Duration.

Staff members may apply for time grants of various duration depending upon the individual activity. The total number of hours for a time grant will not exceed 240 hours.

Use of Libraries facilities and resources.

During the time grant, the staff member may use Libraries facilities, supplies, equipment, and services on a reasonable and occasional basis.

Application procedures.

• A staff member may apply for a time grant at any time through the supervisory line to the appropriate Assistant or Associate Dean who will review the request and forward a recommendation to the Dean of University Libraries.

- Amount and configuration of time grant with beginning and ending dates.
- Description of writing, research or scholarly activity.
- Benefit(s) of the project to the Libraries and to the individual's development.
- Expectations for use of Libraries facilities and resources.
- Anticipated travel time, if any.
- If two or more staff members want to apply as a group, each person must negotiate with their immediate supervisor. The group may submit one application signed by all supervisors or each group member may submit an individual application.

Report of time grant.

The staff member(s) must prepare a brief written report of the results of the activity within a month of the end of the time grant. Included with the report should be a copy of the resulting product, such as an article, bibliography, presentation, or the like.

6 Developing Library Professionals in a Multi-disciplinary Support Environment at the University of Cumbria

Margaret Weaver, Paul Holland, and Lisa Toner

Introduction

Academic library services are diversifying to meet the needs of a new generation of learners, who expect a "one-stop" approach to service delivery and excellent customer service. Notably this is achieved by structural changes, resulting in a convergence of service elements, consisting of library, Information Technology (IT), and associated services (often media, elements of learning support, and, latterly, learning technology). In common with the US and Australia, the United Kingdom (UK) has adopted convergence on a large scale to meet these imperatives.[1] This places new demands on staff in support roles. St. Martin's College (now known at the University of Cumbria) Learning and Information Services (LIS) is an example of how a newly created, "converged" academic library in the UK approached the training of its people following a restructure. A training needs analysis was conducted to assess the learning requirements of staff from variant professional backgrounds.

This chapter outlines the rationale and construction of the training needs analysis, its links with appraisal, and how the results led to the training initiative. The training plan that emerged is specified, including how it was designed to help staff acquire the skills required. Embracing new job roles and understanding the contribution of colleagues from different professions and sites is part of the qualitative evaluation—including the extent to which the training initiative was successful and its perceived value to staff. A literature search on continuing professional development during times of change is presented from a multi-professional perspective. The conclusions are the result of a "whole team" approach to staff development that includes perspectives from participants, trainers, and the LIS Staff Development Group.

Setting

This chapter concentrates on the UK perspective in order to articulate the approaches that are being taken to prepare staff for work in this new learning environment. A case study at St. Martin's College is presented as evidence of how one service transformed itself from a traditional and reactive library service into a proactive and user-centered provider, following a restructure. This development has resulted in a new model of delivery, embracing service integration and enlarged roles for staff. It is first helpful to consider the external factors in the UK brought about this change, before studying the literature on converged library services including relevant staff development contexts that these changes influence. It is a complex picture.

External Drivers Relevant to UK Higher Education

In common with the rest of the world, the UK higher education system is increasingly predicated on the belief that educational opportunity should be inclusive and extended to all. This is reflected in government targets for young people and underpins national widening participation objectives.[2] Students from a variety of backgrounds are now encouraged to see further/higher education as an achievable goal and funding regimes have been introduced to assist disadvantaged groups; opinion is divided on whether the new system of tuition fees, first proposed by Lord Dearing in 1997, inhibits rather than enables take-up.[3] These national trends have contributed to a fundamental rethink about how students from non-traditional backgrounds can be fully supported, with concomitant implications for how universities organize themselves, including their support services, and even a reconsideration of what constitutes a university in the twenty-first century. Student retention and progression routes are therefore a central tenet of university strategies. The 14–19 years policy area[4] and the Every Child Matters strategy[5] are also impacting on the mission and perspectives of institutions like St. Martin's, which is, in the main, a vocational education provider. This expansion of higher education is set against a shrinking unit of resource in real terms, forcing higher education institutions (HEIs) to be more cost-effective and business focused.

The changing nature of students and their lifestyles is also having a profound effect on their expectations of a quality learning experience. Many students combine work with study whether on a part-time or full-time basis and they make increased demand on a range of university services across extended hours of the day and year. They lead busy lives and expect immediate responses and good customer service; they are not interested in service/academic demarcation, but in timely and effective support—often requiring it remotely. It is thought that bringing relevant functions together within a single management structure is of benefit to learners and tutors.

Work-based learning is becoming the norm in many higher education institutions like St. Martin's. The recent Leitch Review of Skills[6] recommended that further and higher education providers more fully embrace the skills required for employability and competitiveness on a global scale; this means increasing skills attainment at all levels by 2020. New qualifications such as Foundation Degrees are enabling students to study and progress in a range of vocational subjects. Institutional learning and teaching strategies are reflecting these changes with more emphasis on students as active learners able to interact in the real world, employable, confident, and Information and Communication Technology (ICT) literate.

The ubiquity of technology is simultaneously shaping university missions, curricula, and service delivery. The term "digital native"[7] is used to describe people who utilize IT in a connected and networked environment that is pervasive in their lives, shaping a new culture of studentship that requires a modern and IT-enabled experience. Increasingly, social and informal learning environments use virtual learning and advanced communication tools to become integral parts of the student experience. In tandem the development of digital libraries, hybrid libraries, and the increased emphasis on information management and records management have contributed to discussions about economies of scale and how best to exploit web-based information and learning technologies. Another kind of convergence is also happening between space and learning, and learning and support. The redesign of the academic library as an "Information Commons" has affected how learning spaces are envisioned and connected to learning and teaching, with significant implications for staff roles.[8]

This complex picture demonstrates that learners are expecting to be more in control of their learning and to be able to make informed choices before, during, and after their course. Realistically this places additional demands on learners, academics, and on supporters of learning, leading to a debate on the very nature of the student experience and what constitutes "graduateness" and the educational purpose of a university. Learning Support has therefore become a greater institutional priority because of a recognition that fundamentally students can only be successful if they are supported via a holistic set of approaches and services.

The join up of higher education in the UK with the entire educational system (from cradle to grave) is evident in government policies[9] and statutes.[10] It is mirrored by bodies such as the Joint Information Systems Committee (JISC), that now serves a unified sector of further and higher education institutions, including academic libraries. JISC is in the forefront of ICT developments in the UK and continues to assist institutions to develop their global information strategies.[11]

Therefore these trends have understandably impacted greatly on institutional missions, strategies, and structures. Bringing functions and services together into a unified managerial framework (convergence) has been seen as one way to address these needs.

Literature Review

The history of and rationale for convergence is well documented in the literature on academic libraries in the UK.[12, 13] Indeed the UK has embraced service integration on a fairly large scale, unlike the rest of Europe.[14] The reasons for this are complex and largely unevaluated. The Fielden[15] and Follett[16] reports of the 1990s first recommended that academic library personnel could and should influence learning support and that they required appropriate training and development to do so. Indeed, most of the studies on converged services highlight the requirement for staff development and training as does Field's seminal work on convergence in the UK.[17] This is true whatever model of convergence is adopted—whether managerial or operational. Fisher also discusses the various models of convergence and the reasons for adoption and points to the creation of multidisciplinary teams being a direct result of service realignments.[18]

Further, the notion of "new professional practice" is now a reality as first envisioned by Fowell and Levy[19] in their article on networked learner support, emerged because of pervasive web-based digital information, and the new pedagogies of e-learning and blended learning. Brophy, writing in 2000, also confirmed the rise of the networked learner and the blurring of roles that would ensue both between information workers and academics, and among supporters of learning.[20] Understandably, new staff development contexts and scenarios develop as a result of these advances.

Staff Development Contexts

Hanson's recent book on the "convergence experience" of academic libraries offers a real insight to the cultural changes that convergence brings about.[21] Using a case study approach, the collective experiences of contributors is presented from the perspective of the Head of Service. The importance of staff development and training as a requirement during times of change is a common theme throughout; it is thought to be an effective way to help bring new teams together to potentially narrow any cultural divide. Delivery of staff development, however, must be set alongside a wider set of strategies such as those concerned with communication,[22] recognition, and support for critical thinking.[23]

The IMPEL Project (arising from the publication of the Follett Report) first suggested that joint staff development and training could promote a shared understanding of service objectives and multi-professional perspectives drawing on the values and behaviors of staff.[24] The IMPEL2 project continued this work, particularly examining the impact of electronic libraries on role perception and educational partnerships.[25] The term "multidisciplinary team" is emerging to describe these multifaceted roles, and while prevalent in health disciplines for some time it has only recently been applied to academic library teams and literature on converged services.   The Society of College, National and University Libraries (SCONUL) Taskforce on e-Learning <http://www.sconul.ac.uk/ groups/e-learning/papers/finalreport.pdf> recommends more research into the development needs of staff who assist learners and tutors with flexible learning approaches. Their report highlights the significance of working with other groups of staff and to the existence of possible professional boundary issues.[26] This suggests that staff require help with role development in these new contexts.

Converged teams bring strategic advantages to an institution, including an expansion of the skills base, and the capacity to support students more effectively and seamlessly. Concerns about deskilling or stifling of identity are a common theme in studies about training in converged services.[27] A training needs analysis is not a new idea but is a practical tool that can be used to plan and implement staff development following a convergence.[28] Further, studies show that implementation of converged teams is better achieved if there is a reassurance that the new identities embedded in new roles will not undermine staff's original professional background and values. According to Haines, "there is a need to help staff recognize different professional cultures and to find ways to identify common values."[29]

What emerges from these and other studies is that irrespective of the institution, the importance of managing change and using the opportunity of the change to put into place a comprehensive and holistic training plan must not be overlooked.

Objective

St. Martin's College LIS is an example of a converged department that met the training needs of staff following the merger of the formerly separate Library, IT User Support, Media, and Learning Technology services. The deciding factors that brought about this particular model of convergence were related to the aims expressed in the Corporate Plan 2004–9,[30] which stated the College's intention to realign its support services to ensure the successful delivery of the student experience in Cumbria, Lancashire, and from its campus in London. The academic strategy was predicated on the assumption that students flourish only if a wide range of pedagogic and blended learning approaches are integrated into a vibrant academic portfolio alongside excellent support. In fact, the creation of a new learning environment was the goal, with a well-prepared workforce functioning within optimum structures.

Taking note of the external and internal factors, the new LIS department was established in January 2006 after a one-year institutional review. In parallel, flexible and distributed learning approaches were being advanced while a new regional university was being created. St. Martin's became the University of Cumbria in August 2007, based on the Harris Report recommendations.[31]

An LIS Implementation Group was set up in April 2006 to oversee the implementation of the new structure. Staff representatives from all campuses and teams were able to meet and agree how the changes would be supported. Staff development and training was identified as essential for all staff. It was obvious that a systematic response was required to meet the revised emphasis of LIS roles and new job descriptions. The modifications to roles centered on:

- a higher profile of ICT and learning technologies within the job specification;
- learning and teaching elements specified in all job descriptions;
- integrated service delivery (front-line roles working across the disciplines for better customer service) on all campuses, harmonizing the current varying managerial structures;
- academic liaison teams to liaise with academic staff about all LIS activities (not just "library" or "IT");
- the use of systems for increased accountability and service improvement, for example, help desk software was introduced for all teams;
- harmonization of service desk functions and opening hours across the three main campuses;
- service availability mapping across core and non-core hours.

It is notable that each of the three LIS campus teams was at a different stage of development as each had been set up at different times. Consequently, each team was inconsistent about the level of convergence. After the restructuring, there was a single service and management model on all campuses.

Methods

A training needs analysis (TNA) was carried out to assess the learning requirements of staff from variant professional backgrounds, who had been brought together into the new LIS department. This section describes how the TNA was designed and embedded within annual appraisal processes and how the outcomes fed into the training plan. Focus groups took place to explore the perceptions of staff who had taken part in the TNA and the staff development sessions. By connecting the strategic purpose of the TNA and the participative benefits of collaborative training design and delivery, the intention was to provide optimal conditions for staff engagement.

TNA in Context

The structure was designed to enable LIS to provide an integrated library, media, and IT support service across multiple campuses, which required staff to broaden their skills in preparation for a wider range of knowledge-intensive activities and responsibilities. The objective of the TNA was to identify any gaps between the current abilities of each individual and future job requirements in the new structure. The proposed structure would require a cultural change, a more integrated approach, broadened roles, and a greater understanding of the services provided by the new LIS. Some staff expressed concern about the complexities of the restructuring process, which coincided with a college-wide role analysis and the harmonization of conditions. There was uncertainty about the impact the changes would have on the day-to-day work of different staff roles. Some staff expressed anxiety about some new areas of responsibility. The analysis of training needs and subsequent training sessions were intended to prepare people for these role-related changes.

Since the LIS team comprised over 100 people working across three campuses, the simplest method of gathering the initial data was to create and issue a TNA form. LIS staff at each campus were asked to incorporate their new staff training programs into the TNA form. Inevitably, in a multi-site organization there were some differences in LIS practice at each campus, often due to a need to meet localized requirements. The form was an opportunity to capture all of these, together with the standardized activities, and to present a comprehensive choice to all LIS staff.

The form listed the full range of skills across all LIS job functions, including library services, audio-visual and media equipment, learning technologies, and basic IT support skills as well as more generic corporate training modules including courses that are mandatory for all college employees. The form was designed to be self-completed by each person. The form (see Appendix 6.A) was e-mailed to all members of staff within LIS. The instructions stated that the form would be discussed during the annual appraisal meeting. Skills areas and existing training courses were categorized to make the form easier to use and to identify mandatory sessions; no attempt was made to steer people toward development opportunities that were solely within the confines of their current or proposed areas of responsibility. A section on the form provided space for recording completed training, together with dates. A separate form was created for line managers to collate the data from the individual TNA forms into one "team form."

The opportunity to self-select areas for personal development was an important aspect of the process. This focus on the learner rather than just the departmental training needs afforded people the freedom to identify areas that needed refresher training, areas that were pertinent to their roles, or topics of personal interest. A learner-focus was recognized by Sloman as something that was necessary in a learning organization, with a subsequent shift in emphasis toward the individual or team taking more responsibility for their own learning.[32]

The completed form was a key part in the forthcoming appraisal meetings between an individual and his or her line manager. This link with the college-wide appraisal process resulted in two benefits:

- **A higher return rate**: traditionally, the return rate for self-completed forms is low and reviewing the forms during the appraisal meeting would counter this.
- **Better balance of development needs**: it enabled a balance to be struck between the areas of development that each person had identified for themselves and additional development areas based on the "bigger picture" of potential future organizational needs that could be suggested by their line manager.

This second element also addressed some of the potential disadvantages that might exist by relying solely on the needs identified from a staff survey. By identifying training needs during the appraisal process, the outcome is a set of personal development plans that meet both individual as well as organizational needs.

One weakness of the form has been identified. Although each campus contributed to its creation, the form does not define the training content, as this is the responsibility of each trainer.

The Role of the Staff Development Group

The Staff Development Group (SDG) is comprised of members from all functions and sites within LIS. SDG has worked to establish a multidisciplinary approach to training and development opportunities, mainly by funding a variety of external courses and conferences but also by organizing in-service training events. The mission of this group includes, "to plan and co-ordinate whole service training events in line with LIS strategic plan." This has partly been achieved by the introduction of a series of half-hour time slots during which different types of training can be facilitated.

Knight and Yorke[33] acknowledge the importance of experiential learning, which can be achieved by demonstrating and learning in different situations. This demonstration of skillful practice in context can enable staff to change and adapt while at the same time promoting the belief that all staff can continue to learn and develop throughout their lives. With that understanding comes self-efficacy and the belief that each individual can make a difference. LIS aims to constantly develop a team of capable staff by stretching, challenging, and stimulating self-reflection within a supportive framework. According to Stephenson:

> Capable people not only know about their specialisms, they also have the confidence to apply their knowledge and skills within varied and changing situations and to continue to develop their specialist knowledge and skills.[34]

As such, LIS training is viewed as a core aspect of work not a "bolt on," or extra. It is a process that all staff engage with, in order to develop personal effectiveness and, as a natural consequence, the effectiveness of the service as a whole. The TNA was seen as an extension of this work. Completed TNA forms were sent to the SDG once the appraisal process had finished. The data was entered into SPSS, a statistical analysis package, which enabled lists to be generated showing which staff had requested which training courses. Once this data was available, the SDG began to plan the course program.

A principal aim of the program was to include as many staff as possible in its delivery, partly to avoid overburdening individuals but also to stimulate ownership from staff in the process of training within their area of expertise. Initially it was hoped that some "train the trainer" courses would be held for those involved in delivery but this was not arranged in time. Instead those who felt the need for support were encouraged to attend external "presentation style" courses. This was of benefit particularly to those at the LIS assistant level who had little experience with the delivery of training. Training from the "bottom-up" has been an inclusive process which has united staff, made the program seem less onerous, and enabled real conversations to take place about aspects of the work changes in a non-threatening way.

The format of the training was left to the individual teaching the session. On the whole, most sessions were half an hour and fitted into existing weekly half-hour training slots. Some courses were delivered over a half or a full day and some were delivered using Blackboard, the college's online virtual learning environment or *Informs*[35] an interactive online tutorial. The mix of delivery methods has proved to be one of the strengths of the program as it has added variety and serendipity to a fairly intensive program. Evaluation forms from the events were distributed via the trainers.

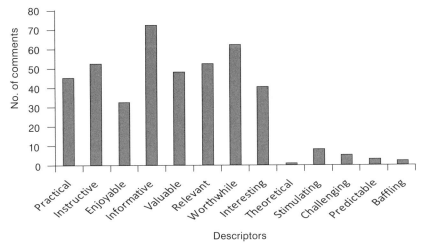

Figure 6.1 Ascribed value of courses

Evaluation

The training plan and program were designed to teach new skills needed as a result of the restructure. Embracing new job roles and understanding the contribution of colleagues from different professions and sites are complex processes. LIS was keen to evaluate both the TNA and the extent to which the training initiative was of value to staff during times of change. Two mechanisms were introduced to collect data from staff: post-training evaluation forms and focus groups.

Post-training Evaluation Forms

The evaluation form was adapted from one designed by the Centre for Development of Learning and Teaching at St. Martin's College. The form has evolved over several years and was shaped by participant research (see Appendix 6.B). The form aims to elicit feedback from a variety of professional disciplines within the college; its style and language have been carefully selected to facilitate this.

Figure 6.1 shows the relevance of the sessions as perceived by staff taking part in the program. Staff were asked to circle words from a predetermined list to reflect the value of the course to the individuals. Most staff replied that the training would help them to advise students more effectively in the future and feel confident about covering for other teams during times of reduced staffing levels. No one circled terms such as threatening, tedious, vague, irrelevant, uninteresting, pointless, repetitive, nothing new, waste of time, or dull.

Focus Groups

To evaluate the TNA process, six focus groups (involving 30 staff in total) were conducted following the training sessions. Each focus group was made up of mixed staff teams and professional backgrounds—two at each campus—to allow for homogeneity but also to capture a variety of opinions as suggested by Krueger.[36] It was important to gauge staff perceptions about the TNA to find out its impact, and also to capture staff views on its future design and use. Audio taping was rejected as it was felt to be a sensitive topic that could affect the level of staff engagement. All sessions were documented by the Service Administrator.

An open questioning technique was used to explore themes. As advocated by Morgan and Saxton,[37] a mix of covert and overt prompts was used. The discussion areas centered on the TNA and its use in multi-professional contexts. Verbal reinforcement was avoided by the facilitator to elicit honest opinions and draw out responses (see Appendix 6.C). The discourse was analyzed using categorization techniques. It was valuable to have the same person record the sessions as it was felt that this provided objectivity. The limitations of focus groups in qualitative research are acknowledged,[38] nonetheless collective phenomena emerged as follows.

Results

Staff views and opinions were analyzed using data from the two instruments. Overall, most staff were positive about using the TNA as a way to identify their training needs. Several cross-cutting themes emerged that prompted further questions:

- Purpose and design of the TNA—did it fulfill its objectives?
- Links with the appraisal process—was it helpful to staff?
- Delivery of training—to what extent did participants and trainers find it of value?
- Professional background—was it a relevant factor?
- Did team dynamics play any part?
- Was training and evaluation of this nature appropriate during times of change?

Each of these is explored below.

Purpose of the training needs analysis

Several people queried the exact purpose of the TNA and felt it needed more clarification during its introduction. The specificity of training was deemed a good thing as the sessions related to St. Martin's jobs rather than being generic. Most categories of training were relevant, although the TNA form did not cover specialized ICT courses.

Staff liked being able to select their own training sessions from the TNA form and felt that more engagement was likely than if they had been told to attend. Self-selection enabled them to tailor training to their need, whether it was job training or personal interest. The TNA form provided a structure to the training opportunities as well as providing an impetus. The deadlines for training completion were also helpful in this respect.

One campus expressed a level of uncertainty about the relationship between the TNA and the LIS restructure process. Since this campus had provided half-hour training slots for some time, there was no distinction between the training provided via the TNA; routine training was seen as addressing the identified training needs at the time. As a result, staff at that campus found it difficult to separate out the TNA from other training sessions and it was seen as only one tool in a range of training opportunities. The reason for this may be connected to the extent that training is embedded into normal working practice.

Design of the TNA

The TNA form was described by staff as a generic but comprehensive list that provided a good breadth of choice. Staff appreciated being involved in construction of the TNA categories, although the use of technical jargon caused some people to be confused. It was felt, however, that the form should have included more detailed descriptions, as the "Categories" might act as deterrents if staff were unsure what they meant. Some felt that there was no one to give guidance when selecting from a wide choice of training sessions, and one person felt that ranking the usefulness of the different training sessions for each job role may have been helpful in determining the level of training. Describing the selection process, staff chose courses that looked interesting or filled as a gap in their own knowledge. They asked themselves, "Do I know how to do that?" when filling out the form. Respondents found it helpful in identifying college requirements for the job. On the other hand, one person commented that the wide range of training allowed her to "spread her wings" and not be confined to the immediate job role and that this was motivating.

Links with the Appraisal Process

Staff said that the TNA was a positive enhancement to the appraisal process and reflected the evolution of LIS jobs especially with relevance to IT. Most staff discussed their TNA forms with their line managers at either an appraisal or probation meeting, and this was described as useful. Discussion at a more formal meeting helped people to focus on their training requirements. Since the appraisal form refers explicitly to training needs, it was the logical time to discuss it. Essential training was the main focus of appraisal discussions but because staff were encouraged to discuss the entire TNA form, they said it enabled them to think about how training is carried out and, importantly, to document systems used within LIS. Day-to-day requirements as well as the elements in new job descriptions were considered. Relevance to the job was high on the list of reasons for choosing a particular training course, borne out by Figure 6.1 (see p. 99).

Staff reported that one of the main benefits of linking training with appraisal was having their manager's knowledge of the "bigger picture" when discussing selected training sessions. Talking about training during the appraisal process led to choosing more sessions than might have been done alone. A minority of staff in the focus groups commented that their discussion at appraisal had not made any significant difference to the selection made. On the whole, staff chose sessions that were not directly related to their own job but that would fill gaps in their knowledge. It was seen as particularly useful for the technical support staff to gain background knowledge in library routines, although this view was not universal.

Delivery of Training

The importance of the trainer in contextualizing the content was mentioned. Having a wider range of staff (than previously) involved in delivery of the training was seen as a benefit. The groups did not think that making staff development "compulsory" was attractive but accepted that certain courses needed to be mandatory. Translating the training into practice was seen as the biggest challenge for staff. The importance of setting aside specific time for training was noted. There was a strong preference for delivering the training during a weekly half-hour time slot. Staff appreciated the small group, informal settings, and the opportunity to mix with others. Overall, staff were fully satisfied with the training that they received.

Trainers' Perspectives

Without exception, the groups questioned how trainers had been chosen, and wondered if this had been done by job title. Some trainers were unsure about whether they were competent to do the relevant training and requested more preparation and discussion about who carried out the training requested. Delivering training sessions was perceived as beneficial to staff's own jobs but more support for trainers would have been appreciated. It was felt that being a trainer offered the chance to "learn how to explain things clearly." It was suggested that trainers should have input about category descriptions, from overview to in-depth sessions on specific subject matter. These results show that some trainers were unused to taking on this role and needed more help, which LIS is addressing.

Professional Background

No one mentioned professional background as being an important factor *per se*, in either choice of course or interactions during training. Focus group participants did find it useful that training sessions were available to all teams and across all sites. There was a feeling in one focus group, however, that staff background would tend to influence the choice of training course taken since gaps in knowledge about the enlarged service would occur both between and across the disciplines. The TNA process highlighted that multi-skilling is necessary in an integrated service. Although some training areas are now blurred and not specifically "Library/IT/Media," the range of training presented on the TNA supported a broader understanding of LIS roles. Participants also thought that the TNA helped avoid staff "stereotyping" and was therefore a supportive tool. The involvement of new staff in the TNA during induction as well as probation was suggested as a future enhancement.

Team Dynamics

The results here varied by campus more than any other category and demonstrated that LIS teams were at different stages of development. At the campus where integrated teams had been established in 1997, working practices did not change much as a result of the restructure, and people that had worked together for some time did not emerge from the process with any different views about the teams or the team responsibilities. This was similar to the situation at the second campus; the TNA did not appear to affect staff views of their roles in the new integrated service as enhanced relationships were underway. Staff were already covering each other's jobs on the front-line service desk and a more holistic team was being developed anyway. Staff expressed the view that they got more job satisfaction from knowing each others' roles in an integrated service and that ultimately this benefited the students. They felt that the integrated service was beneficial to working relationships. The campus that had experienced the most change as a result of the recent introduction of multidisciplinary teams made particular mention of the training's effect on team roles. Staff commented that training allowed people to understand other perspectives, put faces to names, and identify a team's skills gaps. Important points included avoiding variable knowledge in a team, taking a targeted training approach, and limiting variances in staff attending training sessions. The TNA allowed this level of analysis for the first time. Size of teams was not mentioned as a factor but the need to ensure that more than one person has a particular skill was highlighted.

As a Change Tool?

As noted previously, not all staff connected the TNA with a change in culture and practice that the restructure represented. This disconnect was related to different developmental stages of campuses and the perspectives of individuals. It is possible that the way the TNA purpose had been communicated was also a factor. The TNA helped staff become more aware of requirements of other areas within LIS. One person mentioned that it challenged assumptions about staff roles. A line manager who also was a trainer said the opportunity to provide training helped her develop a service-wide role rather than campus-based role, and let others experience this change in her role.

Looking back, staff said that they only had a partial picture of their jobs at the time of completing the TNA; they reflected that they would probably choose additional training if they were completing it now. The role of the line manager was particularly mentioned as a key agent in the process of staff engagement with the TNA and its value in helping staff to see a wider picture. As a training and development tool the line manager discussions were found to increase choice of sessions chosen and to be an effective method of following up training outcomes. However, one group mentioned how feedback from other staff members had also influenced choices of training.

Staff were pleased that technical support members of LIS had chosen to participate in the library training as it was felt that this brought a fresh view and better understanding, even though the extent of this was not even across the campuses. There was agreement that in an integrated service it is good for staff to know as much as possible about other staff roles, and this was seen as important when helping colleagues and customers. To varying degrees, the TNA was viewed as being one of many things that were happening at the time of the restructure, and was difficult to separate out from other events. One member of the staff commented that she had "conquered her personal fear of IT" as a result of completing the training. Staff said that they now felt more comfortable in their new roles.

Value of Training

Did the TNA lead to a better staff training experience? The TNA certainly prompted staff to think about areas of training needed, including areas indirectly relevant to their work, and provided the opportunity for staff to do things that they would otherwise not have done. Staff were satisfied with the results. The opportunity for refresher training was important. This was particularly true for areas with recently updated procedures, or areas of work that changed frequently. An example of this was the Help Desk call logging software. It was felt that the TNA carried out the previous year offered good baseline training so that, in the future, there could be fewer but more focused sessions. In other words, the TNA itself was appreciated and staff felt that they would like to use it again with certain enhancements.

Conclusion

Based on this case study, it is concluded that the use of a TNA and accompanying training program, organized centrally and run locally, has been a helpful tool in supporting staff through periods of change in multi-professional contexts. The multi-campus nature of St. Martin's has added complexity but also yielded rich information about how teams interact over time and within a common service framework. The quality of team relationships before the program took place was as significant as staff readiness for change and comfort with new roles and colleagues. Personal qualities were deemed to be more important to role definition than professional background or technical skills, which confirms previous research.[39]

Several learning points have emerged from this experience. The TNA is an iterative process as is skills acquisition; staff need time to adapt and to understand their response to the change process. Identifying potential trainers and their roles in the new department has led to the emergence of staff expertise and increased confidence. Line managers and trainers need particular support during times of change in order to fulfill their responsibilities as supporters of staff and of institutional change. They are influencers and also part of the change itself. The reflective nature of conversations with line managers is an important aspect of personal growth and development (for both parties) and helps staff to come to terms with changes. Individual responses are valuable indicators of well-being and inextricably linked to personal preferences and expectations of the workplace.

Evaluating the TNA thoroughly and using a participative, flexible design have been parts of the change process itself, leading to a broader engagement with training than would have occurred if this study had not taken place. Significantly, this means that library staff broadly agree on the value of the tool going forward, have ideas for its enhancement, and support its use in practice.

Converged library services bring entirely different staff development needs than traditional library services do. These needs go beyond a simplistic set of training objectives. It is important to engage staff in the design and delivery of training sessions and to evaluate their impact through a "whole team" approach. In this respect, the TNA tool and LIS SDG have important roles to play in developing the multidisciplinary workforce. The evaluation of the TNA process was found to be a helpful strategy in examining the extent to which LIS staff felt empowered in their new roles. The final word rests with a member of LIS staff who wisely commented, "I have more belief in one service now, not necessarily due to the Training Needs Audit, but this is all part of the change process."

References

1. Collier, Mel. "Convergence in Europe Outside the United Kingdom." In *Managing Academic Support Services in Universities,* edited by Terry Hanson. London: Facet Publishing, 2005, pp.181–201.
2. Higher Education Funding Council. *HEFCE Strategic Plan 2006–11.* Updated April 2007. Available: <http://www.hefce.ac.uk/pubs/hefce/2007/07_09/>. Accessed: April 28, 2007.
3. Dearing, Sir Ronald. *Higher Education in the Learning Society – The Report of the National Committee of Inquiry into Higher Education,* 1997. Available: <http://www.leeds.ac.uk/educol/ncihe/>. Accessed: April 28, 2007.
4. Great Britain. Department for Education and Skills. *14–19 Education and Skill.* Cm 6476, 2005. Available: <http://www.dfes.gov.uk/14-19/documents/14-19whitepaper.pdf>. Accessed: May 7, 2007.
5. Great Britain. Department for Education and Skills. *Every Child Matters: Change for Children.* Available: <http://www.everychildmatters.gov.uk/>. Accessed: May 7, 2007.
6. Leitch, Sandy, Lord. *Prosperity for All in the Global Economy – World Class Skills. Final Report.* 2006. Available: <http://www.hm-treasury.gov.uk/media/523/43/leitch_finalreport051206.pdf>. Accessed: May 7, 2007.
7. Gaston, J. "Reaching and Teaching the Digital Natives." *Library Hi Tech News* 23, no. 3 (2006): 12–13.
8. Weaver, Margaret. "Exploring Conceptions of Learning and Teaching Through the Creation of Flexible Learning Spaces: The Learning Gateway – A Case Study." *New Review of Academic Librarianship* 12, no. 2 (2006): 95–107.
9. Great Britain. Department for Education and Skills. *Future of Higher Education.* Cm 5735, (January 2003). Available: <http://www.dfes.gov.uk>. Accessed: May 26, 2007.
10. Great Britain. *Higher Education Act 2004.* The Stationery Office Limited. Chapter 8. Available: <http://www.dfes.gov.uk>. Accessed: May 26, 2007.
11. Joint Information Systems Committee *JISC Strategy 2007–2009.* Available: <http://www.jisc.ac.uk/aboutus/strategy/strategy0709.aspx>. Accessed: May 7, 2007.
12. Hanson, Terry, ed. *Managing Academic Support Services in Universities: The Convergence Experience.* London: Facet Publishing, 2005.
13. Field, C. D. "Implementing convergence at the University of Birmingham." *SCONUL Newsletter* 9 (Winter 1996): 33–37.
14. Collier, M. "Convergence in Europe outside the United Kingdom." In *Managing Academic Support Services in Universities,* edited by Terry Hanson. London: Facet Publishing, 2005, p. 199.
15. John Fielden Consultancy. *Supporting Expansion: A Study of Human Resource Management in Academic Libraries. A Report for the Management Sub-group of the Library Review.* Bristol: HEFCE, 1994.
16. Joint Funding Councils' Libraries Review Group, Report. Bristol: HEFCE, 1993.
17. Field, Clive D. "Theory and Practice: Reflections on Convergence in United Kingdom Universities." *Liber Quarterly* 11, no. 3 (2001): 267–8.

18. Fisher, Biddy. "Converging on Staff Development." In *Developing Academic Library Staff for Future Success*, edited by Margaret Oldroyd. London: Facet Publishing, 2004, p. 75.
19. Fowell, S., and Levy, P. "Developing a New Professional Practice: A Model for Networked Learner Support in Higher Education." *Journal of Documentation* 51, no. 3 (1995): 271–280.
20. Brophy, Peter. "Networked Learning." *Journal of Documentation* 57, no. 1 (2001): 130–156.
21. Hanson, Terry, ed. *Managing Academic Support Services in Universities: The Convergence Experience*. London: Facet Publishing, 2005.
22. Shoebridge, Michele. "A Decade of Convergence: Information Services at the University of Birmingham." In *Managing Academic Support Services in Universities: The Convergence Experience*, edited by Terry Hanson. London: Facet Publishing, 2005, pp. 29–36.
23. Garrod, Penny. "Skills for New Information Professionals (SKIP): An Evaluation of the Key Findings." *Program* 32, no. 3 (July 1998): 250.
24. Day, J. M., Edwards, C., and Walton, G. "IMPEL: A Research Project into the Impact on People of Electronic Libraries: Stage One: Librarians." In *Information Superhighway: The Role of Librarians, Information Scientists and Intermediaries*, edited by A. H. Helal and J. W. Weiss. Essen: Essen University Library, 1994.
25. Walton, Graham, Day, Joan, and Edwards, Catherine. "Role Change for the Academic Librarian to Support Effectively the Networked Learner: Implications of the IMPEL Project." *Education for Information* 14, no. 4 (1996): 343–350.
26. Society of College, National and University Libraries. *e-Learning Taskforce: Final Report*. SCONUL, 2005. Available: <http://www.sconul.ac.uk/groups/e-learning/papers/finalreport.pdf>. Accessed: May 6, 2007.
27. Wilson, Kerry M., and Halpin, Eddie. "Convergence and Professional Identity in the Academic Library." *Journal of Librarianship and Information Science* 38, no. 2 (2006): 79–91.
28. Fisher, Biddy. "Converging on Staff Development." In *Developing Academic Library Staff for Future Success*, edited by Margaret Oldroyd. London: Facet Publishing, 2004.
29. Haines, Margaret. "Convergence at King's College London." In *Managing Academic Support Services in Universities: The Convergence Experience*, edited by Terry Hanson. London: Facet Publishing, 2005, p. 72.
30. St. Martin's College. *Corporate Plan 2004–9*. Available: <http://www.ucsm.ac.uk>. Accessed: May 6, 2007.
31. Harris, Sir Martin. *Initial Proposal for a New University of Cumbria*. HEFCE, 2005. Available: <http://www.hefce.ac.uk./News/hefce/2005/cumbrep/>. Accessed: May 7, 2007.
32. Sloman, Martyn. *Training in the Age of the Learner*. London: Chartered Institute of Personnel Development, 2003.
33. Knight, Peter T., and Yorke, Mantz. *Assessment, Learning and Employability*. Maidenhead: Open University Press, 2003.
34. Stephenson, John. "The Concept of Capability and Its Importance in Higher Education." In *Capability and Quality in Higher Education*, edited by John Stephenson and Mantz Yorke. London: Kogan Page, 1998, pp. 1–13.
35. INTUTE: *informs*. Available: <http://www.informs.intute.ac.uk/informs>. Accessed: May 19, 2007.
36. Krueger, R. A. "Focus Groups: A Practical Guide for Applied Research." 3rd ed. London: Sage, 2000. Quoted in: Wilson, Kerry. M., and Halpin, Eddie.

"Convergence and Professional Identity in the Academic Library." *Journal of Librarianship and Information Science* 38, no. 2 (2006): 83.

37. Morgan, Norah, and Saxton, Julianna. *Asking Better Questions.* Ontario: Pembroke Publishers, 1994.

38. Robson, Colin. *Real World Research.* 2nd ed. Oxford: Blackwell Publishing, 2002, p. 289.

39. Garrod, Penny. "Skills for New Information Professionals (SKIP): An Evaluation of the Key Findings." *Program* 32, no. 3 (July 1998): 256.

Appendix 6.A. St Martin's College – LIS – Training Needs Analysis Form

Key:
E = Essential,
D = Desirable,
C = Completed
[Leave blank if not applicable]
Name .... Date ....

Skills	E, D, or C	Notes (date completed, etc.)
Compulsory Training		
Health & Safety and Risk Management		
Equal Opportunities and Race Awareness		
Disability Awareness		
Freedom of Information Act		
Manual Handling		
Appraisee training		
Library Procedures		
Opening up/Closing down procedures		
Library/LIS tours (inc. Help Desk & Media)		
Converting to Dewey		
Processing materials		
Cash handling, money loaders & daily banking		
Shelving		
Talislist reading list		
Issuing, discharging and renewing books		
Reservations		
Registration of borrowers		
Queried items		
Short loan booking		
Inter-library loans		
Fines and charges		
Till procedures		
Athens		
Operation of copier and risograph equipment		

continued ...

Skills	*E, D, or C*	*Notes (date completed, etc.)*
Basic search operators – Boolean		
Accident book		
Picking lists		
Reciprocal borrowing schemes		
Copyright		
Overview of Faculty Liaison Teams		
Logging requests on Richmond Help Desk		
Learning and Teaching		
Catalogue searching		
Databases		
E-books		
Subject Gateways		
Web searching		
Resources for your subject		
Referencing		
Overview of Information Fluency Framework		
Media & IT Procedures		
Logging, assigning & closing Richmond requests		
Network overview		
Student image overview		
Setting up a multimedia projector		
User names and passwords		
Use of laptops		
Operation of media items eg video cameras		
P-Counter & Print Credits		
Introduction to Blackboard		
Supporting Blackboard		
Smartis		
Booking equipment		
Video editing – Analogue/digital		
Photocopier maintenance		
Teaching Studio – Operation & Production		
Remote desktop assistance		

Skills	E, D, or C	Notes (date completed, etc.)
ICT procedures – account creation, imaging		
Printer maintenance/installation		
Support Pack registration		
Using Interactive Whiteboards		
Analogue and Voice over IP (VoIP) telephony		
Supporting a video conference		
Operating lecture theatre equipment		
Active directory		
Knowledge Base		
Microsoft training – Windows XP		
Microsoft training – Windows XP applications		
ICTS training – Applications team		
ICTS training – Technical Operations team		
ICTS training – Networks team		
Management/Administrative		
Performance Management		
Managing Teams		
Recruitment and Selection		
Enquiry Desk Skills		
Mentoring		
Report Writing		
Improving Memory		
Minute taking		
Emergency procedures		
Managing a Customer Care Environment		
Creating a Project Initiation Document		
Budgets		
Project bids		
Purchasing procedure		
Appraiser training		
Telephone call procedure		

Appendix 6.B: Training Needs Analysis Workshop Evaluation

Title of workshop:

Presenter:

Date:

	Excellent (a)	Good (b)	Satisfactory (c)	Poor (d	Very Poor (e)
Overall Rating					
1. Overall, how would you rate the workshop in assisting you to meet your learning needs?	□	□	□	□	□
Quality of Workshop Organization and Venue					
2. Pre-workshop organization	□	□	□	□	□
3. Organization on the day	□	□	□	□	□

Your Expectations and Realizations

4. What were your main goals for the workshop? In general, did you accomplish this?

5. What were the most interesting and/or useful aspects of the workshop?

6. What were the least useful aspects or those that need most improvement?

	Extremely (a)	Very (b)	Fairly (c)	Not really (d)	Not at all (e)
7. Please indicate how relevant you found the workshop to your area of work	□	□	□	□	□

8. Circle the words which best describe this workshop for you - use as many descriptors as you wish and feel free to add in others:

boring	practical	instructive
enjoyable	threatening	tedious
informative	vague	irrelevant
uninteresting	valuable	pointless
relevant	worthwhile	repetitive
nothing new	waste of time	interesting
dull	theoretical	stimulating
challenging	predictable	baffling

Actions

9. How do you plan to utilise your learning from this workshop in your future activities?

Future Events

10. Do you have any suggestions for future workshops or events relating to LIS?

Contact Information (Optional)

Name:

Site

Appendix 6.C: Focus Group – Question Areas

Area 1

In what ways and to what extent did the TNA meet or not meet your training needs arising from the restructure? What influenced your choice of training and what was going through your mind when you filled in the TNA? What did you think about the self-selection element of the TNA?

Area 2

What did you think about discussing the TNA at appraisal? Can you describe the dialogue you had with your line manager about it? Would you like to see it used again? Yes/No – please explain the reason for your answer.

Area 3

Having had the training, can you talk about the experience, please? What effect did the training have on your own views about your new role in an integrated service? In what ways did your professional background affect your actions or thinking? What did you learn about working relationships (if anything)?

7   Using Grant Funds to Bring Continuing Education Workshops to Central Pennsylvania

Susan Hamburger

Introduction

This chapter will discuss one innovative approach of using grant funds to bring instructors to a central location rather than sending staff off site. Recognizing a need for selected staff members in the Special Collections Library at the Pennsylvania State University to learn basic, intermediate, advanced, and specialized archival principles and practices, one faculty librarian investigated the viability of bringing Society of American Archivists (SAA) continuing education workshops to Penn State to circumvent the high cost of sending professional and paraprofessional staff to workshops at regional or national conferences. She wrote a series of grants funded by the Pennsylvania Historical and Museum Commission (PHMC) that subsidized most of the costs of holding the workshops, taught by subject experts, at the library. The grants covered participation by librarians and archivists in academic libraries throughout Pennsylvania as well as staff in local historical societies—all at the "scholarship rate" of $20 per day; SAA populated the balance of the workshop slots with attendees from across the country.

Setting

Beginning in 2004 with four workshops, and holding three in each of the succeeding years, the ongoing training series has educated 51 individual academic staff members of the 183 registrants (some took more than one workshop) from Penn State and nine other academic libraries in Pennsylvania. The workshops reached librarians and archivists, administrators, teaching faculty, paraprofessional staff, and a few part-time student employees planning to become archivists. The staff have benefited from interactions with colleagues in other institutions, gained insight into professional practices, and applied the acquired knowledge to their jobs. The grant-funded workshops became a successful tool to educate academic library staff *in situ* with high-quality, nationally recognized instructors. Penn State's Special Collections Library has benefited by having everyone engaged in similar tasks working from the same common understanding of the issues.

With the main campus of The Pennsylvania State University located in University Park at the geographic center of a large state, the challenge of providing high-quality continuing education to the Special Collections Library staff has been met by various methods. Hainer differentiates between continuing education and staff development:

> Continuing education implies that the person engaged in obtaining it has previous experience in the field or topic, and is seeking to augment that education ... staff development tends to refer to many kinds of learning opportunities provided by an employer or agency for staff, the end result of which, presumably, is to improve all staff knowledge about a given topic.[1]

Literature Review

The majority of literature on continuing education has focused on awareness of issues (diversity, ergonomics, the Americans with Disabilities Act), skills improvement (time management, performance evaluation, team building), and broadening perspectives (trends in automation, collection development). Authors have discussed access to professional development opportunities, the perceived need for continuing education, costs, and funding sources, but have not addressed topical areas for increasing subject expertise (issues concerning copyright, developing an oral history program, and care of photographic collections, for example).

The literature concerning training for general library staff revolves around who attends continuing education workshops (professional and/or paraprofessional staff) and the best mode of delivery for training (in person, online, remote, in-house). The underlying theme, not always stated, is generally cost-effectiveness. Hegg found that the 120 academic librarians from four Midwestern states she surveyed who attended workshops were more likely to be women, younger, on the job or in the profession for fewer than two years, and have faculty status.[2] An article in *Arkansas Libraries* advocated online workshops as an inexpensive alternative to face-to-face training at conferences but did not discuss actual costs nor address learning styles or topics that would require in-person interaction or hands-on activities.[3] A Canadian study found that there is a preference for face-to-face continuing education; relevance of the topic and geographic location are critical motivators for involvement.[4] Bolt suggested that regional offerings draw attendees from smaller libraries who benefit from face-to-face networking.[5]

As for the substance of training, the majority of articles focus on technological skills and personnel concerns rather than topical issues that would increase the staff's subject expertise. The Health Sciences Library at the University of Pittsburgh, a specialized library, offered basic staff development across three areas: work skills (computer-related), personal development (finances, retirement), and recreational activities (attendance at a professional baseball game), but did not offer topically related workshops on issues such as HIPAA (Health Insurance Portability and Accountability Act).[6] Gracy and Croft, in studying preservation education in continuing education, noted that continuing education aims to close the gap in the knowledge base of library and information science practitioners that cannot be filled by formal education programs or on-the-job training.[7] They observed that the high number of paraprofessionals and entry-level professionals taking continuing education workshops suggest they arrive on the job with little or no exposure to preservation concepts or experience with preservation work.[8]

A top-down approach seems to govern the selection of who gets what kind of continuing education and what is paid for. Historically, management financially supported librarians more widely than staff. A 1987 survey of SUNY (State University of New York) libraries found that administrators tended to make the decision on the distribution of funds for continuing education for librarians; staff training was not included in the survey.[9] Creth cautioned against devaluing staff by neglecting their training and development.[10] Buchanan studied library assistants in all types of libraries in Western New York and discovered that release time and funding correlated significantly with participation in training, especially off site. However, the types of training focused on computer technology, professional skills (supervisory skills, time management, stress management, team building), and software training.[11]

Cost and sources of funding often become the pivotal point in deciding how much continuing education a library can afford and whom it will most benefit. In the late 1960s, the Association of Research Libraries (ARL) identified nine problem areas of management concern for university-based research libraries, including internal and external formalized programs for training and alternative sources of funding.[12] However, the ARL report focused on library management training and in-house training program development and concluded that "training and staff development are traditionally the first thing to be cut when resources are scarce ... Libraries must make a commitment to an ongoing process of development for all levels of staff if they are to successfully meet the challenges of the twenty-first century."[13] In the 1980s, the new director of the libraries at Indiana State University instituted increased support for external and internal staff development opportunities and provided significant increases in staff development and training funds especially for library faculty.[14] With no formal budget, the University of Pittsburgh Health Sciences Library depended on the library administration to provide bookstore gift certificates to outside speakers, and called for in-house volunteers to present programs.[15] Callahan and Watson noted that bringing seminars and workshops to the library is much more cost-effective than sending personnel out of town. They also suggested that possible sources for funding include grants, utilizing imagination, creativity, and persistence in obtaining financial support.[16]

The key article in archival literature is Nancy Zimmelman's report of the 2004 A*CENSUS (Archival Census and Education Needs Survey in the United States) results. Of her eight principal findings, she discovered that continuing education has been the most important route for the primary and ongoing training of individuals working with historical records. She also found that participation is high, needs are changing from basic to advanced or specialized training on a variety of topics, cost is the leading barrier, delivery of education and training will need to be at the lowest possible cost, and the sources of training will need to come from regional, state, and local archival associations more so than national and international ones.[17]

Taken as a whole, the library and archival literature suggest there is a need for continuing education on specialized topics relevant to both librarians and staff, held in geographically accessible areas, at an affordable cost. The grant project discussed in the next section addresses all three points.

The Problem

The Pennsylvania State University is one university that is geographically dispersed. As such, there are twenty-four campuses spread across the Commonwealth of Pennsylvania, a state that is the thirty-third largest in land area in the nation.[18] Providing services to faculty and students in such a situation can be a challenge, but it is equally difficult to offer training opportunities to the faculty librarians and staff, especially those at the main campus in University Park, centrally located but remote from major urban centers.

Central Pennsylvania lacks the critical mass of people and number of local institutions to offer training in contrast to dense clusters of people in and around large cities like Pittsburgh and Philadelphia. Sending staff to regional and/or national conferences for continuing education workshops presents another difficulty—the financial burden of hundreds of dollars per person expense that many of the smaller academic libraries cannot afford. One alternative became a viable option: to write a grant to fund the cost of bringing continuing education workshops to central Pennsylvania.

Since arriving at Penn State in January 1994, the Manuscripts Cataloging Librarian for Special Collections realized that the staff in the three units within the Special Collections Library—Historical Collections and Labor Archives, Rare Books and Manuscripts, and University Archives—relied on in-house training that was delivered differently by each unit. When the units consolidated into one Special Collections Library in 1999, the disparity in knowledge became even more apparent as the staff had to blend duties on the reference desk and merge five databases into one for cross-collection searching and retrieval, as well as standardize how to process, arrange, and describe the archival collections. The need for consistent, expert training became crucial if everyone was to sing from the same page of music.

At Penn State, the librarians and archivists have tenure-track positions. Paraprofessional staff members, while highly educated, may not always have had coursework in subject fields related to their work, or exposure to the continually evolving standards and best practices in archival studies. While the librarians and archivists individually have generous travel budgets, the costs of attending one major conference each year consume the funds in one gulp. Staff must rely on the library's human resources office to provide funding for trainings for all non-faculty employees—a considerable stretch for an always tight budget. Sending staff *en masse* to a regional or national archival conference would be prohibitively expensive. Bringing the workshops to Penn State, however, could centralize the training at home and save on travel, food, and housing costs, but the workshops themselves range in price from $185 to $405 per person per workshop—an expense still beyond the budget.

Two events happened that sparked the idea to write a grant to fund the workshops: 1) a question from a part-time staff member, enrolled in an MLS (Master of Library Science) course, about writing a processing grant proposal for her class, and 2) the October 2003 PHMC annual grant writing seminar coincidentally held at State College. During the seminar, the Manuscripts Cataloging Librarian asked if the PHMC would be interested in funding archival continuing education workshops and received an enthusiastic response. With PHMC encouragement, the cataloger applied for the $15,000 matching grant by the December 1 application deadline.

Planning for a Grant

The cataloger had some success with obtaining grants in the past. She wrote and received funding for a small grant of $1,000 from the President's Fund to print historically significant negatives in the photo archives at Florida State University, and wrote and administered the Virginia State Library and Archives (now the Library of Virginia) portion of a National Historical Publications and Records Commission (NHPRC) multi-institution cooperative grant to catalog manuscript collections.[19] The PHMC grant was her first at Penn State and involved a more complex infrastructure and bureaucracy.

The cataloger quickly revised her original idea of offering archival continuing education workshops to just Penn State staff; she broadened the audience to archivists, librarians, staff, and volunteers in the academic and public libraries, historical societies, and museums beyond the immediate vicinity of Penn State's main campus to the surrounding contiguous counties. There are plenty of smaller repositories with far tighter budgets than Penn State that could benefit from training opportunities within a few hours' drive.

The SAA—the national organization for archivists akin to the American Library Association—contracts with experienced instructors to teach a variety of workshops, and advertises their education catalog online. The cataloger selected twelve workshops graduating in level from basic and intermediate, to advanced and specialized that could be offered over three years, starting with the basics in order to build knowledge incrementally. She did not want to offer workshops blindly and hope that people would attend. She wrote to the repositories' directors outlining her plans, and asked for feedback (without a firm commitment at that time) about which workshops they would be interested in having their staff attend for a nominal fee. A free workshop, she reasoned, would imply lack of worth and a concomitant lack of incentive to attend. A small investment, however, would help ensure attendance and pay for costs the grant funds did not cover such as food for morning and afternoon breaks.

Of nineteen repositories contacted, eleven responded, with only one workshop on business archives soundly rejected. The cataloger e-mailed her idea for the series of workshops to the SAA Director of Education who affirmed her interest in working with Penn State to sponsor the workshops, outlined the costs, and stated what SAA would provide. Based on the workshop costs, the cataloger calculated that $15,000 would cover roughly four or five days' worth of workshops each year. As some workshops are one day in length, and others are two days, she wanted to offer a progression of them within each year. For example, the introduction to archives had to come before arrangement and description.

The cataloger consulted with the Associate Dean's staff assistant to choose and calculate food needs, arriving at $20 per person per day from all "scholarship rate" attendees to cover the drinks and break food for everyone, including the people registering directly with SAA, but not lunch. She wrote back to the repositories' directors with a firm plan and solicited letters of support from them for the grant application. While awaiting the support letters, she worked out an agreement with SAA that fifteen registrants would be the minimum number needed to hold a workshop, and thirty would be the ideal maximum to keep the class size manageable. SAA would supplement the local registrations with national advertising and enrollments to ensure they met the minimum.

In addition to external letters of support, the project needed institutional commitment to host the workshops. The cataloger received the endorsement to proceed from the Associate Dean and the Dean of Libraries. She earnestly began collecting background data and statistics for the grant application. The PHMC requires, if possible, that applicants use their online form to submit grant requests (plus paper copies with supplemental materials). While awaiting budget information for the cost-sharing portion of the matching funds, the cataloger wrote the narrative sections detailing the need for the grant and the work plan. She asked the PHMC to review a draft version and, after taking a few suggestions from them, she prepared the final version.

Most, if not all, academic institutions involved in grant writing have an oversight office through which all grant applications must go. In Penn State's case, the Office of Sponsored Programs (OSP) requires that their own forms to be filled out and signed by the principal investigator and dean before any grant can be submitted. With the requisite signatures, the cataloger submitted the paper and electronic version through OSP before the deadline.

The Grant is Funded

Between December 1 and August of the following year, many grant applicants wait and wonder if all the preparation work will come to fruition or naught. In this case, the grants panel reviewers liked the proposal and funded it at the full amount. SAA agreed to send one bill to be paid immediately following the last workshop. Technically, no work on the grant project could begin until the Project Director had the signed, executed contract in hand but the cataloger (now referred to as Project Director) knew that she could not wait that long to get the workshop dates set up, publicity sent out, and all the arrangements made. She phoned the PHMC and asked if it would be all right to set the workshop dates so she could begin to solicit attendees, and they agreed since Penn State was not hiring any staff to be paid out of grant funds. The Project Director decided that spring would be the ideal time of year—after the major winter snowstorms, and not in conflict with regional conference dates, spring break, summer vacations, or fall football weekends—to host the workshops. As it turned out, the executed contract did not arrive until the first day of the first workshop in March 2004.

The Logistics with SAA

The SAA Director of Education prepared a written contract stipulating what SAA would provide as noted above and what Penn State would be responsible for (meeting room, computer equipment, break food); in return, Penn State received one free registration per workshop. SAA selects the instructors and covers their costs—travel, food, housing, and honorarium—as well as preparing and mailing the on-site workbooks, handouts, name badges, roster, and evaluation forms. A month before each workshop, the Education Office sends out pre-readings as either e-mail attachments or paper copies, depending on the instructor's preference. As an institutional member of SAA, Penn State also received three registrations at the member rate, a saving of $50 to $80 per workshop.

The Project Director created an Excel spreadsheet to keep track of how many grant-funded spaces to reserve for each workshop and how many people SAA registered directly. The spreadsheet listed the name, institution, address, phone, fax, e-mail, date of payment, payment amount, amount due to SAA (non-members paid the full "early bird" registration fee), and break food expenses. Members of SAA received a discounted rate, and the total amount Penn State paid SAA reflected the mix of non-member, member, and free registrations. The Project Director continually adjusted the number of grant-funded slots in each workshop as registrations arrived to ensure that she did not go over or under budget, and to accommodate as many people as possible. One of the conditions of the grant was that if all of the funds were not expended the balance had to be returned to the PHMC. To avoid unexpended funds, the Project Director allocated one or two extra slots in case of cancellations. The "scholarship rate" fees covered the overage, in addition to the break food.

Hosting the Workshops

Workshops do not just happen. In addition to pre-planning which workshops to offer and budgeting carefully to expend all grant funds, the Project Director also had to publicize the workshops to the targeted grant-funded audience. Keeping in mind that library staff members learn about training opportunities from a variety of sources—both printed and electronic—the Project Director devised a plan to expand her network of contacts beyond the institutions originally reached by postal mail. The Project Director provided information for the initial press release to the library's Public Relations and Marketing Office and suggested avenues and outlets for adequate and pertinent coverage to media in the contiguous counties (see Appendix 7.A). Press releases for newspaper, radio, and television get the word out as a public service announcement or a short local interest news item. A website has an even greater potential to reach beyond the coverage area of conventional media. The Project Director drafted the contents for a Penn State Libraries SAA Workshops web page (see Figure 7.1), which the public relations staff turned into an eye-catching website. This site includes information about the workshop series, a page on each workshop adapted from the SAA Education Catalog online, and contains local information on housing and travel, and a link to Penn State's own registration form modeled on the one SAA uses, customized for mail-in to the Project Director.

As of this writing, the website displays third on Google's first screen when one searches for "archival workshops." The Project Director updated the web pages with the help of Public Relations when SAA contracted with one of the campus hotels for a reduced rate, when a workshop filled, and when she scheduled new workshops. The public relations staff archives the previous year's web pages so they can be included in the final report

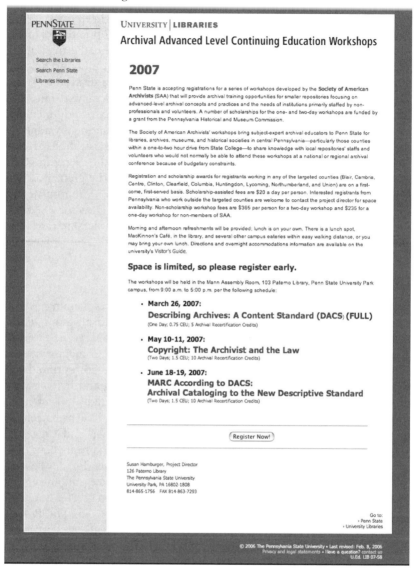

Figure 7.1 The Library's website for the SAA workshops

to the PHMC. Part of the Project Director's mission is to identify the staff members who need the training and reach out to them while waiting for applicants from outside the area.

Proactively seeking registrants takes both person-to-person e-mail and face-to-face contacts. As a member of the Mid-Atlantic Regional Archives Conference (MARAC), the Project Director announced the first workshops at the spring conference (and later potential grant-funded workshops at the fall meeting) to the Pennsylvania caucus members' meeting, and sent an electronic copy of the press release to the MARAC Pennsylvania caucus listserv as well as to the Archives and Archivists listserv, and to the *Mid-Atlantic Archivist*, a printed quarterly newsletter. A library colleague attending the Pennsylvania Library Association meeting recruited one registrant who attended all four workshops. With the goal of providing equitable training to staff in the Special Collections Library, the Project Director announced the workshops on their blog, and distributed the announcement to the unit heads to share with their staff.

As the Project Director began receiving phone calls, e-mail inquiries, and registration forms, she started working on the logistics for actually hosting the workshops: a meeting room to accommodate up to thirty people, tables and chairs for attendees, tables for break food, and computer and projection equipment for the instructors. The library has several instruction rooms, an auditorium, and an assembly room to hold various kinds of high-tech and low-tech meetings. The Mann Assembly Room, adjacent to both Special Collections and the staff lounge/kitchen, offers all the amenities needed to host a small workshop. The Project Director booked the room, asked the computer technician to arrive first thing in the morning on the first day to ensure that the equipment was working, and arranged for the facilities staff member to set up the tables and chairs in the appropriate configuration for optimal viewing of the screen.

To direct the attendees to the location of the workshop, the public relations staff created an eye-catching 11-inch x 17-inch poster (see Figure 7.2) to display in a stanchion outside the Mann Assembly Room. The Project Director made a photocopy reduction of this poster for each of the information desks at all library entrances to alert staff in case participants asked directions. In 2007, public relations staff streamed the workshop information on a new electronic panel display inside the main entrance.

To enhance the learning opportunities for attendees, the Project Director scheduled concurrent tours of the Special Collections Library and the Preservation Department before and after each workshop, and sent out an e-mail to all registrants asking them to sign up for the day and time they wished to join a tour. She notified the appropriate staff in each department about the number of people to expect for a tour on the specific days and times. Each department's representative met the tour groups outside the workshop meeting room and escorted them to the tour sites in different parts of the library. An out-of-state attendee at one of the first year's workshops suggested it would be nice for the non-local registrants to get together for dinner the night before, and/or after, the workshop, especially during multiple-day events. The Project Director obtained an advance copy of the roster for each workshop from SAA and sent out an e-mail in the second year (including Penn State staff the third year) asking for interest in dinner(s) and offering choices of days, keeping track of all events in a spreadsheet.

Archival Continuing Education Workshop
Offered Through the Society of American Archivists:

Preserving Your Historical Records:
An Archival Holdings Maintenance Workshop

Instructor:

Rebecca Elder
Book and Paper Conservator and Instructor
Amigos Library Services, Inc.

Monday, May 2, 2005
9:00 a.m.–5:00 p.m.
Mann Assembly Room,
103 Paterno Library

Funded by a grant from the National Historical Publications and Records Commission through the Pennsylvania Historical and Museum Commission.

PENNSTATE
1855
University Libraries

www.libraries.psu.edu/saaworkshops/

Available in alternative media on request. Penn State is committed to affirmative action, equal opportunity, and the diversity of its workforce. U Ed. LIB 05-121

Figure 7.2 Poster advertising one of the workshops

The Workshops

For the first year, the Project Director selected one two-day and three one-day beginning level workshops: "Understanding Archives," "Leadership and Management of Archival Programs," "Preserving Your Historical Records: An Archival Holdings Maintenance Workshop," and "Arrangement and Description." Both Albright College (Pennsylvania) and Penn State sent staff to all four workshops. Of the 111 attendees, the grant paid for seventy-one persons. Registrants came from small academic libraries from across the country including Lyons College (Arkansas), Anderson University (Indiana), University of Dayton (Ohio), Lock Haven University (Pennsylvania), Lamar University (Texas), Williams College (Massachusetts), and California State University, San Marcos, as well as from museums, religious archives, and private archives.

In the second year, the Project Director selected a mix of three workshops at the intermediate and specialized level. Penn State again sent staff to all three workshops. The grant funds covered fifty-nine of the eighty-nine attendees in "Oral History: From Planning to Preservation," "Archival Perspectives on Digital Preservation," and "Understanding Photographs: Introduction to Archival Principles and Practices." Librarians and archivists from Pennsylvania colleges and universities (Bucknell University, Lycoming College, Albright College, Indiana University of Pennsylvania, Messiah College, Wilson College) joined their colleagues from Ithaca College (New York), Hobart and William Smith College (New York), West Virginia University, Brandeis University (Massachusetts), Lawrence University (Wisconsin), Simmons College (Massachusetts), and Anderson University (Indiana). These workshops also attracted one museum staff member and archivists from government, corporate, religious, and historical society archives.

For the third year, the Project Director chose to offer three advanced-level workshops, building upon the knowledge base created over the first two years. Eight-two registrants (fifty-six grant-funded recipients) participated in "Describing Archives: A Content Standard (DACS)," "Copyright: The Archivist and the Law," and "MARC According to DACS: Archival Cataloging to the New Descriptive Standard." In addition to staff returning from most of the same Pennsylvania libraries who attended in the previous years, librarians and archivists from Wesleyan University (Connecticut), Amherst College (Massachusetts), West Virginia University, Princeton Theological Seminary (New Jersey), Kent State University (Ohio), Temple University (Pennsylvania), Southern Illinois University, University of Maryland, Syracuse University (New York), University of Albany (New York), Duke University (North Carolina), Milligan College (Tennessee), Folger Shakespeare Library (Washington, DC), and the State University of New York at Fredonia joined archivists from private practice, a museum archives, and historical society and corporate archives.

Of the 282 attendees at the ten workshops held over three years, 199 came from academic institutions, and the grant funds covered the majority of registration costs ($5,320) for 157 academic library staff, saving their libraries $40,390.

Evaluations

The instructors asked the attendees at each workshop to complete an evaluation form that the Project Director forwarded to the SAA Director of Education who shared the tabulated data and comments with the instructors and the Project Director. The Project Director also prepared a written evaluation of the host institution's experience. See Table 7.1 for tabulated workshop evaluations for "Understanding Photographs."

A sampling of some of the responses to the question about the most valuable aspect of the workshops includes the following:

Understanding Photographs

- This was the best! The workshop was useful in so many ways.
- PowerPoint with history photographs were delightful as well as informative.
- Hands-on activities were excellent.
- Opportunity to touch (and the gloves were great!) and see different types of photographs was wonderful.
- Pleased so much I can't wait to get back and try it.

Archival Perspectives on Digital Preservation

- The many Web resources, examples and readings were helpful.
- This workshop definitely recharged my digital preservation batteries!
- Oral History: From Planning to Preservation
- The instructor modeled all of the qualities that are essential for a good oral history interview: thoughtfulness, sensitivity, full of good information and practical experience, very well prepared! Also, the practice interviews were very good and informative.
- Group discussions were also very informative and Fred addressed our questions effectively, always reinforcing key points in the course materials.

The tabulated evaluation data became part of the final report the Project Director submitted to the PHMC.

Table 7.1 Tabulated evaluation of "Understanding Photographs" workshop

	1	2	3	4	5	N/A	Total respondents	Real responses	Score	
I. Assess the workshop from the standpoint of what you gained from the experience										
a. Learned to incorporate basic archival knowledge into your work with photographs, whether in an archives, library, historical society or special collections;			2	11	15	1	29	28	4.46	
b. Learned to identify specialized resources, techniques and tools available for managing photographs and identified common photo processes to managing a copy service;			2	13	13	1	29	28	4.39	
c. Learned about risks and concerns specifically related to photos from inherent vice of nitrate and acetate based films to legal and ethical issues;			1	11	16	1	29	28	4.54	4.33
d. Identified and followed standards and best practices when working with photographs;			4	9	15	1	29	28	4.39	
e. Set priorities and made informed choices in your photograph management strategy.		1	4	9	14	1	29	28	4.29	
New knowledge/skills acquired		3	4	8	11	3	29	26	4.04	
Likelihood of applying concepts to your work		2	4	8	13	2	29	27	4.19	
II. Rate the methods and materials relative to their value in accomplishing the workshop										
Clarity of participant handouts		2	3	8	16		29	29	4.31	
Content of participant handouts			4	9	16		29	29	4.41	
Exercises/Group discussions	1		9	9	10		29	29	3.93	4.27
Clarity of audio-visual aids			3	11	14	1	29	28	4.39	
Content of audio-visual aids	1		1	13	13	1	29	28	4.32	
III. How would you rate individual instructor?										
Instructor A										
Knowledge of topic				6	23		29	29	4.79	
Preparation			1	6	22		29	29	4.72	4.56
Ability to handle questions				9	20		29	29	4.69	
Presentation skills		1	2	10	16		29	29	4.41	
Instructor B										
Knowledge of topic			1	6	22		29	29	4.72	
Preparation			2	5	22		29	29	4.69	4.53
Ability to handle questions		1	3	9	16		29	29	4.38	
Presentation skills		2	2	10	15		29	29	4.31	

Post-workshop Reports

Many months after the Project Director received the last workshop evaluations from the SAA Director of Education, and well into the next year's grant-funded cycle of workshops, the PHMC requested a final report of the previous year's workshops. The Project Director wrote a narrative description of the outcome of the project such as attendance as noted above, and included photographs taken during the workshops, copies of the tabulated evaluations, and publicity materials (original posters, press release, printout of the website, and advertising postcards sent out by SAA, for example). The Project Director submitted the narrative online and mailed the supplementary materials with a copy of the report.

The Project Director realized that a professional conference session focusing on continuing education workshops could benefit other academic libraries and archives. She organized a session for the MARAC meeting in spring 2006 including her presentation about sponsoring workshops, an instructor's observations about developing and teaching an SAA workshop, and a participant's reflections from all four of the first year's workshops at Penn State. This session also served as publicity for future workshops.

Recommendations

As in most learning opportunities, what one discovers often comes as a side benefit to the intended outcome. For anyone wanting to emulate this continuing education project, consider the following recommendations:

- Be clear about the outcomes desired.
- Obtain the full support and cooperation of your library administration before proceeding, to save time and avoid frustration.
- Be realistic in what can be accomplished.
- Take advantage of grant-writing workshops to hone your writing skills, and tailor the application to what the funding agency will support.
- Ask staff and potential workshop attendees what they want to learn; "if you offer it, they will come" does not always work.
- Do as much pre-planning as possible to minimize panic and anxiety.
- Develop relationships with support staff to assist with small details such as moving furniture, ordering food, making coffee, cleaning up the room, and tracking down microphone batteries (know who to ask for help and thank everyone who does).
- Create a realistic budget and stay within it.
- Do not be afraid to experiment with different activities (dinners, lunches, tours).
- Be flexible and resourceful.
- No matter how much is planned beforehand, be prepared for surprises (such as last minute requests for child care).
- Learn a lot and have fun.

Continuing education can be a rewarding experience both for the staff members participating in the workshops and the Project Director attending as observer and host. Academic library staff, whether librarians, archivists, or paraprofessionals, deserve equal chances for continuing education so that they can add new skills and knowledge that benefit their library, patrons, and themselves (see Figure 7.3).

Conclusion

Innovative thinking and quick planning resulted in a successful series of continuing education workshops that benefited the staff members of academic libraries as well as public libraries, historical societies, museums, private practitioners, and corporate, religious, and government archives. What started out to be a three-year program of workshops became an ongoing program to offer an assortment of SAA workshops each year as long as the PHMC continued to support the request for grant funds. The Project Director decided midway into the second year to keep writing the grants beyond the original three-year plan. The PHMC approved the fourth year funding and Penn State will host three workshops in

Figure 7.3 Librarians and staff from Penn State Campuses, West Virginia University, and the Philadelphia Jewish Archives Center attending the Copyright workshop. Standing: Heidi Abbey, Meredith Weber, Sarah Sherman. Seated: Michael Furlough, Eileen Akin, Anna Schein, Virginia Lingle, Lee Gruver. Photograph © 2007 Susan Hamburger.

2008: "Encoded Archival Description (EAD)," "Stylesheets for EAD," and "Building Digital Collections." The Project Director is planning for the fifth year of four one-day workshops for 2009, and will continue to offer the SAA workshops until she exhausts their continuing education catalog.

Hosting the workshops was a rewarding experience. The opportunity to sit in on all of the workshops provided the Project Director with a chance to refresh her subject knowledge and learn new information in areas related to her expertise. She also observed each of the instructors' teaching skills, workshop structure, and pacing of instruction—all of which helped in the preparation and delivery of her own SAA workshop.

The attendees benefited from imported instructors from varied backgrounds, experience, and expertise. Participants met colleagues from other academic and historical and cultural institutions and were able to compare experiences. Bringing in outside instructors to introduce new ideas, reinforce existing activities, and demonstrate best practices to a critical mass of staff from one institution afforded those staff members the opportunity to learn together and ask questions of an expert. This was extremely beneficial as the workshops became more highly technical and advanced. The intricacies of digital preservation and copyright law, for example, require expertise beyond what can be learned in a two-day workshop. Rather than sending one person to learn and teach others, the grant-funded workshops allowed several people from one academic library to attend and benefit from the experience first-hand. Bringing workshops to central Pennsylvania solved a financial and geographic problem that seemed insurmountable until one librarian had the vision and interest to help her colleagues by writing an ongoing series of grants to underwrite the costs. She plans to continue writing the grants as long as the PHMC funds them, or until the Society of American Archivists runs out of workshops to offer.

References

1. Hainer, Eugene. "Continuing Education: Where it's Been, Where It (Might Be) Going." *Colorado Libraries* 30 (Summer 2004): 30.
2. Hegg, Judith L. "Continuing Education: A Profile of the Academic Librarian Participant." *Journal of Library Administration* 6 (Spring 1985): 52.
3. "Training Options on a Shoestring." *Arkansas Libraries* 63 (Winter 2006): 12.
4. Black, Fiona A., and Dunn, Judy. "Let's Get Our Continuing Education Act Together." *Feliciter* 1 (2005): 23.
5. Bolt, Nancy. "Staff Development: A State and Regional Perspective." *Colorado Libraries* 30 (Summer 2004): 21.
6. Hartman, Linda M. et al. "Staff Development Planning in an Academic Health Sciences Library." *Journal of the Medical Library Association* 93 (April 2005): 273.

7. Gracy, Karen F,. and Croft, Jean Ann. "Quo Vadis, Preservation Education? A Study of Current Trends and Future Needs in Continuing Education Programs." *Library Resources and Technical Services* 51 (April 2007): 84.
8. Gracy and Croft, "Quo Vadis, Preservation Education?" pp. 88, 91.
9. Parish, David, Chan, Betty, and Arnold, Linda. "Survey of SUNY Library Support for Professional Development. Summary Report." Report No. ED 304 162 (1988): 2.
10. Creth, Sheila D. "Staff Development: Where Do We Go From Here?" *Library Administration & Management* 4 (Summer 1990): 132.
11. Buchanan, Robert A. "Library Assistant Training: Perceptions, Incentives, and Barriers." *Journal of Academic Librarianship* 31 (September 2005): 426–427.
12. Jurow, Susan and Webster, Duane. "Promoting Management Excellence in Research Libraries Through Training and Staff Development." *Library Administration & Management* 4 (Summer 1990): 141.
13. Jurow and Webster, "Promoting Management Excellence in Research Libraries," pp. 143–144.
14. Leach, Ronald G., and Sullivan, Maureen. "Staff Development at Indiana State University: Providing the Competitive Edge." *Library Administration & Management* 4 (Summer 1990): 139.
15. Hartman, Linda M. et al. "Staff Development Planning in an Academic Health Sciences Library." *Journal of the Medical Library Association* 93 (April 2005): 273.
16. Callahan, Daren, and Watson, Mark. "Care of the Organization: Training and Development Strategies." *Journal of Academic Librarianship* 21 (September 1995): 377.
17. Zimmelman, Nancy. "Part 5. A*CENSUS: Report on Continuing Education." *American Archivist* 69 (Fall/Winter 2006): 369.
18. *World Almanac and Book of Facts 2006*. New York: World Almanac Books, p. 445.
19. Hamburger, Susan. "Life With Grant: Administering Manuscripts Cataloging Grant Projects." *American Archivist* 62 (Spring 1999): 130–152.

Appendix 7.A Initial press release for the workshops

PENNSTATE

814-865-0401; fax: 814-865-2344

The University Libraries
Public Relations and Marketing

515 Paterno Library
University Park, PA 16802-1812

November 16, 2004

News

For immediate release

Penn State Offers Archival Workshops

University Park, PA—Registrations are being accepted for a series of workshops developed by the Society of American Archivists (SAA) that will provide archival training opportunities for smaller repositories and will focus on basic archival concepts and practices and the needs of institutions primarily staffed by non-professionals and volunteers. A number of scholarships for the one- and two-day workshops are funded through a grant from the Pennsylvania Historical and Museum Commission.

The workshops bring subject-expert archival educators to Penn State for libraries, archives, museums, and historical societies in central Pennsylvania—particularly those counties within a one-to-two hour drive from State College—to share knowledge with local repositories' staffs and volunteers who would not normally be able to attend these workshops at a national or regional archival conference because of budgetary constraints.

Registration and scholarship awards are on a first-come, first-serve basis. Scholarship assisted, per-person fees are $20 a day. Interested registrants from Pennsylvania who work outside the targeted counties are welcome to contact the project director for space availability. Non-scholarship workshop fees are $365 per person for a two-day workshop and $235 for a one-day workshop for non-members of SAA.

The workshops will be held in the Mann Assembly Room, 103 Paterno Library, Penn State's University Park campus, from 9:00 a.m. to 5:00 p.m., per the following 2005 schedule: Thursday, March 17—Friday, March 18, "Understanding Archives: An Introduction to Principles and Practices;" Monday, April 11, "Leadership and Management of Archival Programs;" Monday, May 2, "Holdings Maintenance: Basics of Housing and Storing Collections;" and Monday, June 6, "Arrangement and Description."

Morning and afternoon refreshments will be provided; participants will be on their own for lunch. MacKinnon's Café, in the library, and several other campus eateries are within easy walking distance, or participants may bring a lunch.

Space is limited, so please register early. To register, go to: http://www.libraries.psu.edu/saaworkshops/ for further information call project director Susan Hamburger (814/865-1755), or e-mail sxh36@psulias.psu.edu.

8 Integrating Electronic Notebooks in Daily Work at Wayne State University

John H. Heinrichs and Bin Li

Introduction

One of the key components of the vision for University Libraries at Wayne State University is to create a learning environment that facilitates the growth and intellectual development of academic librarians. To create this learning environment, Wayne State University librarians are provided with continual training on software productivity tools and for professional development.

Microsoft OneNote 2007 is an electronic notebook productivity tool that can help academic librarians work more productively and can facilitate improved collaboration. To deliver development activities on OneNote 2007, eleven training modules and related helplets were developed to provide the academic librarians with "just-in-time" training and demonstrations of how to use the tool in their daily work. The librarians can take the training through a mixture of learning modes hosted on a website.

Setting

Wayne State University (WSU), located in Detroit, Michigan, is a Carnegie I research university with an urban mission. One of the key departments at WSU is University Libraries. It is composed of five separate physical libraries staffed with professional librarians and a Library and Information Science academic program that provides instruction to over 600 graduate students. University Libraries provides research support to a diverse campus of over 33,000 graduate and undergraduate students as well as to faculty and staff with varied research interests and requirements. The Association for Research Libraries ranked it among the top 60 academic libraries. With its mission of advancing scholarship, student learning, and faculty innovation, University Libraries serves as a national model for a research institution by providing digital access to an expanding source of information.

Yet, providing digital access to information is a growing challenge. In 2002, the worldwide volume of stored digital information exceeded five exabytes, that is, five million trillion characters, of unfiltered data. In 2004, data warehouse projects initiated by various academic libraries and other organizations to store and provide access to this information approached the petabyte range (1,000 terabytes or approximately 250 billion pages of text). The Gartner Group estimated that by 2012, organizations (including academic libraries) will have at least 30 times more data to handle, warehouse, search, catalog, and analyze than they currently have. Given this exploding volume of available information, it is no wonder that respondents to a recent survey indicated that their organization needed to do a better job of searching, handling, providing access, and understanding available information.[1] The sheer volume of available data and the rapid changes precipitated by information technology advances require that academic libraries provide training for their librarians. This training should integrate enhanced software productivity tools into the librarian's daily professional responsibilities.

Background

Wilson describes the future for academic libraries as being determined by how they collectively respond to the requirements for information technology, digitized information, and the anytime, anyplace expectations of the diverse set of customers.[2] WSU University Libraries is one of many academic libraries that are aggressively deploying information technology tools to shape their vision of the future. To create this future, academic libraries can utilize new information technologies to provide innovative and enhanced services.[3]

The academic libraries of the twenty-first century are experiencing tremendous changes brought by the advances of information technologies and the explosive growth of information. An example of change is that academic librarians are evaluating whether they should deploy tablet/notebook computers to implement the various components of a mobile service strategy.[4,5] The expectations from the implementation of this strategy are enhanced communication and improved collaboration among patrons and academic librarians.[6] Further, research demonstrated that the use of computers can affect library patron's problem-solving, critical thinking, and questioning skills thus requiring additional skills and competencies of academic librarians.[7]

University Libraries Vision

To meet these evolving challenges, the University Libraries Dean and her management team developed an overarching vision (see Figure 8.1). The developed vision and the subsequent strategic directions focus on providing an environment where each academic librarian can enhance his or her technical skills and competencies. The Dean envisions the use

---

University Libraries Vision

We endeavor to be seen by our clients and colleagues as a model library serving a pre-eminent public research University with an urban mission. We strive to be 'CHANGED'.

Client Centered	We focus all efforts on the success of our faculty & students
Humane	We treat each other with dignity and respect at all times
Accountable	We use data to make decisions;
	We follow through on commitments
Necessary	We must be the first place our clients go for information
Growing	We learn and work as a way of life
Exceeding Expectations	We go the extra mile
Dependable	We provide reliable service & a consistent message

---

University Libraries Mission Statement

Our mission is to advance scholarship, student learning, and faculty innovation through continuous development of a library that serves as a national model for a research institution.

Figure 8.1 University Libraries vision and mission statement

of leading-edge technology, software productivity tools, and continual learning as a way of life for academic librarians today and in the future. An example of her commitment was the acquisition of Tablet PCs to assist librarians in implementing the mobile service strategy. Another key strategic element to achieve the vision and enhance customer service was to train academic librarians for the information age by developing their software productivity tool skills.

Figure 8.2 highlights the skills development process emanating from the Dean's described vision and strategic direction. The process began with a clear understanding of the strategic plan. Then, a careful assessment of the technology skills of the current academic librarians was conducted. After the analysis of the assessment results, a series of training events and modules were developed and delivered. The immediate evaluations and desired outcomes of this training were assessed and the feedback from each session was used to enhance subsequent training events. The strategic planning team received this feedback for their future reference.

Understanding the Skills Assessment Outcomes

The evolving academic library demands an expanded set of information technology skills and competencies from its librarians. As the demand for technology-related skills becomes crucial to the organization, continual training of academic librarians has become a requirement.[8,9]

To complete the second step of the skills development process presented in Figure 8.2, two unique parts were completed. The first part included a review of the literature of core competencies required of academic librarians. The second part of the process included completing a survey to

Figure 8.2 Skills development process

better understand the academic librarian's current information technology skills.

Core Competencies of Academic Librarians

Competencies are defined as the abilities, qualities, strengths, and skills required for the success of the academic librarian and the academic library.[10] McNeil and Giesecke developed a set of twelve overall competencies for academic librarians.[11] The twelve core competencies are explained below with a brief description of their implications on software productivity tools.

1   **Service attitude/user satisfaction**: this competency refers to the ability of librarians to understand and meet the needs of the users, provide satisfying services, and be helpful when answering user requests.
2   **Analytical skills/problem solving/decision making**: this competency refers to the ability of librarians to recognize patterns, draw conclusions, and use well-ordered approaches to make decisions in gathering and utilizing information.
3   **Communication skills**: this competency refers to the ability of librarians to gather and present information accurately and understandably. It specifies that the librarian write effectively, explain concepts to team members, and seek feedback.
4   **Creativity/innovation**: this competency refers to the ability of librarians to look for and apply new ideas and technologies. It specifies that the librarian tries new tasks and performs them in new ways.
5   **Expertise and technical knowledge**: this competency refers to the ability of librarians to remain current in the technology field. It specifies that the librarians understand the technical components of new technologies and expand their knowledge of productivity tools.

6   **Flexibility/adaptability**: this competency refers to the ability of the librarians to perform a wide variety of tasks and to respond easily to changes. It specifies that the librarians work outside of their ordinary routine and approach situations from multiple perspectives.

7   **Interpersonal/group skills**: this competency refers to the ability of librarians to develop organizational relationships and work together to achieve goals. It specifies that librarians work in group activities including discussions, information sharing, and other communications.

8   **Leadership**: this competency refers to the ability of librarians to model high performance standards and empower teams to achieve the organization's strategic objectives. It specifies that librarians take advantage of opportunities for growth and development to enhance their skills and competencies.

9   **Organizational understanding and global thinking**: this competency refers to the ability of librarians to position and view the organization from a systems perspective. It specifies that librarians work and collaborate in a cross-departmental manner.

10 **Ownership/accountability/dependability**: this competency refers to the ability of librarians to accept responsibility and ensure the required objectives are accomplished. It specifies that librarians focus on project requirements and be responsible for their own development.

11 **Planning and organizational skills**: this competency refers to the ability of librarians to plan ahead and implement initiatives. It specifies that librarians minimize unnecessary errors and develop plans to ensure success.

12 **Resource management**: this competency refers to the ability of librarians to achieve maximum results within existing constraints. It specifies that librarians identify and utilize value-enhancement opportunities.

In addition to these overall competencies, Mahmood reported that seven of the top ten technical competencies he found for academic librarians were in the area of information technology.[12] These required technical competencies included using productivity tools such as e-mail, multimedia, and the Internet as well as file management, security, and website development software. In addition, these competencies involve using technology to alter the existing service delivery process by planning, training, and converting manual functions to automated library systems.

The training developed and delivered to academic librarians needs to incorporate these technical skills and competencies. The training must progress from basic computer literacy to an advanced level of computer competence.

Technical Skill Assessment

To complete the second part of the skills development process, an initial skills assessment survey was developed to determine the existing skill levels and training requirements for all academic librarians. The skills assessment survey was developed based upon the literature review and recent computer support help desk issues.[13,14] The survey examined various perceived skills of academic librarians, and consisted of 22 questions in two categories: information technology skills and software productivity tool proficiency. Various members of the staff development team reviewed the survey questions, commented on the wording, and pretested the survey before it was finalized.[15]

The information technology skills category contained two sub-components: operating the computer and troubleshooting. The survey results revealed that the academic librarians rated their perceived skills relatively high in these two areas (4.86 and 4.69 respectively on a 5-point scale). Five was defined as "can demonstrate all of the time," 3 was defined as "can demonstrate some of the time," and 1 was defined as "can never demonstrate any of the time."

The software productivity tools category contained three sub-components related to the use of these tools in the academic librarian's daily work environment, for communication and collaboration, and the need for advanced usability skills. The survey reported varied ratings in these three sub-components. The reported ratings, presented in Figure 8.3, are 3.79, 4.84, and 2.20 respectively, lower than that of information technology skills rating. The survey highlighted the need to deliver focused software productivity tool training, particularly on the emerging communication and collaboration required skills.

Cohn and Kelsey[16] described the characteristics of a successful development or training program, including the following:

- sustained support from senior library management;
- sufficient funding to support the various training activities;
- training scope to reflect identified assessment goals;
- flexible delivery to accommodate personal needs and schedules;
- conducted by proficient and effective instructors;
- utilization of interactive exercises and practice activities;
- availability of supplemental and supporting materials.

Based upon a review of these training characteristics and the analysis of the survey assessment results, a series of training sessions was developed for various software productivity tools. In May 2006, academic librarians took part in a technology retreat. The retreat consisted of four half-day, face-to-face training sessions on Microsoft Access, Microsoft Project, Microsoft Producer, and Microsoft OneNote.

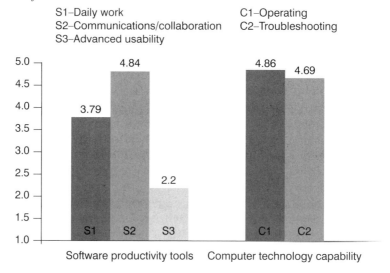

Figure 8.3 Technology skills assessment

Another training session was developed for the fall 2007 time frame. The design of the second training session was based upon the need for continuing and sustained information technology training for librarians; reflections from the first technology retreat indicating the need for a different delivery mechanism; and reflections from the first technology training suggesting more application-specific examples. The primary focus of the retreat was to help librarians use these software productivity tools. Therefore, the second training would focus on integrating software productivity tools into the academic librarian's daily workflow. The fall 2007 training will cover various elements of the skills not covered in the technology retreat by focusing on how new software productivity tools can enhance teamwork and collaboration.

The next training sessions were developed to provide continuing, application-based training with online and just-in-time delivery. Microsoft OneNote 2007 was chosen because it was readily available on all of the librarians' Tablet PCs; it takes advantage of the Tablet PC functionality; it is incorporated in the Microsoft Office Suite of software productivity tools; and it is a powerful software productivity tool that can be used to enhance librarians efficiency and productivity.

Designing OneNote Modules

Microsoft Office OneNote 2007 is a digital notebook that provides academic librarians with one place on their computer to gather their notes and collect information. It contains a powerful search tool to help them find what they are looking for very quickly. It provides an easy-to-use set of shared notebooks so that they can manage information overload and can work together more efficiently and effectively.[17]

Tools with similar functionality have been used in various training sessions by various organizations for several years. The University of Washington developed a classroom presenter tool, which included software to expand the student–instructor interaction.[18] In a 2005 educational technology survey conducted by Lane, Woody, and Yamashiro,[19] students reported the use of Microsoft OneNote 2003 to generate collaborative notes. Amirian reported similar findings of students generating collaborative notes at the University of Pennsylvania.[20] Willis and Mietschin revealed that electronic notebooks such as Microsoft OneNote was an engaging technology, and has great potential to improve their critical thinking skills.[21]

Several key uses for electronic notebooks like OneNote 2007 in an academic library setting include using the tool to take and share notes during meetings, to annotate and mark up documents, to promote critical thinking and questioning, and to facilitate drawing and simple calculations. Based upon the various features offered in OneNote 2007, eleven training modules were developed. The eleven modules include the basics of OneNote 2007, creating notes, capturing unstructured ideas, marking up documents, collaboration, mind mapping tools, note tagging, managing and organizing notes, integration, audio and visual, and OneNote Mobile. These training modules were developed to address and enhance the twelve core competencies highlighted earlier. These twelve core competencies encompass attitudes, personal attributes, and technical knowledge required of librarians. Relevant research from the areas of electronic notebooks and personal information management is also discussed for the modules.

Module 1: Basics of OneNote 2007

Module 1 was developed to provide basic training for using the OneNote 2007 software productivity tool. This training module includes the topics of customizing the OneNote 2007 user interface, creating various notebooks, moving and resizing notes, saving, finding, and protecting notebooks, and navigating around the OneNote 2007 application tool environment. Figure 8.4 highlights one view of the user interface with various toolbars, notebooks, and pages displayed.

This module is the foundation for the other ten training modules. It provides the academic librarians with an overall understanding of and the ability to utilize current technology. This training module focuses on addressing the identified core competency labeled "Expertise and Technical Knowledge."

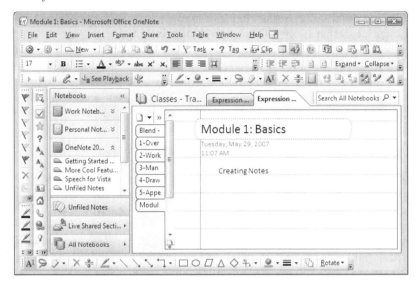

Figure 8.4 Basics of OneNote 2007

Module 2: Creating Notes

Microsoft OneNote 2007 is a very powerful note-taking software productivity application. Academic librarians can enhance their information-gathering experience by using the rich formatting and authoring features found in this product. Librarians can easily change the fonts in their notes, apply colors to the notes, highlight text, and use various numbered and bulleted styles in their lists. In examining ways how people capture short important thoughts, Hayes, Pierce and Abowd noted that participants in their study took notes for day planning, tracking tasks, or storing important information, such as dates and numbers.[22] Many participants liked the benefit of digital information, and often copied their paper notes into digital devices. The researchers argued that a good note-taking system should provide "synchronous, background-aware, pen-and-paper input to a digital repository." Willis and Mietschin pointed out that using the OneNote application, along with its digital ink functionality and the form factor of the Tablet PC, provided students with a natural note-taking experience, in addition to helping them store their notes electronically.[21] Figure 8.5 highlights this capability.

Module 2 was developed to teach academic librarians to create and open notes, create and use various templates (stationery), create and use tables and lists, and how to add web clippings from various sites to their notebooks. This training module was design to address the previously identified core competencies of "Analytical Skills/Problem Solving/Decision Making," "Communication Skills," and "Planning and Organizational Skills."

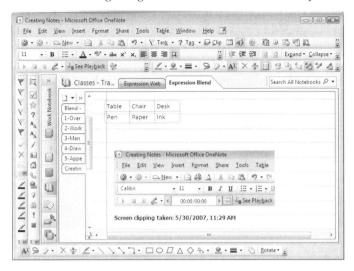

Figure 8.5 Creating notes

Module 3: Capturing Unstructured Ideas

Since OneNote 2007 allows notes to be taken in a free-flowing manner, unstructured ideas can easily be captured. For example, on a Tablet PC, a digital pen can be used to draw diagrams and/or take handwritten notes. These notes or diagrams can be written anywhere on the page and then exported to Microsoft Word 2007 for inclusion in a report or submitted to a blog. Reimer, Brimhall, and Sherve noted that study participants preferred to take notes on devices that allowed them to easily draw diagrams and equations, or to use their preferred layout format, such as writing, annotating, or drawing in the margins.[23]

Module 3 was developed to explain how to use whiteboard features to capture brainstorming sessions while simultaneously taking notes, to take notes through audio/video input, and to use the sticky notes function.

This module addresses the identified core competencies "Analytical Skills/Problem Solving/Decision Making" and "Communication Skills."

Module 4: Marking Up Documents

Wang and Chen argued that annotation software such as OneNote 2007 can be used to increase a customer's online reading experiences.[24] They provided examples of how e-books can be extended with annotation and online support/assessment mechanisms to increase efficiency in learning. The use of this software productivity tool also provides an innovative yet easy way for instructors to integrate live, handwritten material with slides and figures prepared in advance.[25] Students can interact with and mark on the instructors' slides to augment their note-taking experiences.[21,26] Figure 8.6 illustrates this concept.

Module 4 was developed to train individuals to mark up PowerPoint presentations, Word documents, and journal articles. This module addresses the identified core competencies "Analytical Skills/Problem Solving/Decision Making," "Communication Skills," and "Interpersonal/ Group Skills."

Module 5: Collaboration

Working in academic libraries today requires a significant amount of collaboration with other librarians. OneNote 2007 helps librarians work with others by sharing notebooks in a synchronous or asynchronous fashion and from different locations. Shared information space can be used to keep new team members informed, share best practices, and eliminate duplication of work.

Kam et al. studied how cooperative note-taking and discussion supported real-time conversations within small groups of students during lectures.[26] The study reported significant cooperative note-taking benefits, such as higher quality notes, more comprehensive coverage of lecture information, richer variety of whiteboard activity, and powerful small group interaction. As such, Module 5 was developed to teach electronic note sharing (e.g. during meetings), integrating this function with Outlook, and sending e-mail messages. This module addresses the identified core competencies "Communication Skills," and "Interpersonal/Group Skills."

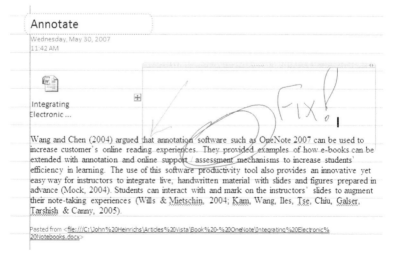

Figure 8.6 Annotating and marking up documents

Module 6: Mind Mapping Tools

OneNote 2007 permits the creation of simple drawings and manipulation of basic shapes to capture and express ideas visually. Willis and Mietschin stated that these tools could be used as a mind mapping tool.[21] Users can graphically present their ideas. These mind-mapping activities can accelerate the development of critical thinking and learning skills. Module 6 was developed to assist in developing concept maps, drawings, charts, and simple calculations.

This module addresses the identified core competencies "Analytical Skills/Problem Solving/Decision Making," "Communication Skills," and "Organizational Understanding and Global Thinking."

Module 7: Note Tagging

Note tags (flags) can be used to highlight key items, urgent notes, or items that need to be reviewed. The customizable flags can prioritize and summarize various tasks and activities. Librarians can become more organized as information is structured; they can review tagged items, and generate summaries (see Figure 8.7). For example, note tags can be used to flag useful references on a particular topic. Later these notes can be retrieved and used to generate a summary note page. Module 7 was developed to assist in note tagging (flagging).

This module addresses the identified core competencies "Analytical Skills/Problem Solving/Decision Making," "Communication Skills," and "Resource Management."

Module 8: Managing and Organizing Notes

OneNote is a very flexible tool that can be used to organize, manage, and navigate notes. Bergman Beyth-Maron, and Nachmias found that the project fragmentation problem is prevalent as project documents exist in multiple formats, such as electronic documents, e-mail messages, and websites. They called for integration solutions that allow users to keep all relevant files in a single folder hierarchy.[27] Jones et al. found that most people wanted to control the grouping of electronic documents, recently viewed web pages, or e-mail messages, and preferred to have all needed and related information in one place.[28] They also liked to use tools that help them visualize information, such as relationships between files, or reminders of things that needed to be done. OneNote offers such a place to organize and gather everything together. It can be used to hierarchically organize notes by color-coded sections, pages, and sub-pages. The notes can be easily reorganized by simply dragging and dropping the notes or pages.

Many times people can become frustrated because they are unable to locate important files. Marshall and Bly, for instance, found that all

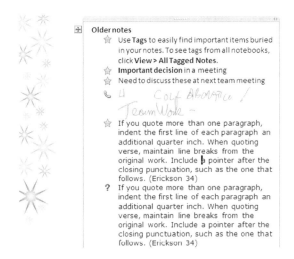

Figure 8.7 Note tags

20 participants in their study intentionally saved portions of published materials but that these clippings were poorly organized.[29] Half of the study participants reported instances of being unable to find a particular clipping later when needed. OneNote, however, can automatically save web clippings or electronic notes, and keep track of their locations. It has powerful search capabilities. When a search term is entered in the "Find" box, the productivity tool quickly locates all instances where the search term appears, not only on the current note page, but in all pages, all sections, and in any open notebook. It highlights all page tabs containing matches to the search term, allowing users to jump through search results. Users can also view all the result pages by clicking the "View List" button, and group pages according to different options.

Module 8 was developed to teach activities such as dragging and dropping components on the OneNote page; grouping and renaming notes; navigating among notes; organizing notebooks, sections, pages, and subpages; moving notes around, managing side notes whether unstructured or structured; sorting notes; and locating (or searching for) specific notes. Librarians can work more efficiently since the notes are easily organized.

This module addresses the identified core competencies "Communication Skills," "Planning and Organizational Skills," and "Resource Management."

Module 9: Integration

OneNote can be used to work freely among different Office system applications such as copying/pasting pictures, text, and/or graphics from

Word, PowerPoint, and Excel into OneNote. Information from websites, including source URLs, can also be copied and pasted, allowing research to be conducted in a more efficient manner. Entire documents can be embedded into a notebook, thereby keeping all components of a research project together. Links to individual contacts can be inserted into calendars to create a unique, individual web presence.

Module 9 was developed to teach linking to and embedding documents; hyperlinking to outside information sources and/or hyperlinking to different sections and/or pages; publishing to the web, blog, Word, and PDF.

This module helps improve the librarian's productivity and efficiency, and addresses the identified core competencies "Communication Skills," "Creativity/Innovation," and "Planning and Organizational Skills."

Module 10: Audio and Visual

Notes can be linked to audio and video presentations. For example, librarians can record conference calls and embed the audio information in their electronic notes (see Figure 8.8). OneNote also provides contextual linkages to captured information.

Module 10 was developed to explain searching audio information and using OCR technology to locate web clippings, business cards, and/or pictures. OneNote ensures librarians do not miss anything that is being said or presented in conference calls, classes, or meetings.

This module addresses the identified core competency "Resource Management."

Figure 8.8 Audio/video capability in OneNote

Module 11: OneNote Mobile

Module 11 was developed to demonstrate how Windows mobile-based Smartphones or Pocket PCs can be integrated with OneNote. Parts of an electronic notebook can be taken on a Smartphone while on the road. Also, new information can be captured on a mobile phone and integrated back into OneNote. For example, the camera feature found on many phones can be used to take pictures and stored in OneNote.

This module addresses the identified core competency "Communication Skills."

Results

The critical components of this online, just-in-time training program include enhancing the technological skills, insight generation, and critical questioning capabilities of academic librarians. The development of these skills and competencies can help serve customers more effectively and support an expanding mobile service strategy. The identified information technology trends clearly point to the need to become educated and comfortable using technology to quickly analyze data, use proven models to focus insights, and create insightful critical questioning skills.[30]

Staley argues that the use of blended learning in training is a good practice. Blended learning deals with the integration of online and in-person learning or the blend of different online learning modes.[31] These online learning modes can help learners with different learning styles, and enrich their overall learning experience. It can provide greater consistency in the content delivery. Instead of segmenting training into something conducted off site, blended learning incorporates into the daily learning activities thereby integrating training concepts into daily work. It can help increase learning retention. In addition, blended learning can reduce the time and cost of updating online learning material and resources, and increase librarian productivity. Based upon this rationale, a mixture of online learning modes, such as online tutorials, multimedia recorded presentations, self assessments, demonstrations, wikis, and others, will be used.

The OneNote 2007 training website was created in response to the academic librarians' request for flexibility for enhancing their OneNote software productivity tools skills. The eleven learning modules were broken down into thirty-six web-based helplets. Each helplet can be completed in a manageable time frame such as during lunch breaks or between meetings. For each helplet, the following was presented to assist librarians learning the information:

- Multimedia recordings that incorporate video recorded demon-strations, PowerPoint slides linked to important websites, and discussions on applying the electronic notebook to daily work routines.

- Screenshots that help librarians perform certain tasks.
- Online text that explains important concepts and provides instructions.
- Quiz questions for each module to help librarians affirm knowledge.

Figure 8.9 displays the OneNote training site with helplets accessible from either from the "OneNote Skill Set" page or "OneNote In Action" page. A Glossary and "OneNote Tips and Tricks" pages were also provided.

Other elements of the training site include a calendar of training events, frequently asked questions (FAQ), wiki sites for sharing innovative uses, suggestions on using OneNote to enhance productivity, links to various sites, news items, Office 2007 features, and a photo gallery. The site was designed to allow easy navigation among the various helplets, self-paced learning, and opportunities to review materials or pursue additional concepts.

The training site was first presented to the librarians' representatives at the March 2007 staff development meeting, in an effort to gain their support. The training modules and OneNote training site were then introduced to all librarians at a monthly staff meeting. Since positive perceptions of an information technology solution may increase actual usage, perceived benefits and relevance to daily work were highlighted at the meeting.[32,33] Librarians were highly encouraged to visit the training site and participate in training. Training incentives were given. Pre- and post-learning assessment surveys were incorporated to determine the level of learning and the design of the next training.

Figure 8.9 OneNote 2007 training

Evaluation

Two facets of the OneNote 2007 professional development program will be evaluated: 1) the reflection on the training development and delivery, and 2) the evaluation of the training outcome. The authors anticipate that the training modules will be successful based upon the fact that the identified characteristics for successful training have been covered in the development and delivery of these modules.[16] The Dean of the University Libraries has provided sustained support. The training provides relevant and applicable examples of how librarians learn and use the productivity tool in their daily work. A mix of training strategies was used, and interactive exercises or practice were provided. The training was delivered in such a flexible and unobtrusive fashion, it can become an inherent part of daily life. The availability of supplemental materials serves as a resource center. It helps librarians explore new features or share new ways to apply the productivity tool, thus creating a community of learning, and keeping the training an ongoing process.

Kirkpatrick's four levels of evaluation will be used to assess the training outcomes.[34] In the first level, the authors will conduct surveys to explore the academic librarian's perception regarding this software productivity tool. In the second level, surveys will be conducted to determine technology tool skills acquired before and after the course to assess learning. In the third level, interviews and observations will be conducted to determine if librarians have adopted more productive behaviors such as note-taking and collaboration. In the fourth level, information can be gathered regarding the academic librarian's marketability and professional development based upon their improved competencies. It is anticipated that some of the surveys will be conducted six months after the training is delivered.

Technology training is an ongoing process at University Libraries. What is learned from this training will be used for the design of future training of other software productivity tools.

Conclusion

To support the technical and professional development of librarians, a training site on electronic notebooks was developed. The project is limited in its current offering of only one software productivity tool, Microsoft OneNote. The next training modules will incorporate the results of the training session. In this project, a skills development process was created to train academic librarians in the use of electronic notebooks to help with their daily work processes. The first major step in this project involved assessing the information technology skills of the academic librarians and required core competencies. This information provided focus for the creation of the eleven training modules in this software productivity tool. Microsoft OneNote 2007 was chosen as the electronic notebook software tool to help academic librarians work more productively and facilitate improved collaboration. This project provided professional development opportunities for librarians to enhance their skills and to meet the Dean's vision for University Libraries.

References

1. King, Julia. "Business Intelligence Skills in Demand." *Computerworld* 38, no. 13 (March 29, 2004): 44.
2. Wilson, Lizabeth. A. "What a Difference a Decade Makes: Transformation in Academic Library Instruction." *Reference Services Review* 32, no. 4 (2004): 338–346.
3. Moyo, Lesley. M. "Electronic Libraries and the Emergence of New Service Paradigms." *The Electronic Library* 22, no. 3 (June 2004): 220–230.
4. Hibner, Holly. "The Wireless Librarian: Using Tablet PCs for Ultimate Reference and Customer Service: A Case Study." *Library Hi Tech News* 5 (2005): 19–22.
5. Smith, Michael M. and Pietraszewski, Barbara A. "Enabling the Roving Reference Librarian: Wireless Access With Tablet PCs." *Reference Services Review* 32, no. 3 (2004): 249–255.
6. Levin, Howard. "Laptops Unleashed." *Learning & Leading with Technology* 31, no. 7 (2004): 6–12.
7. Lowther, Deborah L., Ross, Steven M., and Morrison, Cary M. "When Each One Has One: The Influences On Teaching Strategies And Student Achievement." *Educational Technology, Research and Development* 51, no. 3 (2003): 23–44.
8. Childers, Scott. "Computer Literacy: Necessity or Buzzword." *Information Technology and Libraries* 22, no. 3 (2003): 100–104.
9. Hovde, Marjorie, and Hovde, David M. "Elements of the Expertise Technology Trainers Need to Instruct Academic Library Employees." *Portal: Libraries and the Academy* 2, no. 4 (2002): 601–625.
10. Houghton, Jan, S. "Technology Competencies and Training for Libraries." *Library Technology Reports* 43, no. 2 (2007): 7–12.
11. McNeil, Beth, and Giesecke, Joan. "Core Competencies for Libraries and Library Staff." In *Staff Development: A Practical Guide*, edited by Elizabeth Fuseler Avery. Chicago, IL: American Library Association, 2001, pp. 49–62.
12. Mahmood, Khalid. "A Comparison Between Needed Competencies of Academic Librarians and LIS Curricula in Pakistan." *The Electronic Library* 21, no. 2 (2003): 99–109.
13. The Library Network (TLN) Technology Committee. "Basic Computer Equipment Competencies." 2004. Available: <http://tech.tln.lib.mi.us/basiccompetencies2004.pdf>. Accessed: May 29, 2007.
14. Yale University Library. "The Secretary's Commission for Achieving the Necessary Skills (SCANS) for the Workplace." 2000. Available: <http://www.library.yale.edu/training/stod.archive/competencies.htm>. Accessed: May 28, 2007.
15. Heinrichs, John H., and Croatt-Moore, Carrie. "Transforming the Academic Library by Retooling Employee Skills." *Journal of Instruction Delivery Systems* 20, no. 2 (2006): 17–23.
16. Cohn, John M, and Kelsey, Ann L. *Staffing the Modern Library: A How-to-do-it Manual*. New York: Neal-Schuman Publishers, 2005.

17. Microsoft Office OneNote2007 Product Overview. Available: <http://office.microsoft.com/en-us/onenote/HA101656661033.aspx>. Accessed: May 22, 2007.

18. Anderson, Richard. "Beyond PowerPoint: Building a New Classroom Presenter." 2004. Available: <http://www.campus-technology.com/print.asp?ID=9537>. Accessed: April 9, 2006.

19. Lane, Care, Woody, Karelee, and Yamashiro, Greg. "Mapping the Changing Technological Landscape: The University of Washington's 2005 Faculty and Student Surveys on Educational Technology." In *Proceedings of the 33rd Annual ACM SIGUCCS Conference on User Services,* Monterey, CA, 2005, pp. 154–159.

20. Amirian, Susan. "Putting Tablet PCs to the Test." *T.H.E. Journal* 32, no. 4 (2004): 28–30.

21. Willis, Cheryl, and Mietschin, Susan L. "Tablet PC's as Instructional Tools or the Pen is Mightier than the 'Board'!" In *Proceedings of the 5th Conference on Information Technology Education SIGITE '04*, Salt Lake City, UT, 2004, pp. 153–159.

22. Hayes, Gillian, Pierce, Jeffery S., and Abowd, Gregory D. "Practices for Capturing Short Important Thoughts." In *CHI 2003: New Horizons.* New York: ACM, 2003, pp. 904–905.

23. Reimer, Yolanda J., Brimhall, Erin, and Sherve, Laurie. "A Study of Student Notetaking and Software Design Implications." In *Proceedings of the Fifth IASTED International Conference.* Anaheim, CA: ACTA Press, 2006, pp. 189–195.

24. Wang, Chin-Yeh and Chen, Gwo-Dong. "Extending E-books with Annotation, Online Support and Assessment Mechanisms to Increase Efficiency of Learning." In *Proceedings of the 9th Annual SIGCSE Conference on Innovation and Technology in Computer Science Education*, Leeds, United Kingdom, 2004, pp. 132–136.

25. Mock, Kenrick. "Teaching with Tablet PCs." *Journal of Computing Sciences in Colleges* 20, no. 2 (2004): 17–27.

26. Kam, Mattrew, Wang, Jingtao, Iles, Alstair, Tse, Eric, Chiu, Jane, Glaser, Daniel, Tarshish, Orna, and Canny, John. "Livenotes: A System for Cooperative and Augmented Note-taking in Lectures." In *Proceedings of the SIGCHI Conference on Human Factors in Computing System*, Portland, OR, 2005, pp. 531–540.

27. Bergman, Ofer., Beyth-Maron, Ruth, and Nachmias, Rafi. "The Project Fragmentation Problem in Personal Information Management." In *CHI 2006.* New York: ACM, pp. 271–274.

28. Jones, William, Phuwanartnurak, Ammy J., Gill, Rajdeep, and Bruce, Harry. "Don't Take my Folders Away! Organizing Personal Information to Get Things Done." In *CHI 2005.* New York: ACM, pp. 1505–1508.

29. Marshall, Catherine C., and Bly, Sara. "Saving and Using Encountered Information: Implications for Electronic Periodicals." In *CHI 2005.* New York: ACM, pp. 111–120.

30. Heinrichs, John H., and Lim, Jeen-Su. "Model for Organizational Knowledge Creation and Strategic Use of Information." *Journal of the American Society for Information Science and Technology* 56, no. 6 (2005): 620–629.

31. Staley, Laura. "Blended Learning Guide for Libraries." Web Junctions 2007. Available: <http://data.webjunction.org/wj/documents/13893.pdf>. Accessed May 23, 2007.

32. Li, Bin. *American Libraries and the Internet: The Social Construction of Web Appropriation and Use.* New York: Cambria Press, 2007.

33. Li, Bin, and Newby, Gregory B. "Laptop Requirement Usage and Impact in Graduate ILS Education." In *Proceedings of the American Society for Information Science and Technology Annual Meeting 39*. Medford, NJ: Information Today, 2002, pp. 83–91.
34. Kirkpatrick, Donald L. *Evaluating Training Programs: The Four Levels*. San Francisco, CA: Berrett-Koehler Publishers, 1998.

9 Mission Possible

A Retreat to Prepare Librarians to Infiltrate Upper-level Curricula at the University of Nevada, Las Vegas

Diane VanderPol, Priscilla Finley, Sidney Lowe, and Susie Skarl

Introduction

From its humble beginnings a scant fifty years ago as a small desert school, the University of Nevada, Las Vegas (UNLV) has rapidly evolved into a dynamic urban academic institution dedicated to creating a learning environment that empowers students to become lifelong learners. UNLV's first classes were held in 1957, and its solitary campus building housed all of the classrooms, offices, science labs, and a library of 2,000 books managed by a part-time librarian.[1] Today, the UNLV Libraries include the 302,000 square foot Lied Library, three campus branches, 125 employees, and a book collection that has expanded to well past a million volumes. A multitude of electronic library resources has become a key element of scholarly research and a necessary focus for information literacy (IL) instruction in the UNLV Libraries.[2]

Setting

In support of the University's commitment to a student-centered culture of teaching and learning, the UNLV Libraries' Instruction Department develops creative programs and services to engage students using methods that will enhance their IL skills. Another objective is to collaborate with teaching faculty across a wide variety of disciplines so that they can connect library instruction to their students' learning outcomes. UNLV Libraries' Instruction Department held a day-long retreat for twenty librarians and library paraprofessionals who are involved with library instruction and liaison activities with academic departments. Themed "Mission Possible," the activities and events were designed to help liaisons start conversations with faculty about ways library instruction can support the existing learning outcomes in their upper division classes. This case study offers a detailed blueprint describing retreat activities and reports on the efforts of a typical participant to develop a program tailored to the needs of the discipline.

Literature Review

The library literature describes many efforts of librarians to initiate discussions about the intersections among established curricula, university-wide initiatives, and IL standards and goals, most notably in Patricia Iannuzzi's 1998 piece on establishing campus partnerships.[3] Later work has detailed specific instances of identifying a goal within a program that can be met with IL-related input from librarians, as Lynn Lampert did by addressing plagiarism from a number of perspectives with process-based assignments in a journalism class.[4] This and similar efforts have been successful by many measures, including the student self-assessments and faculty evaluations documented by Alexius Smith Macklin and Michael Fosmire at Purdue when they integrated course content with IL standards and outcomes in science classes.[5]

Helping librarians negotiate possible roles that would provide problem-solving expertise on campus was a main goal of UNLV Libraries' instruction retreat. Several approaches to this potentially delicate positioning have been recorded in the literature. Barbara Dewey identifies the model of the "pervasive campus librarian" as a leader with "special insight on ways to advance the university and achieve its mission."[6] She details strategic collaborations that go beyond the traditional academic curriculum. Other studies have gathered concrete information about the conceptions of IL held by faculty within a discipline,[7] and some librarians have developed programs to introduce concepts of IL to academic faculty, as documented by librarians at the University of South Carolina-Aiken.[8]

In "Reeling 'Em In: How to Draw Teaching Faculty into Collaborative Relationships," Melissa Moore argues that "the destination, or goal, is relationships with teaching-faculty – significant, professional, long-term relationships as peers."[9] The UNLV Libraries retreat combined the approach of developing relationships with an analysis of departmental curricula. By analyzing curricula, librarians were able to target specific faculty members to develop relationships with, and they became conversant with larger curricular goals so that they could interact with curricula in systematic and scalable ways.

Retreating

A retreat format was selected instead of a series of ongoing workshops with the hope that participants would seize the opportunity to be free of distractions such as phone calls, e-mail messages, and other day-to-day obligations. In planning for the retreat, it was decided that invitees should include anyone who taught class sessions for the Instruction Department as part of their responsibilities in the Libraries, along with selected others in administrative or supervisory positions.

Led by the Head of Instruction, a group of interested staff volunteers gathered to plan specific retreat activities. Several of the planners had undergone the ACRL (Association of College & Research Libraries) Immersion experience and hoped to reproduce the immersive aspect of this environment. Retreat planners also took an extremely playful approach by using an espionage theme, which fit well with the goal of gathering information about entities on campus that were important to library liaisons. Participants were called "operatives" and assigned secret code names. After expressing initial interest in attending the retreat, each operative received a mysterious delivery of a CD "dossier," which included background reading, preliminary assignments, and a simple "secret message" to decode that led them to a file folder of information hidden in the library stacks.

Planners played with the theme throughout the retreat day, including beginning the day with a "self-destructing" video describing the mission and periodically "sweeping the room for bugs" when furniture needed to be rearranged to accommodate a new activity. Utilizing the spy premise, retreat sessions were designed to be interactive, to inspire creative thinking and discovery, and also to accommodate a variety of learning styles. The "Mission Possible" theme was useful in breaking the ice and persuading participants to play along with the day's agenda.

Almost half of the participants in the retreat were involved in the planning in some way. The Head of Instruction coordinated three separate teams that planned modules of the retreat. There were many benefits to distributing the planning responsibilities: content was more likely to be relevant to the interests and job duties of participants; planners became deeply engaged in the desired learning outcomes of the retreat activities; and since each planner was involved in preparing and helping lead only one hour, the remainder of the day's events were also fresh to them.

Objectives

Know Your Stuff

The Libraries' Instruction Department wanted to focus on understanding and promoting IL skills development within the academic disciplines. Many students are exposed to basic IL skills and tenets in required general education courses. The instruction librarians believed that the more advanced skills and knowledge of an information-literate student vary from discipline to discipline and that students are expected to demonstrate the ability to engage in a discipline-specific discourse. Librarians need to develop a deep understanding of the disciplines and departments that they serve as liaisons in order to think strategically about when and how students could most effectively develop and demonstrate their IL in their major curricula.

Talk the Talk

After identifying a strategic approach, such as finding an appropriate required course, targeting a receptive and influential faculty member, or integrating IL skills expectations at the curriculum level, librarians needed to develop and rehearse dialogue and approach techniques. Librarians have to feel comfortable in their understanding of both the disciplinary discourse and also of the Libraries' potential roles in the educational mission of the academic departments.

Find Opportunities

The life of the University, its students, faculty and staff, are complex and rich. A psychology student might also be an athlete and a first-generation college student at risk for non-retention due to the lack of social support structures at home. The biology department may be beta testing new course management software. The registrar's office may be developing volunteer training for campus orientation programming. Each individual, unit or department, and college has multiple agendas. When considering IL skills development as a solution to the traditional educational mission and about potential roles for the Libraries, colleagues are well served to broaden perspectives and see if these library staff efforts can support these alternate agendas important to campus entities.

Methods

Know Your Stuff

One multifaceted objective for the retreat involved identifying opportunities for strategic partnerships, locating existing IL outcomes embedded in the curriculum, and outlining broader themes and contexts of the disciplines. A key element for advancing this goal included the use of a curriculum audit, a tool used for systematically examining current curricular practices in academic programs. It was designed to give library instructors a comprehensive overview of the curriculum they serve and how they are currently interacting with their degree programs.

Approximately two weeks prior to the retreat, each "agent" participant received a copy of the curriculum audit grid, a sample grid from a recently completed audit, and instructions on how to complete their "homework assignment" prior to Retreat Day as part of their dossier (see Appendix 9.A). They were given a brief, written explanation of the audit's purpose, and the following guidelines for homework goals:

1   To learn more about a degree program that the librarian supports.
2   To summarize current library practices associated with a given degree program.
3   To establish a baseline of library practices for future assessment purposes.
4   To refresh colleagues' knowledge of basic IL tenets.
5   To identify areas where strategic collaboration efforts and programming can be initiated to ensure that the institution graduates information-literate students.

Detailed directives for completing pre-retreat audits were provided because it was important to emphasize documentation of *current* practices rather than planning or suggesting future strategies and opportunities in advance of the retreat's learning activities. Specific instructions for each participant's homework assignment were outlined.

Participants were encouraged to be candid and creative when completing the audit exercise in response to their particular needs. They were advised that retreat volunteers would have an opportunity to share learning and experiences, but would not be asked to share their audits. One of the intentions of this exercise was to stimulate thinking about what could or should be done in the future within a given degree program. However, participants were advised that they should simply write the response "opportunity" within the appropriate box on the audit grid, and that addressing, brainstorming, and prioritizing their ideas would take place at the retreat.

Since the curriculum audit grid had many blanks, the tendency for some was to try to fill in each space. It was important to assure participants that since there are many courses within a program in which the library has no interaction, it was quite acceptable to leave spaces unfilled. Not every class is a good fit for the five IL areas located along the top of the grid—Identify, Access, Evaluate, Use, and Understand. In these cases, the participants were told to indicate "Not Applicable." If not enough was known about a course to make an assessment of its viability as an IL opportunity, the proper response was "Needs More Research." The sample curriculum audit grid provided for participants was completed for the Women's Studies Department by one of the retreat's leaders and represented a concrete example to assist participants in finishing this task (see Appendix 9.B).

Following the curriculum audit, retreat participants were given an opportunity to talk to upper division undergraduate students about their library instruction experiences at UNLV Libraries. Keeping with the "Mission Possible" theme, it was hoped that retreat participants would extract information from "student informants" about their experiences in school, to brainstorm ways to improve students' exposure to library resources and to learn how to communicate the most needed IL skills in library instruction sessions.

Instruction retreat planners decided to ask library supervisors if their undergraduate workers could participate in the student informant session of the retreat. Two weeks prior to the event, a Retreat Planning Agent e-mailed supervisors of library student workers, and explained the mission briefly. They were told that the retreat planners were looking for a few upper division students who could serve as informants. Student informants would be questioned by library agents about their experiences working with the Libraries, and an hour of paid work time would be granted by their supervisors. Seven willing informants in various majors were recruited. Although these student participants were library workers with some familiarity with library functions, the planning team felt that their range of experiences with library resources and instruction sessions were similar to those of other students.

A few days before the retreat, to prepare them for the interview scenario, student informants were given an instruction sheet (see Appendix 9.C). At the retreat, an agent was assigned to assemble the students in a nearby room (with refreshments) until it was time to escort them into the main arena. They were then seated at tables and grouped with retreat participants based on subject area interest. For example, a science major sat at a table with a medical librarian and others interested in questioning that person. Informants were then interviewed using a pre-planned set of questions. The sessions lasted about ten minutes, and notes were taken for future compilation and assessment. The answers helped library instructors to better understand needed skills and to make improvements in teaching.

Recruiting upper division student library workers worked well for the UNLV retreat, however, strategies for recruiting student informants will vary by organization. Depending on the institution, librarians may want to try other ways to lure interested students into participating, including "man on the street (campus)" solicitations, enticements of food or other rewards, and appealing to various departments or instructors for assistance with enthusiastic students. As IL needs vary with each institution, program, and student, informant questions may differ somewhat among institutions.

Talk the Talk

The predominant current model for instructors to interact with faculty in their disciplines is in one-shot sessions tailored to address the needs of a particular assignment. Faculty who desire a session with librarians are strongly encouraged to discuss their assignment with their department liaison who will teach the session or with a member of the instruction department staff before the class meeting. Faculty requesting generic tours are gently steered into planning a tailored session at the students' point of need. As another retreat exercise, the librarian agents were asked to locate an assignment from an upper-level class in their discipline. In the exercise, librarians reviewed the assignment with a copy of the ACRL Standards for Information Literacy in hand, identifying one outcome that was explicitly addressed by the assignment as written, and proposing a second outcome from the standards that might be achieved by tweaking the assignment in a minor way.

With this preparation made and with the standards fresh in their minds, agents were given a role-playing scenario. Each librarian practiced introducing the idea of IL standards to another librarian playing the role of the faculty member who authored the assignment. They were specifically instructed to compliment the "assignment author" on the IL outcome embedded in their assignment, and then propose a modification to also incorporate a higher-order IL outcome in the class session or assignment. After a few minutes, participants switched roles; after each member of a pair had practiced articulating IL outcomes, pairs were shuffled (based on a "speed dating" arrangement allowing a quick rotation of partners), and instructors had a second chance to refine their "pitch."

For example, a typical assignment to locate three relevant journal articles might correlate with ACRL Information Literacy Competency Standard Two, where the main goal is for students to "access needed information effectively and efficiently." [10] In the retreat exercise, the librarian would note the connection between the teaching faculty member's assignment and this standard, and would then go on to mention an element of a related standard, like Standard Three, which describes ways students "evaluate information and its sources critically." The librarian might suggest a way of coaching students to begin the process of critical evaluation of sources during a library class session or as a follow-up to the assignment. In this way, librarians practiced articulating the spirit of the ACRL Standards to faculty as well as preparing an approach to discussing a potential expansion of the lesson plan. Since the transaction happened as part of a role-playing exercise, it gave librarians a safe place to experiment with different approaches.

The receiving partners also varied their degree of openness to the pitching partner's proposal. The goal of repeating the exercise was to give instructors practice in explaining the concept of IL to faculty members, and help them develop persuasive strategies and anticipate possible types of response.

Find Opportunities

Retreat participants were divided into teams, and in keeping with the spy theme, the retreat leaders asked them to identify their fellow team or "cell" members using code words and signal phrases (see Appendix 9.D). The teams were assigned a campus group such as "faculty" or "undergraduates" and asked to gather "intelligence" about the priorities and agendas of the members of their groups. Prompts or hints for places to look for information and ways to "do surveillance" ("top secret" clues) were provided, and included searching relevant websites, examining committee and governance structures, and reading their group's "propaganda" (newsletters, catalog statements and program descriptions, assessment reports, etc.). The goal was for teams to identify as many issues of import to their target population as possible in the allotted time. Upon regathering, the teams were asked to pick one of the identified issues and to brainstorm ways that IL and/or library expertise/ resources could contribute to a positive resolution of a problem or factor into a collaboration. Essentially, the retreat facilitators wanted staff to ask what the libraries can do for its primary academic constituents—faculty, undergraduate students, and graduate students.

Results

A brief survey was e-mailed to participants in the days following the retreat. The survey asked three open-ended questions:

- What did you find most useful/helpful to you?
- What did you find least useful/helpful?
- List at least one idea/plan that you took away from the retreat for follow-up.

Return rate on the survey was less than one-half of the participants. Survey results varied widely and were heavily informed by each participant's job expectations. For example, several of the liaison librarians listed the curriculum audit as the most useful while other teaching and administrative staff who do not have assigned subject areas listed the curriculum audits that they performed on interdisciplinary programs to be the least useful activity. Several respondents listed the role-playing exercise as most useful, while nearly an equal number listed it as least useful.

Take-away ideas and plans were wide ranging. As his next outreach effort, one librarian planned to target instructors of courses he had identified as key during his curriculum audit. Another made a commitment to collect syllabi and assignments developed by faculty in her department in order to be better informed of faculty expectations for students. Yet another reported she had developed ideas for new faculty seminars to offer.

The curriculum audit, which allowed participants to learn more about a degree program that they support; to summarize current library practices associated with a given degree program; and to establish a baseline of library practices for future assessment purposes, was especially helpful to the Urban Studies Librarian. She had great success using the tool. She focused on the Communication Studies Department, and while auditing the department, she discovered that many of the core courses did not have consistent exposure to opportunities to develop IL skills. Shortly after the retreat, this librarian led an upper division Communication Studies library instruction session that was taught by the Dean of the College of Urban Affairs. During the 300-level workshop, the Dean expressed the idea that every Communication Studies student should be exposed to developing research skills throughout their college career in their major. Following the Dean's comment, the library liaison felt that there may be a prime opportunity to use the new skills and resources learned at the instruction retreat to promote IL competencies across the curriculum. She also felt that the time was right to initiate conversations with the Communication Studies faculty about how the library not only supports the existing outcomes of their courses, but also take these conversations to the next level by discussing a systematic and constructive involvement in the curriculum.

Many Communication Studies faculty take advantage of library instruction to help their students develop and demonstrate information literacies, but some faculty choose not to involve the librarians in their courses. This is presumably based on an understanding that these skills are developed in other coursework, or perhaps are better demonstrated and evaluated in another course. The end result is that student exposure to skills development opportunities is scattershot, non-sequential, and dependent on the electives pursued in their majors. Over the last several years, many librarians teaching Communication Studies (and other classes) have heard from students in research skills sessions that they have not had opportunities to develop IL, especially the more advanced information skills, earlier in their academic career.

The Communication Studies liaison and the Head of Instruction developed a proposal that would address this issue at the curricular level. They began by identifying information competencies they believed the department would like to see Communication Studies students develop in the course of their major. Then, they mapped those competencies to required coursework. The colleagues' initial draft was designed as a starting point for conversation within the department (see Appendix 9.E).

For the initial Communication Studies Department meeting, the librarians included sample assessment mechanisms for select competencies to demonstrate that the inclusion of IL development is, in actuality, nothing new and is a job for librarians and teaching faculty alike. Students demonstrate their skills development, or lack thereof, in the process of doing research, writing, and speaking assignments. The librarians believed that their proposal made pre-existing expectations more explicit by standardizing the student experience with the development and demonstration of these skills and that the sample mechanisms suggested opportunities for instructors to help students succeed (see Appendix 9.F).

The Communication Studies IL curriculum-level proposal is still at the early stages of implementation. During the next summer term, the

Communication Studies liaison and the Head of Instruction will invite instructors who teach the required courses to a brainstorming session to discuss the proposal, which will include the mapped competencies and sample assessment mechanisms.

To be successfully implemented, it was essential to have the support and acceptance of the Communication Studies faculty on this IL curriculum-based proposal. Library instruction sessions, along with the course-driven information competencies and assessment mechanisms, will ensure that Communication Studies majors will be exposed to and will comprehend the basics of IL tenets throughout their college career. Furthermore, faculty acceptance of IL competencies as part of the curriculum will ensure that library instruction sessions will no longer be instructor-dependent in required courses; they will be built into the curriculum on a permanent basis.

Conclusion

The retreat built common ground among participants and laid a foundation for better informed and more strategic conversations with departmental faculty. Retreats are a successful mode of conducting staff training because they let people focus on ideas for a sustained amount of time and in a context that supports both reflection and planning. The librarians at UNLV used a combination of approaches to avoid the small group discussion burnout that can discourage some staff members from participating. The participants documented the retreat's goals and outcomes in advance and offered a variety of structured activities that took different learning styles into account. By distributing the planning among many librarians, the librarians ensured that some activities remained a surprise to most participants, and by incorporating the spy theme, the retreat leaders kept participants laughing as well as cognizant of the larger message of the day, which was to use information about their academic departments to develop a strategy to market library instruction as essential to curricular goals.

Librarians have since requested and received additional training and support for collaborating with faculty. A year later, a follow-up session facilitated by UNLV Libraries Dean, Patricia Iannuzzi, a recognized expert in incubating faculty–librarian collaborations, reinvigorated liaisons by supplying an informal checklist of potential ways to initiate and sustain contact with faculty. Many items on the checklist were activities liaisons engaged in already such as attending presentations and creative events hosted by their departments or meeting for coffee with new faculty and staff in their departments. The checklist provided an opportunity for individual liaison librarians to share tales of their successful efforts and to brainstorm again around their challenges. UNLV Libraries' Instruction Department has continued to employ the curriculum audit process with individual librarians, in particular new librarians. It was revisited by the library liaisons as a group nearly a year later to motivate them to identify additional receptive departments and develop a plan to open conversations about collaboration. The Communication Studies department model offers one way of collaborating on a formal scale, but liaisons have been encouraged to target small, receptive parts of an academic program and see if getting a foot in the door leads to further opportunities within the curriculum.

Retreat participants were equipped with a larger repertoire of approaches when talking with faculty about supporting departmental curricula and planting the seeds of a concrete action plan. Librarians were encouraged to identify receptive programs and learn enough about them to make a persuasive case for reflecting IL skills in the formal outcomes of a departmental curriculum.

References

1. Moehring, Eugene P. "UNLV Celebrating Fifty Years." *UNLV – the University of Nevada, Las Vegas: A History.* Reno: University of Nevada Press, 2007.
2. UNLV Libraries. "University Libraries Fact Sheet." University of Nevada, Las Vegas Libraries, 2007. Available: <http://www.library.unlv.edu/about/facts.html>. Accessed: September 25, 2007.
3. Iannuzzi, Patricia. "Faculty Development and Information Literacy: Establishing Campus Partnerships." *Reference Services Review* 26, nos. 3/4 (1998): 97–102.
4. Lampert, Lynn D. "Integrating Discipline-based Anti-plagiarism Instruction into the Information Literacy Curriculum." *Reference Services Review* 32, no.4 (2004): 347–355.
5. Macklin, Alexius Smith, and Fosmire, Michael. "A Blueprint for Progress: Collaborating with Faculty to Integrate Information Literacy into the Curriculum at Purdue University." *Resource Sharing & Information Networks* 17, no. 1 (2004): 43–56.
6. Dewey, Barbara I. "The Embedded Librarian: Strategic Campus Collaborations." *Resource Sharing & Information Networks* 17, no. 1 (2004): 5–17.
7. Boon, Stuart, Johnston, Bill, and Webber, Sheila. "A Phenomenographic Study of English Faculty's Conceptions of Information Literacy." *Journal of Documentation* 63, no. 2 (2007): 204–228.
8. Little, Jennifer J., and Tuten, Jane H. "Strategic Planning: First Steps in Sharing Information Literacy Goals with Faculty Across Disciplines." *College & Undergraduate Libraries* 13, no. 3 (2006): 113–123.
9. Moore, Melissa. "Reelin' 'Em In: How to Draw Teachinf Faculty into Collaborative Relationships." *Resource Sharing and Information Networks* 17, no. 1 (2004): 77–83.
10. "ACRL – Information Literacy Competency Standards for Higher Education." American Library Association, September 1, 2006. Available: <http://www.ala.org/ala/acrl/acrlstandards/informationliteracycompetency.cfm>. Accessed: September 25, 2007.

Appendix 9.A: Curriculum Audit

Goals

- To learn more about a degree program that you support
- To summarize current library practices associated with a given degree program
- To establish a baseline of library practices for future assessment purposes
- To refresh your knowledge of basic information literacy tenets
- To identify areas where we can initiate strategic collaboration efforts and programming to ensure that UNLV graduates information literate students.

What is a curriculum audit?

A curriculum audit is a systematic examination of CURRENT curricular practices. It will give instructors a comprehensible overview of the curriculum they serve and how they are CURRENTLY interacting with the programs.

Homework instructions

The attached grid is designed for you to inventory the CURRENT support UNLV Libraries provides to faculty and students in raising information literacy skills. To get started, select one degree program that you support. Identify each course in the degree program, the course number and whether the course is a core course or an elective. While reviewing all the courses, note aspects of each course that you may want to remember (e.g. prerequisites, research-intensive, writing-intensive, lab). Using the grid, list the information literacy skill building activities and/or tools that are currently in place to complement the courses (e.g. Libraries instruction session, Tour, Guide/handout, Tutorial, Research assignment). Please complete an audit for at least one of the degree programs with which you work for the retreat. Bring a completed grid with you to the retreat for next steps.

Strategies for how to go about this homework

Be candid. This exercise is a tool BY YOU, FOR YOU. While there will be an opportunity for volunteers to share their experiences completing the homework, no one will be asked to share their audit.

You may have a tendency to start thinking about what you could or should be doing with a given degree program. If you start thinking of these things, note "OPPORTUNITY" in the appropriate boxes. Resist urges to plan and concentrate on simply documenting current practices. The audit should take no more than an hour to complete. If you start to solve the world's problems in this exercise, it will take you much longer. We will brainstorm ways to address and prioritize opportunities at the retreat.

You'll find MANY, MANY courses with which the Libraries have no interaction. Please don't let this discourage you. No librarian is expected to be involved with a degree program at a course by course level. BLANKS (and many of them) are totally acceptable.

Not every class is an appropriate venue to build skills in each of the five information literacy areas. In these cases, you may simply indicate "NOT APPLICABLE."

You may not know enough about a given course to make an assessment of whether it is a viable opportunity or not. In these boxes, you may want to indicate "NEEDS MORE RESEARCH."

Appendix 9.B: Sample Grid

C/E	Course # and notes	Identify	Access	Evaluate	Use	Understand
C	WMST113 Gender, Race, Class Survey course, satisfies general education requirement, lots of non-majors. Introduction to issues of major.	Class sessions for some sections	Class sessions for some sections	Class sessions for some sections		
C	WMST302 Feminist Research Methods Prereq 113	Class session	Class session	Opportunity		Class session
C	WMST401 Advanced Feminist Theory Prereq. 113 Advisors should suggest 302 first.	Class session	Class session	Opportunity		Opportunity
C	WMST497 #Praxis project#Prereq. 113, 302, 401#"Develop skills useful in post-graduate years."	Class session or individual consultation-depends on number of majors	Class session or individual consultation-depends on number of majors		Individual consultation addresses this competency with some students	Opportunity
C	WMST498 or 499 Internship or Independent Study, min. 6 credits. Consult with chair. Prereq. upper division standing.	Opportunity	Opportunity		Opportunity	Opportunity
E	WMST275 Marriage and family Prereq SOC101 or 102; also SOC275					
E	WMST308 Anthropology of women Prereq. 113, ANT101, SOC101. Also ANT308					

Appendix 9.C: What We'd Like You to Do

Student Informants: For about 5 or 10 minutes, we'd like you to tell a small group of librarians a bit about yourself by answering the following questions (the group's interview will follow):

- What is your course of study?
- How did you decide which classes to take during your first year on campus?
- Out of the classes you've taken so far, which have been the most research-intensive?
- What kinds of assignments and research did you have to complete in the one that was the most research-intensive?
- Was there any help offered in figuring out how to do the research needed?
- When is/are the most logical time(s) in your degree program to learn different research skills?
- How do you think the Libraries could improve your education in your discipline?

Appendix 9.D Retreat code words and signal phrases

You will need to identify other members of the Desert Phone Booth cell prior to 1400 hours today. You will do this by incorporating the phrase "Mojave desert" into interactions with fellow participants throughout the day. You will recognize your fellow cell members when they respond to your "Mojave desert" prompt with the phrase, "the park service has disconnected the loneliest phone." Similarly, if a cell member attempts to make contact with you using the code prompt "Mojave desert" be sure to respond with "the park service has disconnected the loneliest phone."

You will need to identify other members of the Sagebrush cell prior to 1400 hours today. You will do this by incorporating the word "stalactites" into interactions with fellow participants throughout the day. You will recognize your fellow cell members when they respond to your "stalactites" prompt with the phrase, "caves may be off limits while bats are nursing." Similarly, if a cell member attempts to make contact with you using the code prompt "stalactites" be sure to respond with "caves may be off limits while bats are nursing." You will need to identify other members of the Ghost Town cell prior to 1400 hours today.

You will do this by incorporating the phrase "pick axe" into interactions with fellow participants throughout the day. You will recognize your fellow cell members when they respond to your "pick axe" prompt with the phrase, "his burro was the miner's best friend." Similarly, if a cell member attempts to make contact with you using the code prompt "pick axe" be sure to respond with "his burro was the miner's best friend."

Appendix 9.E: Proposal for the Integration of Required Information Competencies into the Communication Studies Curriculum

Required Courses for Communication Studies Majors

- COM 101 *
- COM 102
- COM 216 *
- COM 400 ?*
- COM 409 ?*
- COM 408 OR COM 435 ?*

*Courses selected for competency mapping
?*Courses with potential for competency mapping – need further discussion

COM 101 Oral Communication

Theory and performance work in extemporaneous speaking and related speaking experiences. Emphasis placed on developing skills necessary for effective public speaking. 3 credits.

Information Competencies

- Search by author, title, and keyword in library online catalog and locate relevant items
- Conduct a search in an interdisciplinary database (e.g. Academic Search Premier)
- Understand the concepts behind searching simple keywords or phrases and the use of Boolean operator "and"
- Revise topic and/or strategy if search results are unsatisfactory
- Use database features to mark/save/print/e-mail citations and link to full text
- Demonstrate preliminary evaluation abilities; an understanding that audience, bias, author and context play a role in source credibility
- Cite sources properly according to appropriate style guide.

COM 216 Survey of Communication Studies

Analysis of the contexts, principles, and values of human communication grounded in communication theory. Focuses on developing competency in the areas of intrapersonal, interpersonal, small group, organizational, and public communication. 3 credits.

Information Competencies

- Develop a focused topic and strategies for obtaining needed information
- Identify relevant keywords and controlled vocabulary terms for searching a topic
- Interpret catalog and database search results; link from subject headings to find additional resources
- Gather background information in print and online reference-style works
- Identify relevant subject databases, e.g. *Communication & Mass Media Complete* and execute a basic search
- Evaluate information gathered by such criteria as: relevance, authority, currency, peer review process and differentiate between primary and secondary sources.

COM 400 Human Communication Theory

Reviews, compares, and applies contemporary theories of communication. Focus is upon interpersonal, cognitive, and influence theories as they apply to communication processes. Prerequisite: COM 216. 3 credits.

OR

COM 409 The Rhetorical Tradition

Historical and critical evaluation of western rhetorical theory from the classical era to the contemporary period. Examines communication's humanistic traditions on such issues as civic discourse, public advocacy, social interaction, message analysis, and political culture. Prerequisite: COM 216. 3 credits.

Information Competencies

NOTE: These are higher order competencies that might be appropriate for 400-level courses, we would like to discuss further the nature of these two classes to select one, perhaps, that would be the more appropriate place to require the development of these skills.

- Identify relevant subject databases (including those not exclusively focused on communication) and execute a basic search
- Conduct a comprehensive literature review for papers/projects, including books, journal articles, dissertations, technical reports, non-print media, etc.
- Analyze a body of research literature, drawing conclusions and developing new insights

Students are required to take COM 408 *or* COM 435
COM 408 Rhetorical Criticism

Investigation and analysis of public discourse. Students introduced to a variety of critical methodologies used to analyze public messages. Prerequisite: COM 216. 3 credits.

COM 435

Quantitative Research Methods

Survey of empirical research methods in communication including laboratory, field, and survey methods and their applications. Prerequisite: COM 216. 3 credits.

Information Competencies

NOTE: Again, there are higher order competencies that will probably align more directly with one or the other of these two classes. As students are required to take only one of these two, however, we may elect to make these competencies required of both classes. Further discussion needed.

- Use advanced search features of subject databases
- Select and use vocabulary specific to the discipline for searches
- Perform cited reference searches in order to follow a research topic forward and backward in time
- Use citation manager software as appropriate
- Describe how research literature is generated and disseminated in the discipline
- Identify investigative methods in the discipline
- Use research collections beyond the local library when needed (e.g. special libraries and archives)
- Apply ethical and legal principles to the use of information in all formats and contexts (e.g. ethics of using online transcripts; recorded speeches; cost of information barriers, etc.)

Appendix 9.F Library Instruction Assignment

COM 101 Library Instruction Assignment

Name:
Persuasive Speech Topic:

Complete the following to help you prepare for your persuasive speech.

Search the UNLV library catalog for two print and/or media resources in your topic.

• How did you begin your search? What words did you type in the search box?
• Provide the title and the call number of the two sources you found:

Find a full-text article on your topic using the Academic Search Premier Database.

• What keywords did you initially use in your search?
• Did you revise your search based on your initial results? If so, how?
• What is the title of the article you found?
• What is the name of the journal this article was published in?

Analyze the article using the source credibility clues we talked about in our library instruction session. Answer the following questions:

• Who is the author(s) and what is his/her affiliation and/or expertise?
• Is there a bibliography or list of sources cited?
• Do you think this is a scholarly article? Why or why not?

10 How to Survive Your First Term as Team Leader

A One-day Boot Camp at the Purdue University Libraries

*Michael Fosmire, Jane Kinkus,
Rebecca Richardson, and Lisa Rile*

Introduction

In 1999 Purdue University Libraries (PUL) chartered an *ad hoc* team to investigate the difficulties with communication and decision making, especially between technology and public service units in the library. The team discovered that these issues went beyond technology and non-technology units, and were endemic to the entire organization.

Setting

The proposed solution was to create a cross-functional team structure for core library services that would overlay, but not replace, the traditional, hierarchical structure of the organization (see Figure 10.1). These cross-functional units would allow for wide input on core services and new projects, empowering not only librarians but also professional staff to contribute at the system-wide level. Standing teams were chosen on an annual basis, with staggered terms of service of two years for new members. Additionally, *ad hoc* teams were created as needed to address specific projects, such as the implementation of a new service.

The team structure was anchored by the formation of a Libraries Management Team (LMT), comprised of unit heads and through which the standing teams reported, and the Policy and Planning Team, with representation from different library populations and from a selection of team leaders, which addressed more strategic and policy-related implications of the work of the teams. The cross-functional teams were connected to the rest of the organization by having a sponsor in the LMT who was an advocate and conduit of information between the two teams.

As the entire organization was new to team-based work, the original implementation of the new structure relied heavily on self-learning, and some keys to effective teamwork practices were discovered through trial

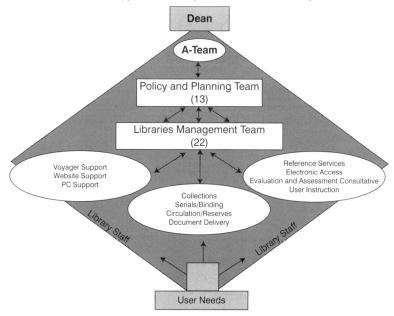

Figure 10.1 Purdue University Libraries team structure in the year 2005 © Purdue University Libraries

and error. LMT devoted some effort to learning principles of working in teams, which they disseminated through team sponsors to the rest of the teams. Unlike the University of Arizona,[1] for example, that created a position of Assistant Dean for Team Facilitation and embedded trained facilitators to help teams function, Purdue University relied primarily on sponsors for that kind of support. As the background and comfort level of sponsors to assist with team dynamics varied, this approach had mixed results.

Needs Assessment

In 2005 at the start of the new cycle of team population, LMT determined that both incoming team leaders and team sponsors would benefit from some formal, systematic training in teaming and leadership skills. Also in 2005, after reviewing feedback from libraries' staff, LMT put special emphasis on considering staff members who had not participated in teams before, for inclusion in this round of team population.

Some library staff had attended past libraries' workshops on team composition and leadership skills, and, indeed, some teams had unilaterally asked for team training. However, many more staff, especially those new to teams, had not had any experience with either being a team member or a team leader. Thus, it was seen as critical that some systematic training in team skills occur to facilitate the work of the new batch of teams. LMT decided that training was needed in order to ensure the success of all team leaders. The single day "boot camp" format was chosen both for scheduling convenience and because the shared experience of all team leaders would create a network of resources, and develop a cohort mentality among participants.

For inspiration on which topics to consider for the systematic team training, LMT drew on its own experiences with team building. During the first year of its existence, LMT members decided to devote some meeting time each month to learning more about how to work effectively in teams. Over a period of several months, LMT members took turns presenting a video that addressed an aspect of teamwork and facilitating discussion afterward. The videos were produced by Video Arts, a company that is committed to training and learning through entertaining and memorable examples. Each video presented a humorous vignette in which the team leader made glaring management mistakes. As the leader discovered new management techniques, sometimes from an omniscient fairy godmother or time traveler, the scenarios were replayed until the leader finally got it right. Topics in the series included how to assemble and develop a team, conduct effective meetings, communicate within a team, and make decisions as a team. As a result of watching the videos, which LMT members found both enjoyable and useful, the group established ground rules for conduct within team meetings and standards for facilitators, such as the requirement for creating and disseminating an action-oriented agenda in advance of a meeting. As the LMT realized a need for broader team training across the library system, the Video Arts management video series provided some inspiration for the kinds of topics that should be covered in a team leader boot camp.

Learning Objectives

In order to determine which specific topics should be covered, LMT spun off a small group to analyze needs and articulate training to address those needs. This sub-group analyzed past LMT work in team building, as well as gathering feedback from sponsors and team leaders about their biggest training needs. Several needs became apparent through this process, which were then translated into learning objectives.

When creating instruction, whether it is a tutorial, one-hour class, or even a one-day workshop, objectives should be developed and distributed to learners as a guide to letting them know what they "should be able to do when they have completed a segment of instruction."[2] Due to the amount of information determined necessary to cover during the workshop, objectives were written as goal statements rather than standard outcome-based objectives. LMT members considered writing the objectives for each module in the standard four-part format of Heinich,[3] in which audience, behavior, condition, and degree would be addressed. However, in a training program of this size there would have been too many to list on one page, thereby running the risk of overwhelming attendees. Instead, during the planning stage, facilitators simply asked the question, "What should learners know or be able to do at the end of this module?" In all, eleven "objectives" were developed to be covered in a day-long "boot camp."

The objectives decided upon asked participants to be able to: explain how teams fit into the organization; interact effectively with the team sponsor/ team leader; locate the various resources available to teams and team leaders; utilize technologies to facilitate teamwork; facilitate expectation and goal setting for the team; facilitate the documentation of the team's activities for reports; conduct a meeting effectively and efficiently; identify common personality types found in teams and explain how those types can influence team dynamics, success, and actions; use a variety of techniques to encourage all members to participate in the work of the team; articulate contributions of individual team members for the purpose of performance evaluation; and employ a variety of methods to manage conflict within a team.

In order to address all of the learning objectives, eight modules were developed, which are described in the following sections in the order in which they occurred. Each module had a duration of between a half hour and an hour, with the longer modules including substantial hands-on activities to help participants engage deeply with team concepts, while the shorter modules were primarily geared toward information transfer, more focused on details that team leaders needed to know from an administrative standpoint.

The Modules

Keynote Speaker and Video

As a fun and inspirational way to begin the day-long boot camp, two keynote speakers were invited to convey the importance of teamwork. The group as a whole was asked to think about what makes a great team, which attributes are necessary, and how teamwork can positively affect an organization. After giving a brief introduction about the powers of teamwork and how an organization can thrive in a team environment, attendees watched an inspirational video titled *Survival Run*.[4] In this video, viewers observed a sight-challenged runner working with and relying on his guide, a sighted runner, to finish a difficult and hilly race. The story of this dynamic duo overcoming obstacles and relying on trust and motivation to achieve a goal was intriguing and inspirational. Key themes throughout the video include risk taking, achievement, motivation, leadership, overcoming obstacles, and trust, all key characteristics of teamwork.

Throughout the video, attendees were asked to write down the characteristics or behaviors of teamwork demonstrated by the runners. Once the video ended, the keynote speakers divided the participants into small groups, where they discussed the video and compared notes taken during its viewing. After debriefing in small groups, attendees then picked five characteristics/behaviors of teamwork and described how these can be put into practice, essentially creating an action plan for accountability. Once the action plans were complete, attendees were encouraged to share their plans with the entire group.

Participants enjoyed not only watching the inspirational video, but also interacting with colleagues in small group discussions and with the group as a whole. As a result, the Purdue University Libraries purchased the video to add to its collection for future team building workshops and activities.

Surviving Your First Year as Team Leader

Facilitators for this module split time between discussing team guidelines and utilizing technology to facilitate team work. Because incoming team leaders may have had limited exposure to the team environment, or have little experience leading teams or working collaboratively among peers, it was important to inform attendees about guidelines, such as team charters, expectations of team leaders, expectations of team members, and the role of the team sponsor (see Table 10.1).

Copies of a handout containing team guidelines and created by LMT members, were provided to attendees for review and discussion. The team charter is the basis for the team. It sets the purpose, goals, and defines the scope of its responsibilities. Elements of a team charter include the following sections: the purpose/goals of the team; desirable/ key characteristics of members of the team; background/relevant history to give the team context of previous work; challenges and considerations the team needs to keep in mind; key responsibilities that need to be addressed; parameters/boundaries of decision-making authority within the organization; an articulation of the measures of success or demonstrated outcomes; communication guidelines (suggestions of who should be consulted and informed about the work of the team); a timeline for the team's work; and a statement of resources the team may tap into and directions for the process of acquiring more resources as needed.

The roles of team members were explicitly addressed, as stated in Table 10.1, since due to the decentralized nature of the Libraries, oftentimes employees do not have the opportunity to work with, or even meet colleagues elsewhere within the system. Providing expectations for team members assists in structuring meetings, communication, and teamwork, all components of a team environment that can cause problems if not addressed. Setting expectations for the team is in the best interest of

Table 10.1 Fundamental expectations for team roles

Team Member	Team Leader	Team Sponsor
Attend meetings and arrive on time	Understand the issues that the team addresses	Serve as liaison in two-way communication between the team and LMT
Come prepared	Willingness to change and adapt as conditions change and as the needs of the organization and the team evolves	Advise the team, as needed
Participate in discussions	Possess people-management skills, especially in facilitating group interaction (member participation, conflict resolution, and consensus building)	Monitor team progress, attending team meetings as necessary
Suggest/propose actions to move team's goals forward	Demonstrate skills in developing and managing relationships with key stakeholders	Mentor the team leader, as needed
Be willing to learn/investigate/test	Facilitate team's annual planning and reporting	Have ex-officio status
Work collaboratively	Have knowledge to obtain necessary resources	
Volunteer for assignments and complete them on schedule		
Have a sense of humor		
Have an avid interest in the Libraries' and the team's responsibilities		

everyone, especially the team leader. Team leaders' roles were also defined, since those chosen as team leaders do not necessarily have prior leadership or management experience. The stated expectations assist the leader when interacting with team members, administration, and team goals. Finally, each team is designated an LMT sponsor. Since this role was completely new to the organization, both sponsors and team leaders needed guidance in determining what the sponsor's role really was. Overall, the sponsor's role is to provide the team direction and facilitation, as needed by the team, as well as serve as a liaison to the LMT.

Once the handouts were reviewed by the attendees, the incoming team leaders were encouraged to discuss the guidelines with the outgoing team leader and team sponsor. Any questions or concerns that the incoming team leaders had could be clarified, and a relationship with the team sponsors established.

To work efficiently and effectively with others and as a group, team members should be familiar with the technologies that foster communication and teamwork. For example, teams are encouraged to utilize Outlook calendar to set up meetings; Outlook e-mail to create a distribution list; and Outlook tasks to delegate and track member responsibilities. To assist in this effort, QuickGuides (one-page tutorials created by PUL Staff Development and Training Department) detailing these technologies were distributed to attendees and demonstrated using a laptop and projector.

Project Management Module

Since team members and team leaders could come from any part of the Libraries, their experience with leading projects varied considerably. Classified staff, for example, largely did not have experience with decision-making authority, and it was a difficult transition to be in a situation where decisions could be made and projects led. Skills for carrying out these activities were not common throughout the system. It was thus seen as important to share some experience with team leaders on how to create an action plan and understand how to "get things done." Since the skills that LMT members wanted to teach were potentially easy in theory but more complex in reality, the kind of training they thought would be effective was a case study for the team leaders to work on. The team leaders were divided into groups of three or four and given the opportunity to create their own action plans under the guidance of the facilitator.

First, an overall orientation to "getting things done" was given, to provide some context for action planning and to discuss some of the ways that ideas get derailed instead of becoming actions. Then an overview of the action planning process was discussed, so the participants would know what was coming and how each step fit together. The training included a sample scenario (baking a cake for a party) that the participants could use for reference while working on their own scenario (planning for a library open house event), and handouts to capture the action plan.

Since the Purdue Libraries have made a commitment to incorporating outcomes-based evaluation of the work of teams, a component of identifying the objectives, outcomes and targets was incorporated into the action planning process. The actual creation of the action plan involved the following steps.

First, introduce the scenario, in this case planning an open house for the library. Then restate the scenario in terms of a specific program or task; identify objectives, that is, what is the purpose of the task; determine desired outcomes, that is, what is expected to change as a result of the task; and set targets, determining how to measure outcomes and what the threshold for success is. Once participants know why they are undertaking a project, the next steps are to figure out what to do in order to complete their objectives and outcomes. The next phase is to brainstorm/mind map a list of activities required in order to complete the task, making sure the list of activities is comprehensive, and organize tasks and create a timeline, in this case in a Gantt chart[5] format. Since plans rarely come off exactly as originally intended, participants were asked to identify challenges that threaten the project, and proactively develop solutions to avoid or overcome potential challenges. Once all the pieces have been laid out and contingencies considered, it is time to create a resource list and assign resources, including determining when resources are needed. Finally, to make sure the project stays on track, accountability checkpoints are set. This includes articulating critical deadlines throughout the project. The final deadline is not always the most critical one.

Each of the above steps was accomplished with a two- to five-minute introduction by the facilitator, followed by about ten to fifteen minutes of small group work, during which time the facilitator and participants discussed specific questions related to the steps. The first five steps were condensed into one exercise because the team leaders planned follow-up intensive sessions with team leaders and other interested team members that involved developing measurable outcomes for the actual goals of the team. After the groups finished their task, the class came together and one group presented their results, while other groups could contribute as well. Since all the groups worked on the same problem, the debriefing process was faster, as all groups had the same background in their discussions. This was important in the limited time allotted to the training.

Lunch

Even lunch included a programming component, albeit in a relaxed, informal manner. After letting participants start on a box lunch for half an hour and network with other team leaders and their sponsors, two speakers who had just finished their first year as team leader gave their insights into what challenges they faced, what they wished they had known, and what suggestions they had to make the new team leaders' tasks easier. This spawned a discussion among participants about being a team leader and assimilating some of the content from the first half of the day's training.

How to Conduct a Meeting

Many team members voiced complaints regarding team meetings: too many, too long, not worth the time. To combat this collective negative opinion of team meetings, and meetings in general, the need to enlighten the staff on the proper way to run a meeting presented itself in this workshop. What better way to promote change and efficiency than to have chairs of habitual "bad" or "inefficient" meetings learn from the always-entertaining John Cleese in *Meetings, Bloody Meetings,* a humorous video about the "do"s and "don't"s of meetings. The viewers learned about the five stages of conducting an efficient and productive meeting: plan meetings in advance, inform attendees of the agenda, prepare necessary supporting documents, structure and control discussions, and summarize and record outcomes.[6]

While watching the video, attendees were instructed to note what John Cleese's character, an inefficient meeting chair, did wrong and what he should have done. The video and activity were followed with techniques that can be used to maintain and restore order, keep attendees focused, and move the team in a positive direction.[6] Attendees then shared anecdotes about meetings that were good or bad, and techniques that were implemented or ignored. Attendees enjoyed swapping war stories while still learning how to run a meeting—or better yet—how not to run a meeting!

Team Roles/Personality Types

One of the topics addressed in the Video Arts management series viewed by LMT members was how to build a team. The main premise of *Selecting the Perfect Team*[7] was based on Meredith Belbin's research that suggested that effective teams have the correct mix of members based on two types of roles: functional roles and team roles. While a functional role is defined by technical skills or specialized knowledge, a team role is defined as a team member's natural proclivity for interacting with other team members in a particular way. Belbin identified nine predominant types of team roles, divided into three categories: action-oriented, people-oriented, and cerebral-oriented. The action-oriented types include the Shaper, who thrives on pressure; the Implementer, who turns ideas into actions; and the Completer Finisher, who spots errors and reminds the team of its timeline. The people-oriented types include the Resource Investigator, who explores opportunities and develops contacts; the Coordinator, who clarifies goals and delegates responsibilities; and the Teamworker, who listens, builds, and averts friction. The cerebral-oriented types include the Plant, known for being creative and unorthodox; the Monitor Evaluator, known for being strategic and discerning; and the Specialist, who provides knowledge and skills in rare supply.

LMT had watched the *Selecting the Perfect Team* video and everyone had completed a team roles inventory, which was included in the accompanying discussion guide. LMT found the concept of team roles to be useful when assigning new members to teams: candidates for a particular team were thus considered not only for **what** they knew how to do, but also for **how** they did it—i.e. how they were perceived to interact with others and whether they would bring an action-oriented, people-oriented, or cerebral-oriented influence to the team. LMT felt that this information was important and worth sharing with the new team leaders. The LMT member who volunteered to lead this module of the training had also presented some staff development sessions on personality types such as the Myers-Briggs Type Indicator and The Platinum Rule,[8] both of which describe sixteen distinct personality types. Myers-Briggs offers a more general, interpersonal model, while the Platinum Rule was designed for use in the workplace. These two typologies were selected for discussion because materials about both were readily available from within the Purdue Libraries. The information about personality types was provided as a way to help team leaders understand how to communicate more effectively with individual team members. Then the concept of team roles was discussed to give team leaders a new perspective on how to get the most out of their team by assigning the right type of work to the right team member. Since the allotted time for the Team Roles/Personality Types module was fifty minutes, both topics were given a brief treatment with a list of additional resources for team leaders to consult as wished. The goal of the module was not to provide in-depth training on team roles or personality types, but rather to introduce the concepts to team leaders to help them think more objectively about their co-workers in a team setting.

Conflict Management Module

The session on "Conflict Management for Team Leaders" was structured as a combination of presentation and participant discussion. This module covered the signs, effects, and responses to conflict in a team setting. Team leaders learned about their role in handling conflict on teams and the types of conflict that can occur. Disagreement over the handling of a particular task is *task conflict.* *Relationship conflict* occurs when conflict is based on issues that are not work related, such as personal and social issues. Disagreements about the use of resources, task delegation, and strategies for accomplishing tasks are examples of *process conflict.* Team leaders should focus not on eliminating conflict, but managing the types of conflict and how they are resolved. If task conflict occurs in greater proportion to process or relationship conflict *and* team members' perceptions on the level of conflict agree, then the teams are more effective.[9]

While conflict is an inevitable part of teamwork, research at a manufacturing facility has shown that teams that properly handle conflict become more productive than teams that avoid or mishandle conflict.[10] The common perception is that conflict is negative and several negative impacts of unresolved conflict have been identified, such as wasted time, poor morale, and the inability to reach decisions.[11] However, there are numerous positive effects of conflict, such as sharing new information, releasing tension, increased involvement, improved understanding of issues, and ultimately better decisions.[12,13] Attendees shared relevant personal experiences and were invited to reflect on those experiences and identify signs of unresolved conflict.[14]

The five typical responses to conflict were discussed along with situations in which each style would be appropriate.[15] The first style, confronting, is used when there is time to work through problems and the desire for a "win" for all involved. This technique requires that both parties work through issues together, and that both parties trust each other. Compromising is best used when time is limited, stakes are modest, and it is important to retain the relationship. Each party gives up something in order to reach a resolution. Smoothing is used when stakes are low and any solution is acceptable. The focus is on the positives, rather than the negatives. Frequently, this can result in one party having an obligation to the other in the future (trade-off). Forcing is used when stakes are high, time is very limited, a decision must be made quickly, and it is more important to make a decision than to maintain relationships. Avoiding, which is also known as withdrawal, is used when you know that you cannot win, stakes are low, or you want to gain time.

After the description of the typical conflict resolution styles, there was a discussion of the team leaders' role in handling conflict, starting with awareness and ending with a six-step process for addressing conflict.[16]

Getting Members Involved/Member Evaluation Module

One of the difficulties encountered by team leaders was eliciting full participation from all team members. This was especially true in functional teams, which had mandatory membership based on members' job descriptions. The primary goal for this module was to share best practices for involving and evaluating members. LMT members decided that a PowerPoint lecture with handouts would be an appropriate technique to use. Examples from George Soete[17] were used to break down large group inhibitions to participation. For example, asking members to brainstorm and write down their answers on notecards, and then share these answers in a round robin fashion keeps a few team members from dominating a brainstorming session. Alternatively, dividing the team into small groups to talk about a topic and do some initial synthesis, allows some of the shyer team members to work in a more comfortable, less threatening environment.

Another topic that many team leaders have been uncomfortable with in the past has been the evaluation of team members as part of annual reviews of performance. Since team leaders can come from anywhere in the Libraries' hierarchy, most team leaders have not been in a managerial or evaluative situation before. Every year during annual reviews, team leaders are contacted about each of their team members to get some feedback on how they have worked and what their accomplishments have been over the course of the year. For this part of the training module, an example of a letter of solicitation of feedback was shared and discussed. The feedback letter focused on levels of participation and on concrete, specific, accomplishments by a team member. This helped the team leaders understand the kinds of feedback they needed to provide to team members' supervisors, and thus the kinds of records they needed to maintain and accomplishments they needed to keep track of. This also allowed the participants to talk about expectations for evaluation and the level of detail needed in their notes. Since the team sponsors attending this event were also typically supervisors of staff, the team leaders got direct feedback about how their evaluations are used in the annual review process and the kinds of information that was most helpful.

Results/Conclusion

To properly assess and evaluate the workshop, a paper evaluation was given to attendees to fill out and submit at the end. The evaluation contained a combination of a four-point Likert-scale statements (Strongly Agree, Agree, Disagree, and Strongly Disagree) about the value of the workshop, and open-ended questions. The open-ended questions enabled attendees to record positive and negative impressions about the workshop, aspects that needed to be changed, how workshop information would be used, and general comments.

Of the twenty attendees, thirteen filled out the evaluation. Of the thirteen respondents, almost all chose Strongly Agree and Agree, revealing positive perceptions. The majority of respondents perceived themselves as having learned the stated skills/techniques/information stated in the objectives, as well as perceiving the workshop as valuable and worth their time.

Critical feedback was provided in the responses to the four open-ended questions. When asked what was found positive about the workshop, statements such as "good information," "material well presented," and "this is helpful in helping me make decisions on how to handle team members who do not cooperate" were provided. When asked what, if anything, could be changed about the workshop, references were made with regard to the length of the workshop, the amount of information given, and the timeliness of the workshop. Participants suggested that the workshop could have occurred as modules rather than an all-day workshop. They also suggested that the workshop content be offered earlier in the year, to coincide with team tenures. When asked how attendees would use the information gained from the workshop, many wrote about utilizing conflict management skills within a team, as necessary, and integrating key documents into planning.

Acknowledgments

The authors wish to recognize the other members of the Purdue Libraries who provided training at the "boot camp": Pat Kantner and Sue Ward. Also, Pat Kantner, Vicki Killion, and Jane Kinkus for creating the handout featured in the "Surviving Your First Year" module.

References

1. Diaz. J. R., and Pintozzi, C. "Helping Teams Work: Lessons Learned From the University of Arizona Library Reorganization." *Library Administration* and *Management* 13, no. 1 (1999): 27–36.
2. Smith, Patricia L. and Ragan, Tillman J. *Instructional Design.* 2nd ed. Hoboken, NJ: J. Wiley & Sons, 1997, p. 84.
3. Heinich, R., Molenda, M., Russell, J., and Smaldino, S. *Instructional Media and Technologies for Learning.* 7th ed. Englewood Cliffs, NJ: Prentice Hall, Inc., 2002.
4. Charlton, Robert, director. *Survival Run.* Santa Monica, CA: Pyramid Film & Video, 1981.
5. Gantt, H.L. "Work, Wages and Profit." *The Engineering Magazine,* 1910.
6. Robinson, Peter, Director. *Meetings, Bloody Meetings.* Chicago, IL: Video Arts, 1993.
7. Garden, Graeme, Director. *Selecting the Perfect Team.* London: Video Arts, 1993.
8. Alessandra, Tony, and O'Connor, Michael J. *The Platinum Rule.* New York: Warner Books, 1996.
9. Jehn, Karen A. "The Influence of Proportional and Perceptual Conflict Composition on Team Performance." *International Journal of Conflict Management* 11, no. 1 (2000): 56–74.
10. Alper, Steve, Tjosvold, Dean, and Law, Kenneth S. "Conflict Management, Efficacy, and Performance in Organizational Team." *Personnel Psychology* 53, no. 3 (2000): 625–642.
11. Capozzoli, Thomas K. "Conflict Resolution – A Key Ingredient is Successful Teams." *Supervision* 60, no. 11 (1999): 14–17.
12. Fussel, S.R., Brennan, S.E., and Seigel, J. "Understanding Effects of Proximity on Collaboration: Implications for Technologies to Support Remote Collaborative Work." In *Distributed Work,* edited by P.J. Hinds and S. Kiesler. Cambridge, MA: MIT Press, 2002, pp. 137–162.
13. Al-Tabtabai, Hashem. "Conflict Resolution Using Cognitive Analysis Approach." *Project Management Journal* 32, no. 2 (2001): 4–17.
14. Association Management. "Spotting Discord Early On." *Association Management* 55, no. 1 (2003): 20.

15. Ohlendorf, Amy. *Conflict Resolution in Project Management,* 2001. Available: <http://www.umsl.edu/~sauter/analysis/488_f01_papers/Ohlendorf. htm#acr>. Accessed: March 12, 2003.
16. Baker, Kim, and Baker, Sunny. *Complete Idiot's Guide to Project Management.* Indianapolis, IN: Alpha Books, 2000.
17. Soete, George J. *The Library Meeting Survival Manual.* San Diego, CA: Tulane Street Publications, 2000.

11 Using Data Analysis Techniques to Focus Academic Librarian Training at Wayne State University

John H. Heinrichs, Kee-Sook Lim, Jeen-Su Lim, and Sandra G. Yee

Introduction

Today, academic libraries exist in a dynamic and highly competitive market-oriented environment. Leading academic libraries that operate within this environment increasingly expect their administrators and staff to generate insights, create and use analytics, and critically assess deployed strategy. To succeed in this emerging evidence-based paradigm, library administrators must effectively utilize the various analytics and insights that are generated. To be effective, these insights must become integrated into operational processes and must support the strategic focus required of each operational unit. This strategic focus sets the direction for the operational units and supports the evidence-based paradigm used by the library administrators and staff during their insight generation processes.

Many library administrators recognize the importance of utilizing all available information and making fact-based decisions. Evidence-based library management systems are rooted in the full use of information and analytics-driven decision making. However, this evidence should not be solely internally focused, as libraries require an external or stakeholder focus. This external focus should drive staff development requirements.

In order to meet stakeholder expectations, library administrators need to develop short- and long-term strategies and plans to address the critical issue of human resource development. This plan needs to consider designated users and must detail information access, usage, and delivery requirements of these users. A staff development plan should address issues related to technical skills training, technical support, personal proficiencies and certifications, and information management skill development. Library administrators know that these skills are critical, and that the resource development plan must support the overall strategic direction and be consistent with the strategic plan of the library. The insights generated from available internal and external data should lead to a complete resource management plan as well as the staff development and training plan.

Setting

Wayne State University (WSU) University Libraries data were used to demonstrate the process of analyzing the data and making recommendations for staff development. This chapter showcases a step-by-step process of using and obtaining data, preparing data for data mining and insight generation, and generating reports, charts, tables, and insights to assess user needs and staff development requirements.

To remain successful and to prosper, library administrators need to understand the key environmental characteristics affecting academic libraries and how to access the ever-expanding availability of information. Information technologies are used as tools to access information about the environment and to integrate this understanding into various operational strategies. These tools provide access to unprecedented levels of data that are used to facilitate insight generation and competitive positioning. It is through the application of these generated insights that the library defines and positions itself in the environment.

The strategic management development process provides focus and direction for the academic library. Providing insights at the various steps of the strategic management process becomes the basis for how library administrators differentiate the academic library's services from other information provider organizations, and thereby create and sustain a competitive advantage. This strategic focus provides the paradigm used by the library administrators to position the academic library in the dynamic environment. In addition, this strategic focus provides the basis of resource management and prioritizing various opportunity areas. Various areas, such as digital content and information acquisition, web and information technology development, and staff development and training, demand ever-scarce resources. It is critical to allocate resources strategically to maximize the efficiency and effectiveness of library operations. The staff development and training process is one of the most important human resource management areas that library administrators must pay attention to in this dynamic and highly competitive global environment. The next section describes the role, process, and implementation issues of analytics and insight generation for library staff development and training.

Reasons for Utilizing Analytics

There are a variety of reasons to develop and utilize analytics. These reasons include improving the productivity and effectiveness of library administrators and staff, promoting collaboration and information sharing, enhancing the evidence-based measurement systems to ensure proper evaluation of library assets, and supporting a learning culture in the library.

Improving Productivity

There have been many changes and much refocusing in the use of information technology in the library. Information technology is a tool or a way to improve productivity and to monitor and improve customer satisfaction. Operating in a productive manner has always been an important objective for the library. Productivity is defined as the use of various inputs such as information or processes to generate the required products and services and thus can be used as measure of progress or efficiency. The challenge facing library administrators is to maintain a positive productivity trend. In order to ensure that productivity continues to increase, available information needs to be accessed and utilized effectively.

Promoting Collaboration and Information Sharing

Collaboration and communication of insights and discovered information is one way to accomplish the objective of continued improvement. The library administrators and staff should be involved in the knowledge discovery and sharing processes.

Enhancing Evidence-based Measurement Systems

Surviving in today's highly competitive global environment requires a different way of looking at and measuring performance. Performance measurements or analytics used in the past may miss or incorrectly assess the library's performance. The library requires a measurement system that recognizes, manages, and assesses knowledge and values intellectual capital.

With the increasing availability of data, storage capacity, and sophisticated analytical tools, more libraries recognize the importance and necessity of evidence-based decision making instead of relying on traditional forms of judgment and intuition-driven decisions.

Supporting a Learning Culture

Decision-making errors and judgment bias are becoming serious consequences in the evidence-based decision-making culture. Insights generated by library administrators can create an advantage or result in a missed opportunity. This shifting requirement demands a skilled, knowledgeable library staff. As a learning organization, the library seeks to be adaptive to the environment and to share knowledge within itself. "In a learning organization ... the conditions are created that enable people to have happy and productive lives."[1] The learning organization has become part of the environment and, according to Peter Senge, seeks to continually expand its capacity to create its future.[2]

A key component to learning and ultimately to the generation of knowledge is the ability of the library to share insights or to disseminate the learned experiences of others. "The radical change is the migration away from courses that are taken or accessed, to learning services that are experienced as a by-product of the real-time work-flow."[3] Conceptually, the library requires analytics on its workforce, workspace, and workflow. As the work processes are altered or reengineered, the demand for training changes. The applications supporting the new processes need to contain intelligence to customize the training provided to each worker. In the library, "the people collaborate in a process to produce goods and services" and as such, the applications need to provide multiple learning opportunities for the library administrators and staff.[3]

The above reasons provide the support for the staff development assessment and planning process driven by data-mining and analytic techniques. Regardless of the analytics techniques and processes used, it is critical that user responses drive library needs and staff development requirements. The next section discusses the four-step process of analytics-driven staff development planning and implementation.

The Four-step Analytics Application Process

Library administrators can follow a four-step process to make fact-based decisions and generate insights. To analyze staff development and training requirements, the following steps can be followed:

- Step 1: Examine analytic questions and type of analytics required for the assessment of library users' needs.
- Step 2: Develop an analytics scheme to identify staff development need areas.
- Step 3: Generate guided analysis insights from the library users' needs and satisfaction data.
- Step 4: Develop alternative solutions and recommend actions for staff development.

Step 1

This first step in the analytic process requires the development of primary managerial questions and related analytic questions. The questions are generated by evaluating managerial decisions and information needs. A simple managerial question is "How satisfied are our library users?" While this is a simple question to ask, it is not an easy one to answer. A question of satisfaction with the library implies an understanding of who the users are and what the users want. The managerial question could be translated into determining the satisfaction level by the various academic roles, by the university's academic disciplines, or by the library the user chose to visit. The question regarding satisfaction could even be investigated by comparing the results to the vision and mission of University Libraries.

After library administrators investigate the analytic problem statement, various solution categories can be evaluated by working through the various external and internal processes. These processes are further refined into various application areas including competitors, human resources, managerial, operational effectiveness, product, promotion, user, and suppliers. As an example, the library administrator can examine the various external analytic processes, which include environmental monitoring, market sensing, user-linking, and competitor analytics.

In the evaluation of the external processes, environmental monitoring is used to develop an understanding of the forces influencing the future direction and requirements for the library. Market sensing provides an understanding of the key needs related to the decision of a student or other user to use the library resources (either electronic or physical). The user-linking analytics support programs, activities, and service delivery recommendations; whereas competitor analytics are used to identify other universities' and public libraries' evaluation factors and their realized strategic directions.

In the research to understand the environment and to perform market sensing, it was determined that the demand for application specific skills is shifting rapidly:

> Librarians not only need technology to improve efficiency in their daily tasks, but also many times are expected by patrons to provide on the spot or classroom training in a variety of computer (applications), some of which may have no direct or obvious connection to the patrons' use of the library. The top four identified technological application needs in libraries are using Microsoft Word, Microsoft Excel, Internet browsers, and Microsoft Access.[4]

> Successful, vital academic libraries are redefining their roles in fulfilling the many goals of both users and higher education. They understand how the increasing importance of electronic resources affects collections, services, and staffing; how scholarship involves a continuum from initial research through the final project; and how information technology is now so essential to the entire research process. While academic libraries have always been involved in the initial stages of academic research, they can now be engaged through its completion. For university students, this means that the librarians provide access to electronic library resources and productivity software applications in the same location. This type of support has become the basis of the information commons concept. The information commons concept focuses on providing a "seamless continuum of … service from planning and research through presentation into the final product."[5]

The environmental monitoring analysis argued for a shift to spending funds on electronic resources and their importance to collections, services, and staffing. These requirements became the basis for the competitive analysis requirements. The outcome from the external review demonstrated a new paradigm in the role of the libraries. Information access has expanded beyond just access to reference and research material. The use of the software productivity tools has become part of the new definition. This insight begins the internal analysis to understand the perceived skill levels of the library's staff and the expected skill requirements for the various productivity software tools offered in the library.

A skills assessment survey can determine skills level for various Microsoft Office products as perceived by the individual employee and their manager. The outcome of this survey can provide the user's desired and the employee's desired and perceived level of skill.

Step 2

In this second step of the analytic process, library administrators identify various dimensions and measures that can be used to determine staff development requirements. This needed information comes from various sources such as existing internal transaction databases, subscribed external websites and reports, and primary survey data collection tools. Many libraries collect user response and satisfaction data through user surveys such as LibQUAL+™. LibQUAL+™ data from WSU University Libraries are used here for illustration purposes.

Dimensions/Members

Several dimensions were created to facilitate insight generation from the LibQUAL+™ satisfaction survey data. These dimensions include the academic discipline and academic role of the respondent, gender and age of the respondent, library visited by the respondent, primary access to the library resources, and library being evaluated. The initial analytics that were created centered on perceived user satisfaction. These dimensions and members were derived from LibQUAL+™ survey data source. Table 11.1 provides details regarding select high-level members from the academic discipline dimension and Table 11.2 provides details regarding the academic role dimension.

The academic discipline dimension consisted of eleven different colleges and two additional categories labeled undecided and other. The academic role dimension consisted of five roles encompassing faculty, graduate students, staff, and undergraduate students and two additional categories entitled no response and undecided. The five academic roles were further broken down to provide additional information for the library administrator. The graduate student member was broken down

Table 11.1 Academic discipline dimension

Academic Discipline	Percentage	Number of Responses		Overall Satisfaction
Business	5%	29	⭨	6.03
Communications	2%	14	⭣	5.57
Education	12%	71	⭡	7.25
Engineering	9%	51	⭧	7.00
General Studies	1%	5	⭡	7.40
Health Science	22%	131	⭧	7.03
Humanities	8%	48	⭢	6.33
Law	4%	22	⭡	7.45
Other	12%	72	⭧	6.89
Performing & Fine Art	4%	20	⭢	6.35
Science / Math	8%	47	⭡	7.21
Social Science	12%	71	⭧	6.80
Undecided	1%	5	⭧	6.80

Table 11.2 Academic role dimension

Academic Role	Percentage	Number of Responses		Overall Satisfaction
Faculty	38%	221	⭨	6.95
Graduate Students	25%	146	⭣	6.63
No Response	1%	6	⭡	8.17
Staff	12%	71	⭨	7.24
Undecided	3%	19	⭣	6.74
Undergraduates	21%	123	⭣	6.80

into doctoral, masters, and graduate status students; whereas, the faculty member was broken down into adjunct faculty, assistant, associate, and full professor as well as lecturer and other academic status personnel.

The gender member was composed of the male and female categories. The age dimension was composed of four age classifications. Those classifications were defined as younger than 22 years of age, between 22 and 30, between 31 and 45, and older than 45. The library visited dimension had the five libraries at WSU as its defined members. These members are Arthur Neff Law library, Vera P. Shiffman Medical library, David Adamany Undergraduate Library (UGL), Science and Engineering Library, and Purdy/Kresge (PK) Graduate Library. The primary access to library resources was divided into electronic usage of library resources and physical usage of library resources. These members had sub-members labeled daily, weekly, monthly, quarterly, and never. The University dimension had four-year research libraries, community college libraries, and medical school libraries as its members.

Measures/Facts

The fact table used in the analysis contains the actual measures. Over 200 different facts/measures were captured and reported in the multidimensional database. These facts include the overall satisfaction of the user, budget of the libraries, and number of students and faculty at the institution. The LibQUAL+™ survey provides the minimum acceptable perceived performance, the actual perceived performance, and the desired level of performance for over twenty-five key survey questions. Additionally, various statistical measures were also captured and stored. These data were cleansed to ensure the overall quality of the data warehouse. Upon completion of these steps, the data foundation was considered sufficiently developed to support the insight generation requirements.

The library administrators can focus on creating analytics to be used in the discovery of insights. They can accomplish this by first converting the general managerial problem statement into a specific analytic problem statement and then defining the appropriate metrics required to answer the analytic problem statement. Then the defined analytics can be created, validated, stored, and accessed. Various data-mining techniques can be utilized to generate patterns and insights that elucidate the analytic problem. Upon completion of these tasks, the library administrators should understand the situation presented by the analytic problem statement and can develop various ideas about required information for and the direction of the potential analytic solution.

Step 3

In the third step of the process, required analysis can be performed to generate tables and charts and to develop related insights. Depending upon the availability of the analytic tools and level of sophistication of the analytic skills, the analytic results can include a wide range of descriptive and inferential statistics as well as predictive models. The results include basic descriptive statistics such as means, frequencies, and standard deviations. Mean difference tests such as t-tests, analysis of variance (ANOVA), and multivariate analysis of variance (MANOVA) can be performed. Variable relationships can be assessed using correlations, regression, and cross-tabulation procedures. More advanced multivariate techniques such as clustering are utilized depending upon the nature of the managerial and analytic problems.

Table 11.3 details the overall satisfaction ratings for each of the seven defined dimensions in the multidimensional database. In addition, for the academic role dimension, the staff member reported the highest aggregate overall satisfaction rating for University Libraries of 7.24 on a 9-point scale (where 1.0 is low and 9.0 is high); whereas the graduate students member reported the lowest aggregate overall satisfaction rating of 6.63. The banding of highest to lowest represented a 9.2 percent difference. From examining this figure, it can be determined that the aggregate overall satisfaction rating for the academic discipline dimension ranged from a high of 7.45 to a low of 6.03 for a banding range of 23.5 percent. Using this information, a sample profile of a delighted user and a needs improvement user can be described. A delighted user was an older individual identified with the law school that visits the law library and uses the library resources electronically on a daily basis. The sample profile of a needs improvement (or dissatisfied) user was a younger individual identified with the business school who visited the Purdy/Kresge library and who had never used the library resources electronically. This profiling exercise can begin to provide an answer to the satisfaction question. Additionally, these profiles provide characteristics of potential members that can be used to create focus groups.

Given the initial response to the question of user satisfaction, two follow-up questions became, "Why are those users satisfied?" and "Why are those users dissatisfied?" To begin to answer these new questions, data needs to be explored through a defined user interface. Geac/Comshare Decision Web software and Microsoft Excel are examples of user interfaces. For example, Microsoft Excel provides PivotTable and PivotChart insight generation functionality as well as Excel Data Mining Add-in. The Microsoft Office Solution Accelerator for Business Scorecards was used

Table 11.3 Satisfaction rating by dimension

Dimension	Delighted	Needs Improvement	Percent Difference
Academic Discipline	7.45 – Law	6.03 – Business	23.50%
Academic Role	7.24 – Staff	6.63 – Graduate	9.20%
Age	7.15 – Older 46	6.52 – 22-30	9.70%
Electronic Usage	7.05 – Daily	6.30 – Never	10.00%
Gender	6.96 – Male	6.30 – Female	2.10%
Library Usage	7.08 – Monthly	6.30 – Quarterly	5.80%
Library Visited	7.30 – Law	6.67 – Purdy/Kresge	10.10%

to develop the balanced scorecards to report the status of key strategies. SharePoint was used to deliver the content to the library administrators and provide discussion room capability. With these tools, the causes of satisfaction or dissatisfaction, and various relationships in the data, can be investigated. Table 11.4 provides various details for understanding the Learning and Growth strategy initiative, based on user responses to four questions from the LibQUAL+™ survey. Library users were asked to rate and provide comments related to:

1 Dependability in handling users' service problems.
2 Employees who have the knowledge to answer user questions.
3 Employees who instill confidence in users.
4 Employees who understand the needs of their users.

The aggregate user response to these questions provided an overall perceived user rating of 6.72 and a desired overall level rating of 8.02 (on a 9-point scale). This rating highlights a performance gap of 1.30 or almost a 20 percent improvement ((8.02 - 6.72) / 6.72) required to achieve the satisfaction level desired by users. The overall profile described by users

Table 11.4 Learning and growth strategy user profile

Dimension	Member	High Perceived	Member	Low Perceived	Percent Difference
Academic Discipline	General Studies	7.20	Communications	5.46	31.90%
Academic Role	Undecided	7.13	Undergraduate	6.45	10.50%
Age	Older than 46	6.96	Younger than 22	6.29	10.70%
Electronic Use	Daily	6.85	Monthly	6.43	6.50%
Gender	Male	6.79	Female	6.66	2.00%
Library Use	Monthly	6.84	Daily	6.54	4.60%
Library Visited	Shiffman	7.21	Purdy/Kresge	6.50	10.90%

Benchmark Questions for Library Visited	High Perceived	Low Perceived	Percent Difference
1. Handling Problems	7.45	6.51	14.40%
2. Knowledgeable Employees	7.35	6.77	8.60%
3. Instill Confidence	6.78	6.07	11.70%
4. Understand Needs	7.28	6.68	9.00%

Learning & Growth Desired Rating	8.02
Learning & Growth Perceived Rating	6.72
Learning & Growth Gap Rating	1.30

was an individual who did not instill confidence when the user was trying to get a problem handled because the individual did not understand the user's needs and was not knowledgeable enough to handle the problem. The profile of the user providing this lower (dissatisfied) overall rating was a younger undergraduate student who used the Purdy/Kresge library's physical resources daily and the library's electronic resources on a monthly basis. Further analysis using the data-mining techniques is required to generate additional detailed insights.

Decision Trees Data-mining Algorithm

The decision tree data-mining algorithm generated from the LibQUAL+™ satisfaction survey multidimensional database highlights that the overall satisfaction with the library is predicated on the user perceiving that the library staff is knowledgeable of his or her needs and requirements. The response to the knowledgeable survey question explains the ratings for the response to the "understands needs" survey question.

Clustering Data-mining Algorithm

The clustering data-mining algorithm was performed on the satisfaction survey multidimensional database. The five dimensions of age, gender, library visited, electronic use of resources, and library use of resources were used in the clustering algorithm along with the five perceived facts of perceived overall satisfaction, knowledgeable, dependable in answering problems, instill confidence, and understand user needs. To prepare the algorithm, three clusters were requested. When analyzing the output of the cluster categories, the results were summarized. The library use and electronic use dimensions were categorized as 1) infrequent use, 2) occasional use, 3) frequent use; gender dimension was categorized as 1) male, and 2) female; age dimension was categorized as 3) older, 2) continuing, and 1) younger; and the library visited dimension was categorized as 3) professional (encompassing Vera P. Shiffman Medical Library, Arthur Neef Law Library, and Science and Engineering Library), 2) continuing, and 1) student (encompassing David Adamany Undergraduate Library and Purdy/Kresge Graduate Library). Based on the interpretation of the clustering algorithm results, the three identified clusters were labeled Older Professional, Continuing Education, and Younger Student.

Assessment Tools

There were a variety of tools and techniques that when combined can generate insights and additional understanding of user satisfaction. Using the balanced scorecard application tool, the staff development rating as assessed by all the users was calculated to be 72.1 percent; whereas the older professional cluster rated the staff at 82.8 percent, the continuing education cluster rated the staff at 69.1 percent, and the younger student cluster rated the staff at 41.9 percent. The next set of questions became, "What should we (as a library) do to improve?" and "What are recommendations for improvement?" The obvious concern was that the younger student cluster is growing at the university and represents the lowest satisfaction ratings for the learning and growth strategy. Unless the younger student cluster requirements are uncovered and acted upon, the overall satisfaction rating is projected to fall dramatically.

Step 4

After library administrators and staff have investigated and developed various patterns, models, and analytics to address the analytic problem statement, they evaluate various analytic solutions and apply them to managerial problems. These developed solution areas further focus the library administrators and staff into various application areas including competitors, customer, human resources, managerial, operational effectiveness, product, promotion, and suppliers. In this final step, decision makers identified alternative solutions, possible managerial actions to be taken based on the analytics results and insights generated from them. The external and internal process review led to a variety of insights and staff development recommendations. The skills development of library staff in the new information age era was a paramount task. There are many recommendations that can be generated from the reports, charts, and insights. In this illustrative example, two primary areas of recommendation are presented. However, the reader can generate many additional recommendations in various areas of staff development and library operations.

Information Commons

The information commons was a prevalent theme in the environmental analysis. Concerns regarding the implementation of the information commons include the ability of library staff to provide adequately capable assistance on new software applications. Staff proficiency with software productivity tools involves substantial redefinition of activities and descriptions. This redefinition raises fundamental issues about the way staff work to fulfill the libraries' mission and how library personnel responsibilities are articulated. It has to determine if library staff should provide a support service for software application productivity tools or if other functions have that responsibility. In discussions during reference services meetings, librarians noted that most of the questions they received were very technical in nature and not necessarily related to their reference expertise, education, and experience. Students asked questions about file transfer protocols, downloading images, web-based e-mail systems, and printing. They did not ask questions about setting up search strategies for specific databases or locating information on the web.[6]

Therefore, the following recommendations focus on enhancing the software application skills of the librarians. These are but some of the many recommendations that can be made. In this case, the Microsoft Office software applications were used for illustrative purposes.

The first recommendation was to focus on Microsoft Office 2007 skills enhancement for all library employees, in recognition that Microsoft Office provides tools and support for collaboration and team building. This collaboration support is fundamental in the enhancement of the identified reference capability provided by the library. The second recommendation was to install Microsoft Office on all library and public access computers. It is recognized that these tools and these skills are critical for the future of WSU University Libraries and should be installed and supported. The third recommendation was to provide and encourage library staff and administrators to earn certification, recognizing that Microsoft Application Specialist or Business Specialist certification could provide the basis for an independent assessment of skill achievement and used to enhance position descriptions. The fourth recommendation was to build a skills database to track current and required skill levels. It was recognized that a baseline skills assessment and future skills requirement are key to ensuring the achievement of objectives and increasing the overall satisfaction rating of the students and faculty. The fifth recommendation was to update the position profiles to reflect the new information age environment. It was recognized that the information commons concept requires a re-evaluation of the current profiles.

In summary, the recommendations focused on expanding the current requisite skills of library employees and were designed to ensure the sustainability of the skills development process. It was believed that these recommendations would begin to address the issues and concerns of the library usage raised by the younger student cluster and the electronic use raised by the continuing education cluster. Additionally, it was believed that the issues that surfaced in the LibQUAL+™ survey would be addressed by these recommendations.

Conclusion

The reports obtained from the insight generation processes provide additional valid analytics leading to evidence-based library management and staff development. This analysis can be extended to other areas of the library operations such as the reference desk, collection development, database services, and interlibrary loan.

A skills database, staff development training, and individual skills assessment are required for all staff development programs. The capture and update process, in the skills database, is an area of potential enhancement that will ensure that individuals are in the right positions and doing the right jobs with the correct tools and proper training. As new skills are acquired, the responsibilities assigned to the individual can be expanded. The skills capture process requires the identification of the skills and competencies required by the library, tracking of the individual's skills, measurement of the specific skills and competencies, and improvement of those identified skills with specific training programs.

WSU University Libraries' LibQUAL+™ survey data were used to illustrate and demonstrate that data-mining tools and techniques can provide focus when used in the context of the library's strategic plan.

References

1. Starkey, K., Tempest, S., and McKinley, A. *How Organizations Learn: Managing the Search for Knowledge*. 2nd ed. London, UK: Thomson Learning, 2004.
2. Senge, P. *The Fifth Discipline: The Art and Practice of the Learning Organization*. New York: Doubleday, 1990.
3. Adkins, S. "Radical Learning Technology." T+D 57, no. 11 (2003): 65–73.
4. Eastmond, G. "Technical Training: from 'Eeek!' to 'Ooh!'" *Library Administration and Management* 16, no. 2 (2002): 73–78.
5. Bailey, R. and Tierney, B. "Information Commons Redux: Concept, Evolution and Transcending the Tragedy of the Commons." *Journal of Academic Librarianship* 28, no. 5 (2002): 277–286.
6. Cowgill, A., Beam, J., and Wess, L. "Implementing an Information Commons in a University Library." *Journal of Academic Librarianship* 27, no. 6 (2001): 432–439.

12 You Came for the Snacks, But What Have You Learned?

Evaluation of a Staff Learning Program at the University of Maryland Libraries

Maggie Z. Saponaro, M. Sue Baughman, and Jennifer Kinniff

Introduction

As a team-based learning organization, The University of Maryland (UM) Libraries, places importance on the development of individual staff as well as the organization as a whole. In order to grow as an organization that remains an excellent resource to students, faculty, and staff, library staff need to acquire the critical skills and tools that allow them to become key players. The Libraries hold high the value of learning and education for its staff.

Setting

The Learning Curriculum was created as a comprehensive curriculum for knowledge and skill development. Introduced in 2001, this program seeks to provide educational and developmental opportunities to all library staff members to develop skills needed to support the Libraries' goals. The Curriculum is divided into ten components and the entire learning plan covers approximately 150 contact hours. The Curriculum is designed to allow flexibility in implementing modules from the various components depending on the needs of staff.

Needs assessment and evaluation both play critical roles in the development and implementation of Learning Curriculum activities. In order to measure the impact of the programs, a number of evaluation activities occur. These include "on-the-spot" online post-session evaluations, as well as long-term evaluation via Outcome Based Evaluation (OBE). The Libraries began using OBE in earnest to assess the impact of participation in Learning Curriculum activities in 2005.

This case study describes the philosophy behind the development of the learning program and highlights the process used for creating the comprehensive curriculum, evaluation processes used to assess the program, and future plans for completing an extensive review of this program, now finishing its sixth year. The use of the OBE method and how it has impacted the program are also described.

The UM Libraries as a Learning Organization

The UM Libraries began a systematic change process in 1998, which was based on the recognized need to serve the University's faculty, students, and staff more efficiently and effectively. Changing information services and technologies and the need to work differently to better meet user needs set the Libraries on a path to become a more dynamic organization. The Libraries wanted to create a work environment that focused on the customer (i.e. faculty, staff, and students); was committed to quality service; encouraged teamwork and collaboration; continuously improved practices and procedures; and emphasized continuous learning. Creating this new environment also meant accepting that change would be ongoing, both outwardly and inwardly.

The Libraries adopted Peter Senge's definition of a learning organization, which is an "organization where people continually expand their capacity to create the results they truly desire, where new and expansive patterns of thinking are nurtured, where collective aspiration is set free, and where people are continually learning how to learn together."[1] This new path of becoming a dynamic learning organization led to several major changes: the creation of teams throughout the Libraries to do the work and the acknowledgment that knowledge, skills, and tools were critical to the development of staff and their ability to be successful in their work. The foundations of a learning organization helped the Libraries identify the resources needed to accomplish this task.

Creation of the Learning Curriculum

Building a shared understanding of and agreement for the goals of the Libraries' learning organization were the first steps in creating a framework. The Manager of Staff Learning and Development and the Assistant Dean for Organizational Development wrote *Working Paper 3: Becoming a Learning Organization,* which provided background information about a learning organization, described key elements that would support the goal of becoming one, and identified initial content categories for building a learning program.[2] An outside consultant, Maureen Sullivan of Sullivan and Associates, assisted in framing the Learning Curriculum around five content categories, which were detailed in the *Working Paper.*

The first category was designed to focus on the development of the organization by addressing issues such as visioning, systems thinking, change management, and leadership. The second category paid attention to the development of individuals and teams by focusing on how to work in a team environment including decision making, problem solving, and how to conduct effective meetings. Further exploration of leadership and followership was the third category.

With the creation of teams and new working groups, there was not only change in leadership assignments, but also a new expectation for working differently. This category was designed to focus on developing leadership and facilitation skills of all staff. While the Libraries felt it already provided good service, there was agreement that defining customer service was an important category to address. Improving how customer service was provided was the fourth category. The last category focused on ways to increase self-awareness and improvement by supporting development of skills such as the Microsoft Office products, project management, time management, etc. Following the release of the *Working Paper*, staff focus groups were conducted to review the five categories in order to gather additional ideas and feedback. Other critical questions discussed in the focus groups included how staff liked to learn, how participation could be encouraged, and how to measure the success of the program.

Using data obtained from the focus groups, the Learning Curriculum was expanded to ten components with specific workshops created for each. While an initial listing of workshops was identified, from the outset, the intent was that the Learning Curriculum would be an evolving framework. In this way, it allowed for flexibility as new needs were noted or particular topics became more important to staff. The Learning Curriculum was not intended to replace on-the-job training occurring for specific jobs, but rather to supplement skills development for library employees. It was also realized that implementation of a comprehensive program would take the time and effort of a number of people, which was reflected in the inclusion of a train-the-trainer element in the Curriculum. The revised Learning Curriculum contains the following components:

- **Introduction: Development of the Organization**: this component covers an introduction to the Learning Organization, how to deal with change, and dealing with differences.
- **Defining Customer Service**: customer service is key to meeting users' needs. Modules within this component address the service philosophy as well as working with internal and external customers.
- **Measurement, Evaluation, and Continuous Improvement for Planning and Decision Making**: data-driven decisions are critical for successful performance. Workshops that develop skills in the areas of assessment, tools and techniques for collection and display of data, grant writing, and performance review are included in this component.
- **Development of Self, Teams, and Workgroups**: workshops in this component are designed for individual growth and team development and focus on giving and receiving feedback, meeting management,

tapping creativity, decision making, stress management, time management, and mentoring.

- **Exploring Leadership**: how roles as supervisors and leaders change over time is an important concept. Thinking about leadership styles and working in a team-based environment are two of the issues tackled in this component.
- **Individual Improvement**: this component includes workshops that are required for library staff: Sexual Harassment Prevention, and Safety and Security Measures. Other programs in this component cover such topics as presentation skills, project management, and understanding learning styles.
- **Computer Skills**: an array of computer workshops is included in this component, with emphasis on the Microsoft Office Suite and web creation/design.
- **Library Basic Skills**: workshops in this component cover a variety of basic skills necessary for library staff to do their jobs.
- **Leadership Development**: leadership, as a key value in the UM Libraries, is an overarching component in the Learning Curriculum. Workshops that focus on leadership have been developed within other components, and cross-referenced to Leadership Development. While all staff are eligible to participate in any workshops provided, some workshops are highlighted as particularly useful for supervisors and team leaders.
- **Train-the-Trainer**: this is a five-day training program offered as a way of teaching library staff to be trainers and to assist in the delivery of Learning Curriculum workshops.[3]

Once the ten components were developed, the Manager of Staff Learning and Development and the Assistant Dean for Organizational Development continued to work with Maureen Sullivan to create objectives for the workshops within each component. Contact hours were tentatively assigned, resulting in a program of approximately 150 contact hours.

The Learning Curriculum was unveiled to library staff in May 2001 during a library-wide staff meeting. University of Maryland Professor Henry P. Sims, Jr., kicked off the meeting with a presentation on leadership titled, "Company of Heroes: Unleashing the Power of Self-Leadership." The first workshop offered to staff was "Learning to Thrive in an Ever-Changing Workplace" with over 115 participants in six sessions. Since its release, fifty workshop titles have been developed and offered, and the Learning Curriculum framework has been periodically reviewed and updated. Most workshops are conducted by library staff, while others are facilitated by on-campus experts in the subject matter or by outside trainers.

Staff Training Needs Assessment

As noted by Charles Kratz, "successful staff development programs are relevant to the needs of the staff."[4] More specifically, training activities can be considered relevant when they are tied to types of needs identified by Barbara Allan. *Implementing* needs are those that arise in the process of bridging a gap between present and desired performance, while the process of *improving* performance to raise standards brings about the second training need. The final need (*innovating*) arises as libraries seek to do "new and better things."[5] Any or all of these needs can be addressed in a staff training program, however, in order to identify the most critical needs, the scope of the need must be assessed. This assessment allows those involved with the training program to better target learning opportunities and develop appropriate objectives and outcomes.

A wide variety of information-gathering methods were used to determine specific needs of staff and develop appropriate programming via the Learning Curriculum. In addition to the focus groups that were conducted to create the Learning Curriculum, two library-wide assessments were conducted in 1998 and 2000, with the resulting data providing useful insights into the training and development needs of library staff. The 1998 assessment focused exclusively on staff learning needs,[6] while the 2000 Organizational Culture and Diversity Assessment focused more generally on the organizational climate and culture.[7]

Additional information-gathering activities included computer training surveys completed in 2000, 2002, and 2005, and supervisory focus groups and a writing workshop survey conducted in 2003.[8] The 2000 and 2002 computer training surveys and the 2003 writing workshop survey were administered in paper format, while the 2005 computer training survey was made available to staff online. To this day, assessment and evaluation continue to play a critical role in the development and implementation of Learning Curriculum activities.

Evaluation

Evaluation of learning activities can be viewed in a number of ways. One such method was developed by Donald Kirkpatrick, who promoted a four-level scheme for program evaluation, designated from lowest to highest as reaction, learning, behavior, and results. The first level focuses on the "customer satisfaction" aspect of training. Simply put, those participants who have a negative experience in a training activity are less likely to put to practice the skills presented in that program. Kirkpatrick's second level of learning relates to how participants choose to change attitudes, knowledge, or skill, as a result of a training activity. The third level similarly focuses on willingness to change behaviors. Kirkpatrick's final level focuses on results that occurred as a result of participation in a training activity, which "can include increased production, improved quality, [and] decreased costs."[9]

Evaluation, like learning, is intended to be a never-ending process. In order to measure the impact of programs sponsored by the Learning Curriculum, a number of evaluation activities occur, including "on-the-spot" program evaluation surveys, and a long-term critical evaluation, via OBE.

On-the-spot Reviews: Program Evaluation Surveys

While participation in Learning Curriculum activities is tracked via an online database, this admittedly measures attendance at a session rather than learning that may take place. To further capture initial reactions to sessions (Kirkpatrick's first level of evaluation), session participants are encouraged to complete a post-workshop evaluation survey. The surveys were print-based until 2003 when they were made available online. Surveys were switched to an online format to allow attendees time to reflect on the attended program, rather than asking attendees to complete an evaluation at the end of a session. Online surveys also facilitated data entry and analysis by eliminating hand-keying of survey responses.

These surveys assist in measuring a number of aspects of the training activity, including the degree to which program objectives were clear and met, workshop organization, overall reactions, suggestions for improvements, additional workshops on other topics, and the most important outcomes from the workshop (as reported by the participant). An illustration of a sample session-end online survey appears in Appendix 12.A.

The Office of Staff Learning and Development compiles survey results, which are shared with session facilitators as a means of immediate feedback. Facilitators frequently use these data to fine-tune their programs as necessary—and as such, preliminary survey results are provided when there is a week or more between multiple offerings of the same program. Program evaluation summaries are also reviewed by Staff Learning to determine whether or not additional offerings of a particular program should be scheduled.

Long-term Critical Evaluation

While program evaluation forms and surveys are extremely useful in providing immediate feedback and reactions to individual sessions, it is equally important to determine the impact of Learning Curriculum programs over time. There have been several instances where the long-term impact of a session has been measured via a longitudinal assessment, such as surveys completed by individuals attending Meeting Management training (1999) or participating in all three Customer Service workshops offered (2003). An additional "post-workshop" survey was distributed in

December 2003 to those who attended any of the programs developed specifically for supervisors (known as the "Summer for Supervisors" series) that year, in order to determine the value of these sessions in terms of behaviors and attitudes changed. These long-term surveys were completed online, and results were tabulated and shared with the Library Executive Committee (LEC). This was done in order to keep LEC aware of the results of programmatic offerings, as well as to remind them of their commitment and need for continued support to encourage staff from their units to participate in future Learning Curriculum offerings.

Each of these individual efforts at short-term and longitudinal evaluation yielded useful data, however, there was no systematic means in place to assess the overall impact of the Learning Curriculum. A new approach was needed to fill this void. At the suggestion of the Manager of the Library Management Information Systems (MIS) office, OBE was investigated as a possible means of addressing this need.

Outcome Based Evaluation

OBE has a long history in not-for-profit institutions, including United Way and the Kellogg Foundation. The Institute of Museum and Library Services (IMLS) instituted OBE evaluation methods in 1997 in order to help grant recipients

> articulate and establish clear program benefits (outcomes), identify ways to measure those program benefits (indicators), clarify the specific individuals or groups for which the program's benefits are intended (target audience), and design program services to reach that audience and achieve the desired results.[10]

Since that time, OBE methods have become a requirement for all grant recipients. Using this assessment method, outcomes themselves are viewed as participant benefits, "specifically, achievements or changes in skill, knowledge, attitude, behavior, condition, or life status."[11]

Since OBE can easily be applied to measure the results of training activities, programs, or materials, and the University Libraries regularly submit proposals to funding agencies such as IMLS, the Learning Curriculum appeared to be an excellent candidate for applying this evaluation method. Through OBE, systematic data collection is employed in the short term, intermediate term, and long term, thereby addressing levels two through four of Kirkpatrick's matrix. One way to easily track the OBE progress is through the development of a Logic Model (or evaluation plan), which focuses on six discrete components:

• **Inputs**: the resources and materials used in the activities or process of the program, which are easily identifiable.

- **Activities**: processes or actions used in the program to meet the needs.
- **Outputs**: the measure of those served through the program.
- **Outcomes**: the actual benefit/impact or change for the participants during and after the program.
- **Outcome targets**: the number and percentage of participants needed to achieve the outcome(s).
- **Outcome indicators**: observable and measurable "milestones" toward an outcome target.[12]

In a Logic Model, outputs are considered measures of the volume of a program's activity. Examples of program outputs can include products created or delivered, the number of attendees at a program, the number of times a workshop was offered, etc. In contrast, outcomes are the "people" or the "so what" piece—what happened *because* of the outputs. For example, the number of participants at a Learning Curriculum HTML 101 workshop is considered an output, while the ability of participants to construct a web page after attending the workshop is an outcome. In the end, the chosen indicators measured show to what extent a program achieves its goals.

OBE Applied to the Learning Curriculum Programs

In 2003, Staff Learning and Development and MIS began looking at OBE as a tool for assessing the intermediate-range impact of Learning Curriculum programming. The original vision was to create individual OBE Logic Models for every Learning Curriculum program based on the model used by IMLS. Logic Models were initially developed for three workshops and tested through a pilot survey in 2004 that targeted a library-sponsored customer service workshop. This pilot study included two different surveys—one for participants and one for their supervisors. The goal of the evaluation was to determine whether the workshop met stated objectives, which elements of the workshop were critical and which were missing, long-term benefits for workshop participants, and any added value.

Surveys were designed to be completed online in a brief amount of time, and contained a maximum of five questions. Participants and supervisors were each given two weeks to complete the survey. Survey response rates were lower than anticipated, with only 14 percent of workshop participants completing the OBE pilot survey (in contrast to a 100 percent response rate for the initial session-end survey). Further, supervisors indicated they did not understand why they were being surveyed six months after the initial training program (despite being given notice at the time of the workshop that they would be asked to complete surveys for their staff at a later date). Given the staff reaction to the survey and the low survey results, OBE surveys for the Learning Curriculum were put on hold and retooled.

Revising the OBE Implementation Strategy

After analyzing the results of the 2004 pilot survey, Staff Learning and MIS decided to develop a new approach to OBE. Instead of creating Logic Models for each individual Learning Curriculum workshop, a single Logic Model was developed to encompass the Learning Curriculum as a whole (Appendix 12.B). As a result, the *target* audience for the combined Logic Model is defined as UM library faculty, staff, and graduate assistants. *Inputs* include assembling a cadre of trainers, developing and providing training sessions, creating publicity, and producing handouts for each session, among others. The *desired outcome* is that participants will be able to successfully practice the skills gained through training programs. The Logic Model's intended outcomes span three time periods:

- **Immediate**: participants benefit by learning a new skill or improving upon a current skill.
- **Intermediate**: participants begin to comfortably use the information or techniques over a period of time.
- **Long term**: participants continue to use acquired skills and to attend Learning Curriculum sessions.

In the revised OBE program, evaluation goals remained the same as in the pilot program. Targets were set for immediate feedback of 90 percent for the session-end survey and 50 percent for the six-month (OBE) follow-up survey. Staff Learning and MIS chose these as reasonable targets based upon common standards for OBE implementations. The long-term target outcome of the Logic Model is that 100 percent of library staff attends at least one Learning Curriculum program each year.

With the assistance of MIS, Staff Learning developed survey questions to determine the degree to which participants are able to practice the skills gained through attendance at training programs in the intermediate term. The revised OBE survey (Appendix 12.C) contains a mix of yes/no, Likert scale, and free-answer questions. Sample questions address knowledge or skills learned at the particular workshop, and whether or not those skills have been used or applied since the time of the session. The survey also gives respondents an opportunity to indicate whether or not there were any other skills or topics of interest.

OBE Results

In summer 2005, the retooled implementation plan for OBE was launched. All workshops taught since July 1, 2005 were included in the plan, with participants receiving a session-end evaluation as well as a follow-up (OBE) survey six months after the workshop. Due to poor supervisor response during the pilot, surveys are currently sent to program participants only, but are still completed online within a two-week time frame as in the pilot program. In order to publicize the OBE surveys, a "kickoff" article was included in the library staff newsletter[13] and workshop presenters or members of the Staff Learning Office remind workshop participants of the OBE surveys at the conclusion of every workshop. Participants were sent a reminder e-mail message that included the URL to the follow-up survey.

A total of 29 OBE surveys were conducted from January 2006 to March 2007, with 145 surveys completed. An average of 32 percent of attendees responded to the OBE survey for each workshop (compared with 66 percent responding to the session-end surveys). While both averages fall short of the desired response rates outlined in the Logic Model, the OBE response rates for individual workshops covered the full spectrum of possibilities, from the occasional 0 percent or 100 percent response rate to many in between. When evaluating whether to continue the OBE program, Staff Learning and Development and MIS plan to consider the reasons for the lower-than-expected OBE response rate. Was the initial response rate goal set too high? Did the participants experience "survey fatigue" from being asked to complete too many evaluations? Is there another issue that needs to be addressed?

Information Gathered from OBE

Although the overall response rate to OBE surveys was lower than anticipated (see Figure 12.1), the surveys continue to provide valuable information. The response to many OBE survey questions affirmed that the Learning Curriculum team is selecting appropriate training topics for the staff. For example, 67 percent of respondents were able to apply skills learned to their work.

Those who were not able to apply skills taught at workshops often cited reasons such as "I have not yet had the opportunity" or "I have been too busy to work on this project," indicating that the problem in application was not with the training itself, but with the changing nature of their

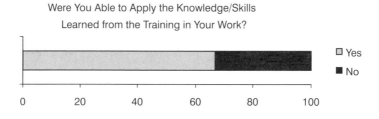

Figure 12.1 Applying workshop skills response rate

workflow. When asked, "Are there other skills you wish had been taught at this workshop?" 80 percent of respondents selected "No"—indicating that, overall, they were satisfied with the skills that were taught. When asked if the workshop would be helpful to others who do similar types of work, responses averaged between "Agree," and "Strongly Agree."

Application of Results

Staff Learning and Development have applied the results of all assessments in a variety of ways. Many comments on the session-end evaluations concern issues that are easily addressed by the team when conducting subsequent trainings. Room set-up, the times that sessions are offered, and refreshments, for example, can all be modified with minimal effort. Based on feedback, session facilitators can also modify the contents of workshops and handouts before the next training session.

One of the most useful features of the OBE survey is the free-response questioning (see Figure 12.2). These questions include, "What other skills do you wish were taught at this workshop?" and "What other topics would you like to see Staff Learning and Development offer?" While open-ended answers can be difficult to measure quantitatively, they do provide more training-specific data that can be analyzed. For example, if several survey respondents indicate they would like more information on sizing images in the Intermediate HTML class, the team will consider revising the workshop content before the next session. Likewise, when the team notices a growing trend of requests for certain workshop topics, a repeat of a popular session can be offered, new content can be developed or a session with an outside consultant can be scheduled, depending on which response best meets the employees' needs.

Sample Responses to the Question "Are there other skills you wish had been taught at this workshop?" for the "Presentation Skills" Workshop:

- "As hard as it was, I think the impromptu speech-giving exercise was great practice and would have been okay with doing another one later in the day."
- "I think it would have been nice if it was customized more for library instruction and not just presentations in general."

This workshop was taught by an outside consultant, so the team will share this feedback with him and suggest that the training content be revised for future sessions.

Figure 12.2 Sample survey responses

When feedback concerns the content or materials for training that is taught by an outside facilitator or consultant, this information is passed along to the consultant. The team also retains information so that, should the same training with the same trainer be offered, the team can revisit the comments and request that trainers address the suggestions from the previous session.

OBE feedback is also useful for medium- and long-range planning. The Staff Learning team shares OBE survey results with its advisory Staff Education and Coordination Team and also revisits information (such as suggested future topics or ideas for additions to existing training) when scheduling future sessions or in strategic planning. Some suggestions for future topics are addressed using resources other than training sessions. Online tutorials, informative articles, or one-on-one consultations with staff might be used as alternative ways of fulfilling these requests for programming. Information from the OBE surveys has proven useful along the entire spectrum of planning and evaluating staff learning activities.

Conclusion

The Learning Curriculum has reached significant milestones including the roll-out of the 200th workshop and development of the 50th program title. As of August 2007, total Learning Curriculum workshop attendance exceeded the 3,000 mark. Given the wide range of programs offered, and the amount of staff time and energy devoted to the Learning Curriculum, it is vital to assess its impact and utility. OBE has been a useful exercise to apply to the Learning Curriculum as a whole. As noted by IMLS:

> All libraries ... strive to provide excellent services, to manage programs effectively, and to make a difference in the lives of their audiences. Any kind of systematic evaluation contributes to project quality. The OBE process supports these goals by focusing programs and providing tools for monitoring progress throughout a project.[14]

Certainly, the Learning Curriculum is no exception in terms of having an overarching goal of providing excellent programming that improves the productivity of library employees. One aspect of Logic Models—such as the one designed for the Learning Curriculum—is that they should be adaptable. According to the Kellogg Foundation:

> As a program grows and develops, so does its logic model. A program logic model is merely a snapshot of a program at one point in time; it is not the program with its actual flow of events and outcomes. A logic model is a work in progress, a working draft that can be refined as the program develops.[15]

Given this, it is time for Staff Learning and Development and MIS to review and revise the Learning Curriculum Logic Model. In particular, one component of the Logic Model that will be closely considered is the target response rate. An additional aspect that has yet to be analyzed is the long-term outcome target of 100 percent staff participation in at least one Learning Curriculum workshop annually.

In addition to reviewing and revising the Logic Model, another area in need of further attention is the OBE survey itself. Consideration must be made to whether or not the right questions are being asked and if the time frame for sending out the long-term survey is sufficient in order to provide useful data. It is also necessary to look at the data being mined to see if enough insight is being gained in order to make improvements in Learning Curriculum offerings or to assure that staff needs are being met in a timely and effective manner. Beyond continued monitoring of session-end and OBE evaluations for suggested program revisions and additional topics to address via workshops or other training support, the time has come to conduct a comprehensive review of the Learning Curriculum itself. The last time the Learning Curriculum was examined was in 2005, at which point nominal changes were made to workshop titles and descriptions. The goal of a comprehensive review is to assure that Staff Learning and Development is meeting the current needs of the total library staff and continuing to assist them toward achieving their professional development goals.

References

1. Senge, Peter M. *The Fifth Discipline: The Art and Practice of the Learning Organization*. New York: Doubleday, 1990, p. 3.
2. Baughman, Sue, and Hubbard, Bette A. *Working Paper #3: Becoming a Learning Organization*. College Park, MD: University of Maryland Libraries, 2001. Available: <http://www.lib.umd.edu/PUB/working_paper_3.html>. Accessed: September 14, 2007.
3. *The Learning Curriculum*. College Park, MD: University of Maryland Libraries, 2005. Available: <http://www.lib.umd.edu/groups/learning/curriculum.html>. Accessed: September 14, 2007.
4. Kratz, Charles E. "How to Design and Conduct a Needs Assessment." In *Staff Development: A Practical Guide*. 3rd ed. Chicago: American Library Association, 2001, p. 26.
5. Allan, Barbara. *Training Skills for Library Staff*. Lanham, MD: Scarecrow, 2003, p. 121.
6. *Needs Assessment Survey Results: November 1998*. College Park, MD: University of Maryland Libraries, Staff Learning and Development, 2004. Available: <http://www.lib.umd.edu/groups/learning/surveyrep.html>. Accessed: September 14, 2007.
7. Nishii, Lisa H., Raver, Jana L., and Dominguez, Alexandra. *Results of the University of Maryland Libraries' Organizational Culture and Diversity Assessment: Final Report, August 2000*. College Park, MD: University of Maryland Industrial/Organizational Psychology Program, 2000. Available:

<http://www.lib.umd.edu/PUB/diversity.html>. Accessed: September 14, 2007.

8. *Writing Workshop Survey*. College Park, MD: University of Maryland Libraries. Staff Learning and Development, 2003. Available: <http://www.lib.umd.edu/groups/learning/writing.html>. Accessed: September 14, 2007.

9. Kirkpatrick, Donald. *Evaluating Training Programs: The Four Levels*. San Francisco, CA: Berrett Koehler, 1998.

10. *Outcome Based Evaluation: Frequently Asked Questions*. Institute of Museum and Library Services. Available: <http://www.imls.gov/applicants/faqs.shtm>. Accessed: September 14, 2007.

11. *Outcome Based Evaluation Overview*. Institute of Museum and Library Services. Available: <http://www.imls.gov/applicants/basics.shtm>. Accessed: September 14, 2007.

12. Dillon, Irma F., and Saponaro, Maggie. "The Use of Outcome Based Evaluation (OBE) to Assess Staff Learning Activities at the University of Maryland Libraries." In *Proceedings of the Library Assessment Conference: Building Effective, Sustainable, Practical Assessment*. Washington, DC: Association of Research Libraries, 2007, p. 390.

13. Saponaro, Maggie. "Your Thoughts Please! Learning Curriculum Launches Six-Month Evaluation Program." *Library Matters* (February 24, 2006). Available: <http://www.lib.umd.edu/groups/learning/lmarticles/lcevaluations.pdf>. Accessed: September 14, 2007.

14. *Outcome Based Evaluation: Frequently Asked Questions*. Institute of Museum and Library Services. Available: <http://www.imls.gov/applicants/faqs.shtm>. Accessed: September 14, 2007.

15. *Logic Model Development Guide*. Battle Creek, MI: W.K. Kellogg Foundation, 2004. Available: <http://www.wkkf.org/pubs/tools/evaluation/Pub3669.pdf>. Accessed: September 14, 2007.

Appendix 12.A: Learning Curriculum Session-end Online Survey

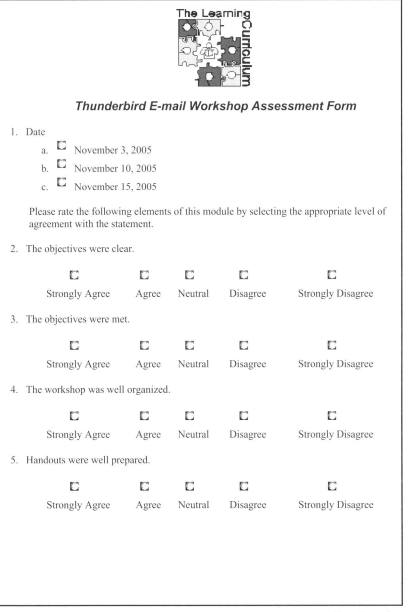

Thunderbird E-mail Workshop Assessment Form

1. Date

    a. ☐ November 3, 2005

    b. ☐ November 10, 2005

    c. ☐ November 15, 2005

    Please rate the following elements of this module by selecting the appropriate level of agreement with the statement.

2. The objectives were clear.

☐	☐	☐	☐	☐
Strongly Agree	Agree	Neutral	Disagree	Strongly Disagree

3. The objectives were met.

☐	☐	☐	☐	☐
Strongly Agree	Agree	Neutral	Disagree	Strongly Disagree

4. The workshop was well organized.

☐	☐	☐	☐	☐
Strongly Agree	Agree	Neutral	Disagree	Strongly Disagree

5. Handouts were well prepared.

☐	☐	☐	☐	☐
Strongly Agree	Agree	Neutral	Disagree	Strongly Disagree

Continued...

6. Overall, I found this workshop to be valuable.

☐   ☐   ☐   ☐   ☐

Strongly Agree   Agree   Neutral   Disagree   Strongly Disagree

7. Help us improve this workshop! Please explain any items you rated Neutral or lower.

8. What worked well in this program?

9. What did you expect to learn from this training that was not included?

10. What do you think are the most important outcomes of this workshop for you as an individual?

11. Please use this space for any additional comments.

Appendix 12.B: Learning Curriculum Logic Model Excerpts

Organization Name – *University of Maryland Libraries*

Project/Program Name – *Learning Curriculum*

Need Identified	Sources of Information
The Library faculty, staff, graduate assistants and student assistants (where applicable) should have the necessary knowledge, skills, and abilities for individual and organizational advancement.	Anecdotal information from trainers and Library Executive Council (LEC), library staff, Staff Education Coordinating Team (SECT), and previous staff surveys.
Program Influencers	*What Information Do They Want*
Learning Curriculum Team	Are individual Learning Curriculum (LC) programs meeting stated objectives? Do programs have long-term benefits for participants? Why is program used or not used? What are the critical elements of programs – what is missing?
Library Staff Instructors	Skills to assist in performing their jobs. Did sessions meet needs of attendees?
LEC	What added value does this bring to the Libraries? Can staff efforts in developing and maintaining long-term program be justified?
What Outcomes Do We Want?	Participants will be able to successfully practice the skills/abilities gained through training programs.
For whom? (Target audience)	Library faculty/staff/Graduate Assistants.
What will the program provide?	Opportunities for the staff to increase their knowledge, skills and abilities in various components of the LC – including computer skills, development of self and teams, and measurement and evaluation. Opportunities for professional and personal growth through on the job training sessions provided through the LC.

Continued…

Inputs (Materials/Supplies/staff/building or other resources needed to support the program)

Trainers (Staff Learning, MIS, Grants, Digital Collections, ARL, others)

Learning Curriculum Team support – publicity, registration, monitoring sessions

Refreshments for workshops

LEC – encourage individuals who would most benefit from particular sessions to register; funding for outside facilitators (ARL – July 21st)

Facilities support – room setup/cleanup

Handout packets
Web access to materials

Target Audience	Target Audience Characteristics That Might Impact the Success of the Program
Library faculty/staff/graduate assistants	Staff Time Staff Interest Schedule of training

Outputs (Quantities of things that represent program productivity)

Number of participants

Number of sessions held

Outcome #1 Participants will learn use of methods/tools discussed in the session.

Indicators	Data Source	Applied to whom	Data intervals	Target
All participants will understand how the tool/skill discussed could be applied in the work setting.	Participant Self-assessment (online)	Participants	Link to online assessment sent after conclusion of program. Participants given one week to submit responses.	90% of participants complete online survey

Outcome #2 Participants are comfortable applying techniques learned.

Indicators	Data Source	Applied to whom	Data intervals	Target
All participants report they have applied or are applying skills and tools learned at the session attended.	Participant Self-Assessment (online)#	Individual Participants for specific sessions#	6 months	50% of participants submit surveys#

Appendix 12.C: Learning Curriculum Outcome Based Evaluation Survey

E-mail Follow Up Survey

1. What knowledge/skills did you learn at this workshop?

2. Have you used or applied the knowledge/skills from the workshop?

   ☐ YES ☐ NO

3. If yes to question 2 above, how have you used the skills?

4. If no to question 2 above, why not?

5. Are there other skills you wished had been taught at this workshop?

   ☐ YES ☐ NO

6. If yes to question 5 above, what skills? If no, go to question 7.

7. This workshop has made a positive impact on how I do my job.

☐	☐	☐	☐	☐
Strongly Agree	Agree	Neutral	Disagree	Strongly Disagree

8. This workshop would be beneficial to others who do similar types of work.

☐	☐	☐	☐	☐
Strongly Agree	Agree	Neutral	Disagree	Strongly Disagree

9. What other topics would you like to see Staff Learning and Development offer?

13 Course Management Systems for Staff Development at Pennsylvania State Great Valley School of Graduate Professional Studies

Dolores Fidishun, Julie Meyer, Mary Murray, and Carol Riley

Introduction

Any librarian or library paraprofessional is extremely aware of the rapidly changing environment found in today's libraries. Michael Gorman summarizes the state of libraries today saying that "we are deep into an era in which digitized information and electronic resources dominate our working life and professional discussions."[1] New technology and advances in service as well as online environments that change daily make it necessary for libraries to continually train staff. As Westbrook points out, "in a field whose unofficial motto is 'the only constant is change,' serious efforts at ongoing library staff development constitute fundamental concern for all levels of management."[2]

It has become important for staff to have access to just-in-time learning or to be able to review information on new processes or policies at a moment's notice. This environment is coupled with the requirements of library staffing, which mean that employees work days, evenings, weekends, and in some academic libraries, into the night. As much as library staff want to turn to the person next to them to ask a question, there are many times when staff work by themselves or the authority on a specific technology or topic has long since gone home. Library workers are therefore faced with learning new technology on the job and in situations where there are few human experts present to answer questions.

Penn State Great Valley Library answered this challenge by creating a course management system site for library staff. The site was developed using ANGEL software and permits staff to access resources for training, important procedures, memoranda, staff schedules, etc. Individuals with a Penn State Access Account can access the site twenty-four hours per day, seven days per week from any Internet-accessible location.

Course management systems (CMS) such as Blackboard and ANGEL are frequently used to offer library instruction to students and faculty but these systems can offer more than course-related instruction activities. This case study explains how CMS can be used for library staff development, communication, and training.

Using the *Great Valley Library Staff* User Group site created by the Penn State Great Valley School of Graduate Professional Studies Library staff as an example, this chapter will briefly explain course management systems, discuss the rationale for using a CMS site for Library staff development, and explain how these systems can be created, implemented, and used to improve access to important processes, procedures, and documentation. Advantages and challenges of using this technology will be covered. The chapter will end with a discussion of future trends that may influence the development of CMS sites.

Setting

Penn State Great Valley School of Graduate Professional Studies is a graduate-only campus of Pennsylvania State University, located near Philadelphia. Part of Penn State University Libraries, the library is open sixty-five hours per week including evenings and weekends, and employs a staff of twelve (full- and part-time professional and paraprofessionals). Although the staff are fairly savvy about technology, they still face continual changes in technology, policies and procedures, as well as situations in which a staff member performs a function that is not part of his or her normal routine, such as opening or closing the library.

In both staff meetings and individual conversations with the Head Librarian, staff had expressed the need for a more flexible and accessible way to consult training materials and copies of policies and procedures. Although the Circulation Desk included a number of notebooks filled with information, a bulletin board for important items, and "red memos" for notices of high importance, the staff were seeking better ways to locate and update materials as needed. The ability to access just-in-time training or immediately get information on a policy or a procedure when needed during the course of a patron interaction or performance of a task were high priorities in staff conversations. During a general staff meeting discussion, ANGEL was suggested as a possible way to increase communication. This idea was made easier by the fact that the campus Instructional Designer reports to the Library and she was well-versed in the ANGEL system because of her work with faculty and students. She understood the various tools that were contained in the CMS and how these tools could be used to get staff the information they needed when they needed it.

The Head Librarian appointed a task force consisting of the Instructional Designer, Library Assistant for Technology, Head of Circulation, and Reference Librarian to put together a site and to start to populate it with information. The Head Librarian served as a resource as necessary and added suggestions related to site content when applicable.

What is a Course Management System?

CMS is software designed for teaching and learning. Library staff may be familiar with the acronym CMS in other contexts. For example, in web development, CMS stands for Content Management Systems. In the area of instructional technology, CMS is used to represent Course Management Systems, which are also commonly called Learning Management Systems (LMS) and Learning Course Management System (LCMS). These systems are designed primarily for use by faculty or corporate trainers to create online or blended instruction. Many educational and corporate institutions also use this software as a centralized location to share asynchronous and synchronous educational materials.

This CMS environment allows users to self-pace through materials or access just-in-time materials that are needed for daily work. CMS sites serve as locations to share educational materials, but can also act as warehouses or centralized repositories where staff and co-workers can share documents and materials in addition to educational information. A CMS can also act as a knowledge management system, becoming a place for collaboration and communication in the process of teaching and learning, as well as a place for the use of other electronic media.

A group within a CMS creates a common environment where materials can be shared without the knowledge of HTML, so anyone can be the creator and editor. Use of a CMS allows the editors to manage shared knowledge or training materials and other important documents among a staff of many. This facilitates training especially when there is little overlap of schedules. It also allows editors to develop a centralized location to store important materials and documents. A CMS is also a location for communication. It provides e-mail to group members, discussion boards, chat rooms and note-taking locations for members of the group.

Great Valley Library staff use a software system called ANGEL, which is an acronym for A New Global Environment for Learning. As the ANGEL Learning site explains, ANGEL provides "engaging communication and collaboration capabilities" that "augment instruction to deliver leading edge teaching and learning."[3] This product was developed by a faculty member from Indiana State University for use by other faculty members. It was sold to CyberLearning Labs, which is now ANGEL Learning. ANGEL is continuously monitored and upgraded by ANGEL Learning but was also customized specifically for Penn State. Not only is ANGEL a location in which to place course materials, but in addition to those resources, faculty, staff, and students (members of the Penn State community) can build a Group. Groups can be built for study, interest groups, or projects. It was decided that an ANGEL Group would be the perfect vehicle to support the Library's learning needs. All library staff and librarians were entered as members of the Library Group. Similar to student and faculty who use the system, each library team member uses his or her ID and password to access ANGEL. Groups can be set to public or private, limiting who can access the site, an important concept when internal library procedures are to be posted as part of the content. Currently this site is set to private and a moderator enrolls members of the staff. If one is interested in setting up a similar site, CMSs are commonly accessible on college campuses. If one is not available, open source CMSs such as Moodle can be used via the Internet. A new trend configures a blog into a CMS but privacy issues may arise with this solution as documents are open to the public.

Rationale and Goals

As the ANGEL site developed it soon became evident that it provided a number of advantages for staff training. First, it was available anytime and anywhere. This is very important because Great Valley Library staff report to Penn State University Libraries, whose administrative offices are located three hours away in State College, Pennsylvania. Librarians and library assistants frequently travel to the University Park Campus. While in discussions at that campus, they sometimes require access to library procedures or need to troubleshoot a situation from other locations when attending a conference.

ANGEL's flexible access also promotes just-in-time learning, particularly when new policies and procedures are implemented or if a staff member faces an infrequent situation that has a set policy. This just-in-time learning also promotes cross-training as it easily allows staff to learn procedures that are not normally in their skill sets. The procedural documentation found in the ANGEL site ensures that all staff can access the same information and that no one is faced with "winging it" because the expert in a particular area is not currently in the library.

The site also promotes better communication by allowing staff access to materials they may not normally see. Librarians can create *ANGEL Pages,* online pathfinders that are attached to a faculty member's course. These pages are only available to other librarians, and the faculty member and students in the specific course. If students ask questions that involve information in the pathfinders, normally library staff would not be able to look at the pathfinder. By adding copies of the ANGEL Pages to a folder in the Library ANGEL site everyone on the library staff gained access to these pages.

Finally, the site provides access to schedules making it is easier for those not in the library to know who is working at any one time. This is crucial at times of emergency closure or when a staff member suddenly becomes ill and the Head of Circulation, Head Librarian, or other responsible party tries to figure out how to keep the Library open.

Adult Learning and the CMS

In addition to the practical advantages of using a CMS to provide access to training information, the tool provides a number of benefits related to work-based and adult learning. Work-based learning is important because it permits staff to learn processes in a situation that is, as described by Allan, "closely linked to the needs of the library, contextualized to the workplace, and flexible in terms of time, place and staff involvement."[4] As Library staff use the CMS, they understand more about how University Libraries and the Great Valley Library function as well as gain the ability to serve patrons immediately without asking for assistance from another staff member.

Adult learning theory contributes several concepts that make the use of the CMS effective.[5] First, adults want to use what they learn today to make their lives easier tomorrow. Use of the CMS not only permits staff to obtain answers to questions immediately but also helps to reinforce concepts if a person looks up the same information a number of times. Adult learners also want to be able to use their already acquired experience. The CMS allows staff members to link what they already know about the library to new knowledge that is included in the content area. Finally, adults learn more effectively when they are active participants in their learning. By connecting to the content of the CMS as they perform their job, they have the opportunity to interact with a learning environment that meets their immediate needs.

Creation Process

As discussed in a previous section, Library staff had numerous means of acquiring information including a binder full of printed e-mail alerts about technology problems, policy memoranda from the Head Librarian, and telephone numbers and other general information covering library operations. The staff would try to verbally inform other staff members about issues and staff members would leave the ubiquitous post-it notes with news. However, often a staff member looking for specific information would not remember that something was in the paper file or would not be able to locate it. Post-it notes get lost and there was always one staff member that "didn't get the memo." Using ANGEL seemed to be an appropriate means of communication since it would be the one place to seek answers, and if organized properly, locating information would be less cumbersome. Additionally, it would be easier to quickly add, update, and change information.

Before the Library Staff User site could come into existence, several issues had to be addressed:

- Who would be responsible for creating, maintaining, and updating information?

- Who would train the rest of the staff to use the site?
- Besides the "content feature" would any other elements of ANGEL be utilized?
- What information should the site contain?

Initially, editing rights to the site were given to the Head Librarian and Reference Librarian, Head of Circulation, and Assistant for Technology. A current review indicates that all staff should have rights to insert new information as needed. All members of the editing team can create files, upload documents, and add web links, etc. The Assistant for Technology became the site moderator, enrolling others, and keeping the content current.

ANGEL Training

The Assistant for Technology instructed staff members in the use of ANGEL. Training consisted of hands-on, one-on-one instruction with each staff member. Staff members who had not previously used ANGEL were taught how to fill out their "profile," which consisted of identifying information. A demonstration of the "theme selector" showed staff how to customize the look of ANGEL if they wished. Training also included a demonstration of accessing the information in the "Content" folder as well as a discussion of the other features available in ANGEL.

In addition to the content feature, ANGEL also provides e-mail, message boards, and a calendaring feature. The "My Files" feature is a convenient means of transporting files between computers. The library staff have access to a university-wide e-mail system and its accompanying calendar system, so the e-mail and calendaring features on ANGEL have not been utilized by the group. The message board has been used for discussion of projects.

The Content area is the feature most extensively used by the group. As a starting point to creating content, the Head of Circulation and Assistant for Technology discussed information that is usually communicated to a new staff person. It was decided that the site should include the basics such as opening and closing procedures, contact information for other staff members, circulation desk procedures, and information about equipment maintenance. The pair decided to prepare Word files with the types of instructions normally communicated verbally to new staff members. In addition, links to existing University Libraries web pages with circulation, acquisitions, and course reserve procedures were added to make access easier for the staff.

Once procedures were written, the written instructions were distributed to team members and asked for input to ensure the inclusion of all steps of each process. Then the procedures were placed into ANGEL. Other staff members were asked to access ANGEL and proofread the postings.

Having many eyes read the ANGEL postings reinforced procedures and also made sure that all process steps were included.

As library team members became more familiar with using ANGEL, the decision was made to include more circulation procedures. The circulation system had been upgraded and was quite different from the previous Telnet system. An informal survey was conducted to identify the most troubling or confusing new circulation procedures. Screen captures and dialogue were used to assist staff and circulation trainers in realizing the process of the new procedures for themselves.

Faculty members asked the librarians to prepare ANGEL Pages for courses. These pathfinders contained database and text resources that could be used for student research and projects. Only students who are class members can access these pages. As mentioned earlier, the pages were loaded into the library staff site in the event of student questions.

Sometimes the obvious takes a bit more time to become obvious. An unexpected snowstorm closed the library for the day. The evening before the storm, the Head of Circulation revised the phone list to include a new staff person. The information was hanging on the staff bulletin board and saved on her computer, which was not helpful since she was snowed in at home. After that snow day, it was decided to add the staff phone list and staff schedules to ANGEL; ANGEL could be accessed remotely and the inclusion of the staff phone list is a significant improvement in communications for the library team in case of emergency.

Since all staff members could access the site on a regular basis the team also decided to use it to upload items that could be used for their professional development. Web sites of interest, blogs, articles, and other materials to enhance professional development were posted for the staff to read (see Figure 13.1 and Figure 13.2). Links to Webinars were also included.

Advantages beyond Basic Training

As discussed, the system has many advantages for training and serves as an important resource for staff but there are important by-products of using it that are not directly equated with library training. The first is that since ANGEL is used by many faculty members and students, using it as a training site gives staff a better understanding of what a course management system is and how it can be used. When students talk about ANGEL, everyone in the library has experienced it. In addition, the staff get to know the vagaries of the CMS. For example, for a while it was not possible to use Firefox to print from ANGEL. Links to electronic reserves on faculty ANGEL sites give students instant access to course reserves. Since students ask all kinds of questions including how to use the CMS, the staff are better prepared to answer these types of questions. Finally, the use of ANGEL allows the Library to incorporate a number of technologies in one place. The CMS permits linking to important websites, such as

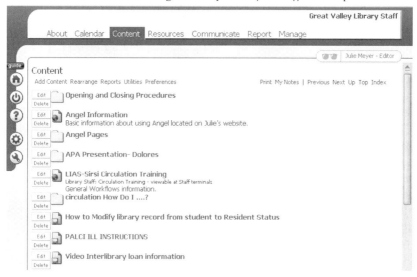

Figure 13.1 Main page of Penn State Great Valley Library ANGEL training site

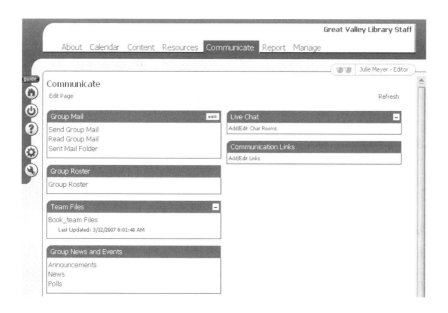

Figure 13.2 ANGEL site communication resources

suggested external blogs or Webinars as well as internal Penn State sites. Although some of the communication tools such as threaded discussions have not been used very much, these resources will be valuable later for brainstorming or other information sharing.

Challenges

The Great Valley Library ANGEL page has given staff immediate access to just-in-time learning, provided them with up-to-date information and opened lines of communication about policies and procedures. There are some disadvantages. Although the current Library staff are very technologically savvy and willing to try anything new, there have been times in the past when staff members were not as comfortable with new technology. For those people this was one more product they had to be willing to learn.

A second issue is that ANGEL is not as available as the Libraries' home page and the circulation system, both of which are up and ready on terminals at the Circulation Desk at all times. A staff member must remember to go into ANGEL and login at the appropriate time. This means that employees, particularly new ones, must occasionally be reminded that the site exists. Using ANGEL does require some training and this must be added to the training list for new employees.

Another issue, at least in the beginning is remembering to consistently add to the site when policies, etc. are announced. The Head of Circulation routinely uses the site to add new procedures and information and the Library Assistant for Technology uses it as a working tool, but not everyone is as diligent. For the site to be successful it must be kept up to date and everyone must contribute to it.

Finally, occasional upgrades of the ANGEL system require retraining just as any online library tool would. Most of these upgrades are minor but sometimes new versions create a need for training.

Future Considerations

Future training and environments for sharing materials are changing and growing every day. Sites need to be dynamic, and users need to be able to interact, collaborate, and communicate within systems. ANGEL allows users to become creators and editors. The CMS will grow into a portal as environments become blended and tools are accessed through the course management system. Some of these tools include synchronous conferencing solutions, blogs, wikis, and podcasts. Even virtual environments such as Second Life[6] will become important resources that permit just-in-time learning opportunities that meet staff's learning styles. All of these factors will impact the use of a CMS in the future. This information is also becoming mobile and users will want to interact with systems using Blackberry and Smartphone devices. Learners are now synching MP3 players and iPods to connect to resources and accessing audio and video distant from Internet connections. It will be important to monitor how the CMS can be used by those who use such equipment. Finally, as with any technology, it is important to ensure that the ANGEL site is fully accessible for those with visual impairments or other learning concerns; this step is in process now that the site is up and running and content has been added.

Conclusion

Decades ago, the ability of computer programs to create a paperless workplace was predicted. There would be no more overflowing file cabinets. The printed paper item would become obsolete. While the computer works well as an individual personal filing system, many people still have overflowing file cabinets stuffed with backup copies. The problem with a computer file accessible only by one is that it reduces the efficiency of communicating information to a team or group. The Penn State Great Valley Library ANGEL (Course Management System) site provides the staff with a place to instantly access resources needed for just-in-time training. As with any technology, one must deal with issues of training and software upgrades. This system gives staff flexibility in locating updated policies, procedures, and resources and provides staff development opportunities. Barbara Allen said that "libraries require a flexible and skilled workforce if they are able to maintain and develop relevant services."[4] The implementation of this CMS training site has not only taken Great Valley Library staff training into the 21st century but has provided staff with a way to keep up to date on topics of importance as they perform their daily work.

References

1. Gorman, Michael. "Technostress and Library Values." *Library Journal* 126, no. 7 (April 15, 2001): 48–50.
2. Westbrook, Lynn. "Problem-based Learning: A Staff Development Model for Tight Budget Times." *Technical Services Quarterly* 23, no. 1 (2005): 27–33.
3. *ANGEL Learning.* 2007. Available: <http://angellearning.com/>. Accessed: May 30, 2007.
4. Allan, Barbara. *Developing Library Staff Through Work-based Learning.* Lanham, MD: Scarecrow Press, 2003.
5. Fidishun, Dolores. "Teaching Adult Students to Use Computerized Resources: Utilizing Lawler's Keys to Adult Learning to Make Instruction More Effective." *Information Technology and Libraries* 19, no. 3 (September 2000): 157–158.
6. Linden Research, Inc. *Second Life: Your World. Your Imagination.* 2007. Available: <http://www.secondlife.com/>. Accessed: May 30, 2007.

Exercises

Elizabeth Connor

Table E.1. Learning activities for staff development in academic libraries

Thinking levels	Learning activity
Knowledge	• Define staff development. • Define organizational culture. • Define culture of research. • Define needs assessment.
Comprehension	• How can experiential learning be adapted to library staff development? • How do generational differences affect the quality and quantity of training given to new and current employees? • How does knowledge about an academic library's client base affect library staff training or development? • How do focus groups yield qualitative and anecdotal data?
Application	• Review philosophy or vision statements related to library staff development. One notable example is Yale University Library <http://www.library.yale.edu/training/stod/lhrphil.html>. • Develop teaching goals/objectives for a potential orientation session for a newly hired entry-level librarian, or on-the-job training for a mid-career librarian promoted or transferred laterally into another position. • Use <http://www.instructables.com/> to develop and share a simple set of illustrated instructions for opening or closing the library, verifying a citation, or other common procedures. • Write a brief script for a library orientation session planned for a newly hired reference librarian. How would this script differ if the new hire worked in cataloging? • Based on goals/objectives for a current or hypothetical staff development program, develop three questions that can be used to assess learning of key concepts for library staff orientation and/or training.

Analysis	• Review various staff development policies from small, medium, and large academic libraries. How do they differ? Do these library policies resemble staff development policies developed for non-library faculty/staff at the same institution? • Locate and compare the orientation schedules for new librarians hired at small, medium, and large academic libraries. • Review The National Staff Development Council Standards <http://www.nsdc.org/standards/index.cfm>. How can these standards be used or adapted by academic librarians? • Search the library literature to find articles about the effectiveness of staff development programs in academic libraries. How do academic libraries differ from other academic disciplines in this regard? How are non-library faculty or technical staff oriented at similar institutions?
Synthesis	• Based on analysis and application of policies, standards, and philosophy statements developed by other academic libraries, write a brief philosophy statement, set of standards, or release time policy for an actual or hypothetical academic library. • Write a hypothetical e-mail message inviting academic library colleagues to participate in the planning of a staff development retreat. What are the goals and objectives of this event? • Develop a set of criteria that can be used to measure the success or failure of a staff development program.
Evaluation	• Using the criteria developed above (in the synthesis section), develop an evaluation instrument for orientees, trainees, or supervisors to rate the quality of orientation or staff development efforts. • Seek permission to attend an orientation session for new employees (not librarians or library staff) at your current or potential academic institution. What are the similarities and differences? Which components can be adapted to an academic library setting? • Test and revise the instructable created above (in the application section), through the use of focus group and survey techniques. • Test and revise the content of the script created above (in the application section), through the use of focus group and survey techniques with inexperienced and experienced librarians.

Adapted from E. Connor, *Evidence-based Librarianship: Case Studies and Active Learning Exercises*. Oxford: Chandos Publishing, 2007, p. 35.

Index